Pacific Asia 2022

The cosponsors of this project wish to thank

Asia Pacific Agenda Project

Pacific Asia 2022

Sketching Futures of a Region

Japan Center for International Exchange
Tokyo • New York

The surnames of the authors and other persons mentioned in this book are positioned according to country practice.

Copyediting by Elmer Luke and Pamela J. Noda.
Cover and typographic design by Patrick Ishiyama. Typesetting and production by Patrick Ishiyama.

Printed in Japan
ISBB 4-88907-064-8

Distributed outside Japan by Brookings Institution Press (1775 Massachusetts Avenue, N.W., Washington, D.C. 20036-2188 U.S.A.) and Kinokuniya Company Ltd. (5-38-1 Sakuragaoka, Setagaya-ku, Tokyo 156-8691).

Japan Center for International Exchange
9-17, Minami-Azabu 4-chome, Minato-ku, Tokyo 106-0047 Japan
www.jcie.or.jp

Japan Center for International Exchange, Inc. (JCIE/USA)
274 Madison Avenue, Suite 1102, New York, N.Y. 10016 U.S.A.
www.jcie.org

Contents

Foreword

This publication is the final report of the Asia Pacific Agenda Project (APAP) research endeavors on the "Vision of Asia Pacific in 2020," a joint research project among seven leading scholars from six countries in Asia Pacific. When members of the APAP Steering Committee gathered toward the end of the twentieth century to discuss the first topic APAP should address in the new century, they agreed that APAP should lay out a vision for Asia Pacific in the first twenty years of the century. The Steering Committee also agreed to ask one of the younger members of the APAP circle, Dr. Simon Tay of the Singapore Institute of International Affairs, to lead a project team.

Dr. Tay accepted the challenge and identified six perspectives from which a blueprint of the region could be drafted: the security environment, trade and investment, sustainable development, governance, demography, the IT revolution, and institutions. Subsequently, Dr. Tay, with the help of the Steering Committee, assigned young experts to tackle each angle. The research team, thus organized, met twice among themselves to share a sense of mission and consolidate the division of labor as well as to review their preliminary drafts. In the course of the deliberation, the author of the security environment chapter had to resign. We are truly grateful to Dr. Yoon Young-kwan, who graciously and courageously agreed to join the project at the very late stage when other members had already completed their first drafts. After submitting his paper, Dr. Yoon was appointed minister for foreign affairs and trade of the Republic of Korea, thus confirming our choice of an appropriate expert.

So many things have happened since this project was first envisioned, including the tragedy of September 11, 2001, wars in Afganistan and Iraq, and the rise of international terrorist threats, which, in the context of Asia, highlight the need of peaceful coexistence between the Muslim and non-Muslim populations. The APAP secretariat apologizes for the delay of the completion of this otherwise timely project due to a variety of reasons.

Nevertheless, we believe that the analyses and insights incorporated in this volume are still very much valid and relevant in putting current developments in a longer-term perspective.

The APAP Steering Committee wishes to express its deepest gratitude to Dr. Simon Tay and all the other members of the project for their excellent contributions. The Steering Committee also wishes to acknowledge the generous financial assistance provided by various sources, but most notably Japan's Ministry of Foreign Affairs, without the assistance of which this project could never have been launched.

Yamamoto Tadashi
Director
Asia Pacific Agenda Project

President
Japan Center for International Exchange

PACIFIC ASIA 2022

1

Introduction: Sketching a Regional Future

Simon S. C. Tay

Talking about the future offers both temptations and difficulties. The last years of the twentieth century and the first years of the twenty-first have produced a series of surprises and discontinuities for Asia, Pacific Asia, and indeed the world.

The first and most traumatic of these for most Asians has been the so-called Asian financial crisis that began in 1997 with the devaluation of the Thai baht. The crisis deflated the idea of the East Asian "miracle" that was projected to bring the region on a par with North America and Europe. The speed with which this "contagion" spread and the precipitous fall of the economies of almost all of Asia were shocking. The subsequent years of slow or no recovery to the pre-crisis levels have added further disappointment.

The second trauma has been the tragic events of September 11, 2001, or 9-11, that has quite fundamentally shifted the sentiments of Americans about their sense of security and their place in the world. From this rupture, a U.S.-led war against terrorism has been waged across the world. There have been campaigns in Afghanistan and Iraq, as well as changes in both foreign policy and internal politics—not just in the United States, but also in many countries in Pacific Asia.

A third set of changes has occurred in relations among countries in Pacific Asia. In the 1980s and early 1990s, it seemed that the economic growth of Japan would come close to being on a par with that of the United States. With the growth of the newly industrialized economies (NIEs) of Hong Kong, Singapore, South Korea, and Taiwan, as well as the near-NIEs of Malaysia, Thailand, Indonesia, and the Philippines, it also appeared that intraregional relations in Pacific Asia might achieve more equality as a community emerged. Instead, Japan has been mired in a "lost decade," still rich but without reforms—or the political will to carry them out—to spark new growth. With the Asian crisis, the promise of the NIEs and near-NIEs has also faded.

Contemporaneously, the United States has discovered a rich seam of growth that has lasted for more than a decade and has reinforced U.S. primacy in economic terms, security, as well as soft power. On its part, China in the 1990s accelerated its economic development and kept on growing throughout the crisis, thus altering the competitive environment in Asia. With these and other factors, the United States has emerged, more than ever, as the determinant in the shaping of the Asia Pacific community, where U.S.-China relations are the most critical.

Understanding these changes and debating the necessary responses are not easy tasks. Amid the present storms, visibility is limited. There is no clear horizon, no path ahead that can be discerned. To many, the past of Pacific Asia may have been perfect, but the future is tense, and surveying the next twenty years may seem an impossible undertaking. It is nevertheless important to try, in order to better understand what options we can and should pursue for the future of the region.

TALKING ABOUT PACIFIC ASIA: THE PAST PERFECT, THE FUTURE TENSE?

From the vantage point of the early twenty-first century, Pacific Asia in the twenty-first century is a very different place from the perspective of it a decade earlier.

Predictions for Pacific Asia in the 1990s were based on the idea of an Asian miracle. Japan would lead the way for the "flying geese" of the NIEs, which, in turn, would be followed by the near-NIEs.

The rapid growth rates in Japan, the NIEs, and the near-NIEs drew attention to what the World Bank deemed "the East Asian miracle." East Asia seemed to possess a formula that had thus far eluded countries in Eastern Europe, Latin America, and Africa. In comparison to import substitution strategies and centralized economic planning, that formula mixed economic basics—such as markets, exports, and foreign capital—with social and political poli-cies—including an emphasis on education, savings, and community stability. The example the miracle set in utilizing global markets, foreign capital, and export-led industrialization would, predictions went, be followed by the much larger, less booming Asian economies of China, India, and Vietnam.

The Asian model was praised not only in contrast to Soviet and import-substitution economies. Some saw it favorably in comparison to the United States, which seemed in relative decline in the 1980s, and Europe, which seemed spent and introspective. The picture of the United States that emerges from this period, from observers within and without the United States, is critical of U.S. society and U.S. economics—with concerns for the lack of family values, the low levels of personal savings, and the high crime rate. The view of Europe was one of a world stuck in slow growth, no jobs, and an overly generous welfare state.

Asia, on the other hand, had growth rates that were extrapolated into the twenty-first century as catching up with and overtaking those of the United States and Europe. Rapid economic development would encompass the whole of Asia. The twenty-first century would be the Asian century.

This prediction was not politically neutral. Asia was seen to have a model of politics and society distinct from that of the West. "Asian values" were articulated to legitimate its differences as regards democracy and human rights, leading to considerable debate between East and West, belying their increasing economic interdependence.

The balance of different components in the East Asian miracle varied according to interpretation. Some emphasized the role of government, industrial policy, or the importance of "culture." Others stressed the importance of free markets and the "soft" nature of the authoritarianism in states that, they predicted, would evolve with the maturing of society and the rise of a more educated middle class.

From this, ideas about governance, human rights, and democracy came to be debated in terms of how Asian values differed or where they might indeed be superior to values of the West. Asian views about the balance between the environment and development, the concept of security, and the modalities and institutions for cooperation in the region gained credence.

This picture changed, quite suddenly and irretrievably.

In this, the Asian financial crisis that struck in mid-1997 has been a historic watershed. No one had predicted the crisis.[1] The relatively brief but intense crisis witnessed large and rapid falls in investment, currency values, jobs, and companies. Most countries that sustained damage have yet to recover to pre-1997 levels. In some, complex and large-scale political and social changes are still unfolding.

In the aftermath of the crisis, observers per force revised their views on the Asian miracle. This revisionism has identified weaknesses in economics, politics, and society. Systems of governance are now seen to have been

5

Simon S. C. Tay

wanting, with cronyism, corruption, and nepotism in both the public and private sectors. Markets for Asian investment have lacked, and consumer expenditure has been low.

More broadly, environmental and human factors have come into focus. It is now acknowledged that the price Asia has paid for its rapid growth has been in terms of the environment, with increased pollution levels and a downturn in natural resources. As a result, attention is now paid to the development and security of human beings as regards, for example, education, the inclusion of women, the rights of ethnic minorities, and worker protection. Despite analysis of the problems, however, reform at the national and regional levels has been slow. Indeed, many Asians still harbor the notion that international institutions let them down and call for reforms at the international level.

But, although critical, the 1997 crisis is not the only factor that Asia today must consider. While the worst of the crisis has passed, effects linger and there is no easy recovery to rapid growth and the idea of a miracle. Some countries continue to face considerable economic and political challenges, especially in Southeast Asia. The NIE model and the leadership of Japan have been discounted. Asia's halo has been knocked off. Meanwhile, the world has not stood still, waiting for these countries to recover. Indeed, the external environment has become more challenging and difficult.

From late 2000, the economic slowdown experienced by the United States has rippled through Asia. The region's countries had relied heavily on the U.S. market to stimulate their recovery, and, as that demand declined, so did their rates of growth. That countries had not proceeded with reforms of their economic and political structures became evident.

The terrible events of September 11, 2001, have also taken their toll on countries in Asia Pacific. While the targets of the terrorist attacks and of the U.S.-led response lie outside the region, Asia Pacific has not gone unaffected in terms of either economics or security. The terrorist attacks sharpened the economic downturn in the United States and the world, and the U.S. war on terrorism has brought changes in security policy throughout Asia. In some cases, new economic and political instabilities have been added to those unresolved from the crisis.

Against this backdrop, were the miracle years of growth in Asia but a mirage? Will they not return? Will this, the first ten years of the new century, be a lost decade for Asia, especially for some in Southeast Asia?

The continued growth of China has stood out in sharp contrast to other countries in the region. China rode out the Asian financial crisis, something now seen to have been assisted by its refusal to devalue the yuan, thereby avoiding further instability. At the start of the first decade of the twenty-first century, China's growth rates seemed even to be surviving the global downturn. Already there is talk of China becoming a new great power that will dominate Asia and be on a par with the United States. This has caused some to suggest the notion of a Chinese century, and others to consider the need for the containment of China.

But in the larger current picture, the new century seems to belong not to China, but as did much of the latter part of the twentieth century, to the United States. The position of Pacific Asia has, in the judgment of most, returned to one of subordination. The future of Asia as a region seems to depend mainly on the prospects of U.S. foreign policy and the rise of China.

Revisionism of the Asian miracle, while a necessary exercise, can go too far. There has been a tendency to rubbish Asia and—with the exception of China—to write it off. In the face of such pessimism, the fledgling Pacific Asian markets and institutions have suffered with little growth and diminished attention. There is every reason to look to China with interest. There is, however, no reason to transpose dreams of an Asian miracle to those of a Chinese miracle.

The future of Pacific Asia, as that of other regions, extends beyond financial crisis and terrorist attacks. The past of the region is by no means perfect, but the future, while tense, is not fated to work against it.

THE FUTURE OF METHOD OR MADNESS

When we look back at the 1990s, we may ask how we could have been so wrong. There are no easy answers.

The methods of predicting the future of Pacific Asia are diverse. For simplicity, however, most may be characterized as belonging to either a "Nostradamus" approach or a "Naisbitt" approach.

Somewhat in the tradition of Nostradamus, many have emphasized the importance of a vision for the region. The word "vision" can be found in almost every report or analysis by an eminent person—and especially in conjunction with the Asia-Pacific Economic Cooperation (APEC) process. Like those of the sixteenth century "prophet," some of these writings were cryptic. They were less about what the visionary hoped for the future, than about the paths to be taken and the wherewithal for the journey. Political will was a given, as were the capacity and centrality of government action. But the underlying assumption was growth—continuous, heady growth.

Such assumptions tie to what we might call the Naisbitt school of prediction—after the futurist, John Naisbitt, who in *Megatrends* used a method of news analysis to identify the directions of history. Obviously, the approach is dependent on the media as a market for accessing, assessing, and finally envisioning events. Using his method, Naisbitt wrote in 1994 of "the dragon century," where he saw Asia, and Latin America too, as "new areas of opportunity." In 1996, he concentrated his thoughts on megatrends in Asia.

Naisbitt's observations, and those of others that are similar in approach, were not without useful insight. But whether visionary or analytical or media-based, it is clear that many of these predictions about Pacific Asia have proved to be too optimistic. Unexpected events and discontinuities have surprised leaders, analysts, and ordinary citizens alike.

One methodology that may deserve more consideration in the future is the use of scenarios, as suggested by Louis Lebel in his chapter here. Scenarios enable thinking that reaches beyond present facts and trends to consider unexpected, extraneous events. This is helpful in contemplating the impact of sudden shocks, such as the financial crisis, 9-11, or severe acute respiratory syndrome (SARS). Yet, if not handled correctly, scenario building can descend to the realm of bad science fiction. Much also depends on the participants—and their interaction—in the scenario-building exercise, especially if there are elements of role playing involved. Perhaps it is telling that while scenarios have been employed by companies and governments, none has predicted a scenario such as that which the region has encountered since 1997.

With this in mind, this volume must be offered with greater caution and humility than others in the past. The methods used to obtain the information have been relatively simple and direct, drawing from a project that has engaged scholars from seven fields of study: demographic changes and challenges; the consolidation of trade and investment regimes; information technology (IT) and its impact on the region; the challenge of environmental protection and sustainable development; issues of governance at the national level; the need for a new security order; and the needs, likely shape, and modality of regional institutions. The scholars were asked to prepare preliminary papers and then to discuss their findings with each other, seeking to link their thinking across different fields of inquiry. The selection of younger scholars from different countries in the region was another element of the project.

Thus, this volume depends on neither vision nor content analysis. Instead it surveys a limited but relatively broad range of disciplines that seem of relevance to developments at the national and regional levels, and offers thoughtful scholars an opportunity to share their perspectives from different disciplines. It then seeks to cut across these disciplines. Thus, while the writer of each chapter may be steeped in a particular expertise, his or her challenge has been to make that knowledge and its concerns understandable and pertinent to others.

A LOOK AT DIFFERENT SECTORS

Demography

Trends in population growth, aging, and migration in Pacific Asia are the focus of Yu Xuejun as he looks toward the next two decades.[2] In each of these areas, there is a considerable difference among the countries of the region, and their policies will necessarily have to reflect their stage in the demographic transition from high to low fertility.

Thailand, Indonesia, and Malaysia are in the middle of this transition. In the wake of the Asian financial crisis, they have faced declining government budgets that have adversely affected population and health programs. But some countries are already in the low fertility band. These include developed countries like Australia, New Zealand, Japan, the NIEs, and Brunei, which have implemented various national family planning programs. Through sometimes controversial means, China's population growth trend is similarly low. The population policies of these countries have succeeded at the same time as they have been accompanied by such social changes as a rise in income and a rise in literacy. In fact, Japan and Singapore have been so successful that they are facing an aging population and labor shortages, and they are currently formulating pro-natalist policies to encourage a rise in birthrate.

This is not a small concern. Although lower fertility and a shrinking population have been welcomed, they come with their own set of challenges. These include the need for adjustments in national expenditure and allocations, investment and consumption patterns, as well as labor and employment policies, all in order to accommodate larger numbers of the elderly. In this respect, the countries with the most successful population control policies, like the NIEs, China, and Japan, will paradoxically be most adversely affected.

Simon S. C. Tay

The region is also divided on the issue of migration, both international and rural-to-urban migration. International migration is a considerable factor in the regional transfers of labor. Countries such as China, the Philippines, Indonesia, and Vietnam are identified as sources of labor for countries such as Japan, the NIEs, Australia, and New Zealand. The problem is not confined to circumstances affecting richer and poorer countries. It is perhaps most acute in mid-level economies like Malaysia and Thailand, which are each host to a million illegal workers from less-developed Indonesia, Cambodia, Laos, Myanmar, Vietnam, and, even further afield, South Asian countries.

Large-scale illegal migrations cause a range of social problems. Malaysia's situation is made worse by an administrative system that cannot adequately prevent illegal migration or deal with the workers once they are within its borders. There is also the sense in some countries—such as Japan and Australia—that immigrants of a different race, legal or illegal, are less than welcome.

Movements of people can be expected to increase with globalization and the increasing economic integration of the region. Political integration remains unlikely, however, and policies will continue to restrict the movements of people between countries even as their desire and ingenuity test the wherewithal of governments. Political and social tensions can arise from this, as seen in Australia regarding its dealing with boatloads of those seeking refuge.

One possible development will be bilateral arrangements that address the issues of inter-country migration. These issues could be quite specific, such as the concerns expressed by the Philippines to countries accepting Philippine citizens for domestic work and other blue-collar jobs. Another might be arrangements allied to trade and economic agreements, where the focus is likely to be on higher-level jobs in business and the professions. But underlying this will be a contest—in the region, and the wider world—for talent. In countries like Singapore, for example, economic strategy will suggest a relatively open system to attract higher-value foreign workers. Elsewhere, nationalistic sentiment may limit the acceptance of such workers to instances when no locals can be found to fill positions.

Within national borders, rural-to-urban migration is increasing as well. A subset of this involves a significant portion of the young female population, as their status in the family is enhanced when they become wage earners. Together with others seeking jobs in the cities, these young female migrants, by virtue of their fertility, will become part of a growing urban society in the region; within the next two decades, more than half the population of Pacific Asia will live in the city.

This migration contributes to the growth of mega-cities, placing huge burdens on infrastructure, resources, and the environment. By 2015, predications are that there will be twenty-three mega-cities in the region; nineteen of which will be in developing countries. This is a rapid change to the face of Asia, when we consider there were just three mega-cities in 1975, and that many still have an image of Asia as being predominantly agrarian.

A major challenge, therefore, is to develop an informed response to these changes and to implement effective management of urban settlements. China will be the country most tested in this respect. While the international community has focused attention on many of the issues, Yu believes that regional institutions must play their part and national governments will likely be the main actors to respond.

Trade and Investment

In the wake of the financial crisis, patterns of trade and investment in Pacific Asia have changed, as Okamoto Yumiko discusses in her chapter on regional economic arrangements. The period has been marked by, first, the rise of China as an economic power and, second, proposals for regional trade agreements, which although initially controversial are now being received favorably. Underlying these changes is the real and continuing need to strengthen the environment for trade and investment in Pacific Asia.

Countries in the region differed in their post-crisis economic record. Some managed to record strong growth before the worldwide U.S.-led downturn in late 2000. Others were unable to shrug off the ill effects of the crisis. Indonesia has perhaps suffered the most, but similar concerns were felt in the Philippines, Cambodia, Laos, Myanmar, and Vietnam. In a very different way, Japan—the once economic leader and model of the region—remained mired in a decade-long period of slow, if any, growth.

Where countries did do well post-crisis, the pattern of growth was brought about by domestic fiscal stimulus; a favorable export environ-ment led by electronics; competitive currencies after the 1997 devaluation; a boom in information technology; and intra-Asian investment by Japan and the NIEs. With the global slowdown and events of 9-11, the pattern of growth ended, especially for the IT sector, revealing the vulnerability of Asian economies to global business cycles and U.S. markets.

China, however, has stood out as an exception. China managed to avoid the financial crisis, in contrast to the miracle economies, and its economy has gone forward intact even in the face of the global slowdown and 9-11. The world now watches the rise of China as both an economic and political power. In Asia, the country seems to be the only bright spot. China fever has reached new heights. After a rocky period, U.S.-China relations seem to have improved. China hosted the APEC summit in 2001 with some success and is now a member of the World Trade Organization (WTO). Beijing will, in another vaunted symbolic gesture, host the Summer Olympics in 2008. Signs of success are evident in foreign direct investment (FDI) as well. Among the world's developing countries, China now attracts the lion's share of FDI, surpassing the Association of Southeast Asian Nations (ASEAN), the previous strongest magnet for FDI.

China's immense internal market has held the promise of continuing dynamic growth even amid the global slowdown. Accordingly, China provides both opportunities and challenges for its Asian neighbors. Its WTO membership opens up the Chinese market to Asian imports, on the one hand, but, on the other, it will also compete with its neighbors for exports to markets in the developed world—as well as for FDI. Another attraction of China is its pool of low-cost and lower-value-added labor, which competes directly with the labor force in Vietnam and Indonesia. The more developed regional economies—like Japan, Singapore, and Taiwan—are engaged in finding advantages and opportunities, as companies relocate much of their industrial activity to China.

It is conceivable that China's competitiveness—within the region and indeed with the rest of the world—will extend to sectors beyond the production-value chain. This is because of the differentiation among different centers in the country: cities like Shanghai and Hong Kong can compete with the world's leading cities as a hub for business, while coastal cities can compete for middle-value activities and inland areas can focus on lower-cost jobs. High technology and research-based activity in China also has considerable potential, given its core of well-educated, scientifically trained workers.

The challenge that faces countries in the region is how their economies—both present and hoped for—will fit with China's development. Early trade figures for some—Australia, Singapore, Malaysia, and even Thailand—suggest that they are already adjusting to and benefiting from

China's growth. Economic activity can, after all, be a win-win proposition. Other countries will have to consider similar strategies of cooperation as well as competition.

It is in this context that the second major trend in the region has emerged: bilateralism and subregionalism in trade and economic agreements. Some have already proceeded—the Japan-Singapore Economic Agreement for a New Age Partnership, the New Zealand–Singapore Free Trade Agreement, and the Singapore-Australia Free Trade Agreement. There are also discussions of regional and subregional arrangements—an ASEAN-China Free Trade Area is under negotiation, there are prospects that Japan will proceed with more bilateral agreements with selected Southeast Asian countries, and there is talk of an eventual East Asian or Northeast Asian free trade agreement.

These efforts are not necessarily incompatible with regional efforts that have been made through the APEC forum, nor are they always contrary to the global obligations of the WTO. Nevertheless, these bilateral and subregional efforts may betray some impatience or distrust of these processes.

APEC's collective voluntary liberalization and promotion of free trade through individual action plans failed due to Japanese reluctance to open up agricultural sectors. The initiative to open up APEC trade within the WTO framework also failed due to deep divisions between the United States and Japan. In this breach, Japan, Singapore, and South Korea sought to conclude bilateral free trade agreements of their own.

The flurry of free trade agreements in the region is the result of Pacific Asian countries, excluded from the North American Free Trade Agreement (NAFTA), scrambling to get into a bloc of their own. It has also seen the revival of the idea of an East Asian economic group, which was initially rejected by Japan and the United States. While the group may not now be feasible, the subregional and bilateral efforts may be building blocks for just such a regional agreement.

A regional free trade agreement affords maximum trading benefits. Basic to such an agreement is the mechanism it provides to maintain the momentum for free trade and to enable liberalization beyond the provision of WTO rules—and within a shorter period of time. But there are drawbacks as well: the proliferation of, and argument over, rules of different origins, as well as retaliation by disadvantaged nonparties to the agreement.

Clearly, Asians must give first priority to continuing the multilateral free trade initiatives under the WTO and the General Agreement of Tariffs and Trade (GATT). With the increasing global trade linkages and the open trading nature of many countries in Pacific Asia, this would be necessary and wise. The regional free trade agreements that are forged should be more proactive than negative; that is to say, rather than excluding nonparties to the agreement, they should embrace them progressively—on a kind of most-favored-nation basis.

A trading regime in East Asia may be unlikely in the short to medium term. A free trade area requires both extensive technical cooperation and strong political will. The European community found it had both, but in East Asia the time is not yet here, at least for the next decade. Before something of an East Asian economic group or an effective APEC free trade agreement can materialize, there remain such sticking points as the coordination of ASEAN countries' trade policies with China and the liberalization of Japanese and South Korean agricultural sectors. Until there are strong common interests, Okamato believes, there seems to be no strong incentive for a regional free trade area.

Nevertheless, we see that national policies on trade and investment have shifted in a number of leading economies in the region, others have followed, and regional cooperation (as well as competition) is increasing. In this context, the China-ASEAN free trade agreement and the expansion of the Japan-Singapore Economic Agreement for a New Age Partnership provide competing paradigms that can be healthy for all parties. While China-Japan rivalry may increase in the short term, the hope is that these disparate efforts may eventually encourage greater interdependence and cooperation between the two great Asian nations in a wider regional context.

Information and Communication Technology

In their chapter "Digital Dreams and Divergent Regimes," Jamus Jerome Lim and Yap Ching Wi find a clear, growing digital gap exists in the region between developing countries, on the one hand, and developed and newly industrialized economies, on the other. Regional efforts can assist in addressing this gap, but the elements that will be critical to the resolution of these differences are the policies of each country toward information and communication technology (ICT). For it is infrastructure at the national level as well as economic development that are fundamental to a country's ICT development.

In terms of infrastructure, developing countries have low Internet penetration and personal computer (PC) diffusion rates. When viewed on a national basis, even middle-level economies like Malaysia and the Philippines, which have sectors of strength in ICT, lag behind. E-commerce activity is similarly low or nonexistent in developing countries due to inadequate support infrastructure and a small pool of ICT manpower. Most developing countries have only a small ICT export base, if any.

Policies that foster the ICT sector are still lacking in many developing countries. This is the case in two main areas: enforcement of intellectual property rights and consolidated ICT education. Taken together, this deficiency translates into lower ICT literacy rates and higher levels of piracy, therefore triggering concerns among regional and international investors, and encouraging a downward spiral in the field. If a developing country wishes to have any chance at closing the digital gap, a national concept of ICT development is essential.

In comparison, the developed economies and NIEs of the region are quite well poised to take advantage of ICT. This is due not only to their overall economic development and income level, but also to coherently conceived blueprints, such as Japan's Global Information Infrastructure, Singapore's ICT 21, and Hong Kong's Digital 21. The upshot is that Japan and the NIEs have built an ICT infrastructure that has seen results in high rates of PC penetration and e-commerce activity. An example of governments' promoting ICT development may be seen in the adoption of ICT in their procurement procedures (business-to-government, known as B2G) and their provision of public services (government-to-consumer, known as G2C); this has spurred the private sector to go online, creating a critical mass of consumers and a market for e-commerce.

Because of strong policies regarding intellectual property rights, Japan and the NIEs are able to attract foreign investment and are major exporters of ICT products due to the existence of a large pool of literate ICT manpower. They also have vibrant ICT private sectors that capitalize on the ICT infrastructure; the research and development policies of South Korean chaebols and Taiwan's small- and medium-enterprise–led innovations in Taiwan are two such examples.

Why is there an urgency to close this digital gap in the region? ICT can be a tool for gains in national productivity in much the same way that the now-developed countries of the region put technology to their advantage during the 1980s and 1990s. It can be a tool for countries to make important progress economically, educationally, and in infrastructure.

The urgency is greater when one considers the ICT competition represented by China. Many parts of the giant economy of China show progress toward ICT development that is on a par with that of Japan and the NIEs. China has its pool of talent, and no less advanced are its infrastructure and its development policies. The shortcoming in China at the moment remains its failure to protect intellectual rights, which has been troubling for foreign investment in the sector. But this has not proved to be a complete roadblock, given China's other significant attractions. Moreover, protection of intellectual rights in China is expected to improve now that the country has acceded to the World Trade Organization as well as, in the medium to longer term, with the development of its own, indigenous software that will also seek to enjoy such protection.

A fundamental challenge for Asian governments in developing an ICT economy is manpower. Countries need to revamp their economic models to encourage inflows of human talent. Singapore and Hong Kong have taken steps in this direction, while other countries have remained cautious. Japan has been reluctant—a fact that has only slowly been addressed—but its shortfall in ICT talent has hampered its ICT development.

A second challenge lies in a country's education policy: the teaching of mathematics and science in particular need to be upgraded in many countries in the region. Japan and the NIEs have begun working on education reform, as have Thailand, Malaysia, and several mid-level economies. Others, however, have continued to focus on basic education for the masses and on more general education at tertiary levels; these social and political choices will have impact on ICT development.

The third challenge is for each state to promote a national innovation system that reaches into the workplace. Governments could help by efforts to coordinate science and technology policies, promote research and development, provide a sound legal framework, and develop venture capital financing for ICT.

Fourth, while ICT is a priority for economic development, there are also social dimensions that governments must address. The digital gap that exists between rural and urban dwellers could be diminished through welfare policies and educational opportunities, use of ICT's interconnectivity and real-time capabilities for communication, and new rules of engagement between the government and people at both global and national levels.

Fundamentally, however, just focusing on ICT will itself be a challenge to many developing Asian countries, given their many competing priorities since 1997. Yet doing so is critical because of the avenue toward the next stage of economic development that ICT affords.

International and intraregional assistance must be extended to assist developing countries in this regard. Japan's offer at the Group of Eight meeting in 2001 is a step in the right direction. The e-ASEAN effort at the subregional level is also promising. Efforts must also be made to bring in the private sector, which in many cases is working across borders for manufacture, as well as other aspects in the ICT sector. The economic interdependence of the region—in ICT, as in other fields—should be fostered and nurtured. In terms of human talent, capital, markets, and infrastructure, elements for information and communication technology in Asia Pacific are present. Lim and Yap also call for political cooperation to be extended to achieve these complementarities.

Environmental Protection and Sustainable Development

Over the past decades, many parts of East Asia have experienced fast economic growth. This fast growth, together with rapid urbanization and industrialization, has placed a strain on East Asia's environment. This, as discussed by Lebel in his chapter on environmental change and transitions to sustainability, has had a number of negative environmental consequences.

First, atmospheric emissions are on the rise. In Thailand, for example, sulphur dioxide emissions from the industrial sector doubled during the 1980s, while in Malaysia, sulphur and nitrogen oxides nearly doubled as emission of particulates increased threefold. Second, urbanization has become a coastal problem with rapid migration from upland rural areas to the major coastal cities. The infrastructure for water, electricity, and roads has struggled to keep pace with demographic and consumption changes.

Third, in order to feed the growing mega-cities, agriculture has expanded and intensified. This has resulted in widespread deforestation, commercial logging, and the increased use of pesticides, contributing to an increased vulnerability to floods and to losses of biodiversity. Fourth, environmental problems now extend to the sea, where there is overexploitation of fisheries and coastal ecosystems. Industrialization has led to chemical pollution in mangrove swamps. There has been not only pollution of water where fish thrive, but also shortages of potable water for human consumption. Among the needs of agriculture, industry, electricity generation, and the domestic sector, the competition for water is fierce. This problem is exacerbated by drought.

With these and other environmental problems looming, countries in the region need to act responsibly and expeditiously before the situation becomes irreversible. To anticipate what the future holds under various circumstances, Lebel's chapter employs a scenario analysis. For Pacific Asia, three scenarios are envisioned: "conventional worlds," which suggests continuity; "barbarization," which envisages fundamental and negative social change; or "great transitions," in which there is fundamental but positive social change. Under the "conventional worlds" scenario, Lebel pictures three variants: business as usual; policy reform, where attempts are made to address problems; and an Asian renaissance, which reasserts Asia-centeredness. None of these scenarios, however, portends fundamental change to the way things are now or the direction things seem to be heading.

Under the "barbarization" scenario, two variants that Lebel sees are "gated communities" in which the majority are affected but a small elite stands protected from the harms that arise, and "security collapse," in which the environmental, social, and economic foundations for the security of the state and the people living in it are undermined. Under the "great transitions" scenario, Lebel imagines that the change is positive: Local livelihoods are affirmed and real transitions to sustainability are made in society and the environment.

Trends have emerged in the region that can make an impact on how these scenarios play out. While decentralization and democratization seem to be on the rise, public access to information and involvement in planning processes is still limited and needs to be enhanced. Public disclosure of the environmental performance of companies is necessary and will help to ensure that society and the environment are both protected.

Attendant upon this is a growing interest in more comprehensively addressing the consequences of regional environmental issues. Lebel suggests this may betoken a future trend away from emphasis on military conflict and toward understanding notions of human rights and quality of life. With greater access to information, there are greater possibilities for learning from experience to improve environmental management.

Governance

The Asian crisis has been a watershed in thinking not only about economic activity, but also about governance in the region, as Ake Tangsupvattana demonstrates in his chapter. The causes of the East Asian crisis have made us rethink how economic globalization and cultural values interact. The crisis has also created opportunities for Asian reformers to challenge and change the old systems of governance in their countries. This has sometimes been in tandem with the reforms for good governance suggested by international financial institutions (IFIs). At other times, the two have been in tension, and domestic reformers have found the international agenda to be problematic. What many hope will emerge in the next two decades is an ongoing dialogue about good governance in the region.

The first factor that contributed to the economic crisis was economic globalization. This allowed rapid financial flows to take place in global markets. Far from perfect, the markets were shown to be volatile, unstable, irrational, and uncontrollable. The openness of Asian markets to capital flows, their interdependence, and the volatility of the global financial markets affected the state of Asian economies. So did, fundamentally, the way that capital was utilized domestically and the way government agencies sought to govern or influence markets.

Market failures, together with cultural values influencing the way Asians do business, created the financial crisis. For example, in the case of Thailand, capital inflows were misallocated to borrowers in a way associated with Thai cultural values. In another example, loans in South Korea exceeded 60 percent of the country's total external liabilities. The misallocation of funds in these two cases arose partly from Asia's Confucian tradition with its emphasis on *guanxi* (connections or relationships), which was twisted to encourage cronyism, nepotism, patron-client networks, and corruption.

In Southeast Asia, these values are often spread by overseas Chinese as well as by indigenous concepts of the rights of rulers. The colonial monopolies and distortions of power also did not help. In Northeast Asia, because of a Confucian heritage, many similar cultural roots were shared, resulting in paternalistic developmental states in Japan and Korea.

The misallocation of funds clearly indicated the want of good economic governance. In this sense, the financial crisis has created an opportunity for Asian countries to reform their economic sectors and to create structures for governance. Indeed, when the International Monetary Fund (IMF) offered its rescue package to aid the Asian countries struck by the financial crisis, good governance was a condition of assistance.

Good governance connotes certain values, like greater participation, transparency, openness, and accountability, that will help to deepen domestic democracy. Greater participation refers to the empowerment of nongovernmental organizations (NGOs), introduction of greater local autonomy, and reduction of state power. As a result, NGOs and local powers have arisen to challenge the old cultural values of the state, pressing it toward greater accountability. Indonesia is perhaps the clearest example of this. Such universal values must be incorporated in a vision of good governance for the region.

The danger for Asia at present is that the topic of governance remains only an issue for national audiences, if at all. Interstate commentary and interaction on the issue has generally been taboo. The only exception to this has been the actions of the IFIs during the Asian crisis, and this has been perceived as foreign intervention. International scrutiny over national governance was resisted by some even during the crisis and now faces more domestic resistance than ever.

It is therefore necessary to look beyond international efforts. We need to focus on the domestic roots and constituencies for the reform of governance. For this, Tangsupvattana urges that civil society, NGOs, and academics must play their part. They can help to make the public aware of governance in the private and public spheres. The effectiveness of NGOs is increased proportionately by globalization, and networks of NGOs and academic activists can thus be fostered. Localization, or the devolution of authority from the capitals, is another important measure that can help to weaken the state's cultural hegemony. If this succeeds, with the help of the media, people will become more aware of the economic situation and seek to curb excesses created at the local level. Such examples can be.built into effort at the national level.

Security

In his chapter on security in Pacific Asia, Yoon Young-Kwan addresses the changes that the end of the cold war brought to the environment of the region. There has been a rise in flashpoints and disagreements among states, and this has led to an increased level of mutual suspicion.

During the cold war, the United States played an important role, alongside South Korea, Japan, and China, as a deterrent to the former Soviet Union, but now that the threat has disappeared, the nature of the U.S. commitment to the region has changed from deterrent to stabilizer. The United States has many bilateral alliances with countries in Pacific Asia, and these alliances have filled the vacuum left by the lack of multilateral institutions, which would ordinarily provide the norms, rules, and standards regulating state behavior and international relations.

In the face of that lack, the ASEAN Regional Forum (ARF) was established in 1994 as a multilateral institution to address the security issues in Asia Pacific. It has been an important forum for dialogue, and this has helped build the confidence of its membership. However, the ARF is little more than a forum for dialogue, with limited influence on national behavior. This is a reflection of culture and the long tradition of noninterference in the internal affairs of another country to which most if not all states in the region adhere. But to defuse tensions and to increase cooperation, Yoon argues that Asia needs a more effective body, something in the order of the Commission on Security and Cooperation in Europe (CSCE).

Within Asia Pacific, there are ongoing events certain to affect significantly the region as a whole: the rapid rise of China's economy, Japan's search for a more responsible role, the volatility of North Korea, and political changes in Indonesia. The current bilateral alliances between the United States and individual Asian countries may not be equipped to address these regional events. If an effective multilateral institution existed to monitor developments, then the security of the region would be greatly enhanced.

Such an institution will have to complement the current bilateral security situation in Asia, where most security procedures are heavily skewed toward the United States. The disappearance of the Soviet threat, however, has reduced the incentive for China to cooperate with the United States. The U.S.-China relationship has also suffered from the inconsistency of different U.S. administrations. In the wake of the 9-11 events, however, the United States and China have improved their relationship through the war against terrorism, but how long this new relationship lasts is uncertain.

Perhaps by engaging the United States and by inducing China to join its ranks, a multilateral institution might be in the position to offer these two powers a forum for better cooperation. A multilateral institution might also help improve the strained relations between China and Japan. China remains suspicious of Japan, a feeling that has grown as Japan, with the end of the cold war, searches for a larger security role in the region.

At the moment, there are three main security concerns in Pacific Asia: the Taiwan Strait issue, North Korea, and terrorism. The most urgent of these is the third. Since 9-11, the region has been in the limelight due to the discovery of terrorist networks with ties to al Qaeda. Countries in the region have been resolute in their opposition to terrorist cells, taking strict measures against radical fundamentalist groups. Indonesia, having weak government will and fearing a Muslim backlash, has been the exception. Although the region is united in countering terrorism, most countries believe it prudent for individual countries to take the counter-terrorist initiative themselves, rather than to invite direct U.S. intervention. The major test is the coordination of individual governments' policies, as they all differ. Again, the need for a multilateral institution becomes evident. Of the existing institutions, ASEAN and the ARF seem best poised to strengthen collaborative counter-terrorist efforts.

Establishing a new multilateral institution will take time, energy, and political capital. Yoon suggests that it might therefore be expedient to extend the role and function of APEC, or ARF, and develop it into something akin to the Organization for Security and Co-operation in Europe (OSCE). At a time when current events have made countries predisposed to cooperate, such a proposal should be given serious consideration.

Regional Institutions

Finally, in my chapter on attempts at developing regional institutions, we arrive at the rising sense of East Asian identity today.

ASEAN leaders and their counterparts from China, Japan, and South Korea sent a strong signal at the informal ASEAN summit at the end of 1999. In the summit of 2000, the leaders agreed to upgrade their meeting to an East Asian summit. Functional cooperation is starting in different areas, most notably in finance. A system by which ASEAN countries exchange information and comment on each other's policies is being expanded to include China, Japan, and South Korea. In March 2000, finance ministers from these ASEAN + 3 countries agreed to stand by arrangements for currency swaps and to help each other in the event of sudden raids on their currencies.

Some academics and think tanks suggest further, grander measures. The idea of an Asian Monetary Fund, first proposed by Japan in the early days of the crisis and summarily dismissed by the United States and others, is being reconsidered. Some suggest that Asia should aim for a common currency and even adopt the vision of an East Asian union.

These developments point to something of a change. In the past decade, Asia Pacific has been the preferred framework. APEC embraced the United States, Canada, Australia, and New Zealand, in addition to Asian countries, in its design to build a community spanning the Pacific Rim for trade and other issues. In security, the ARF again included these countries as well as some further afield—Russia, the European Community, and India. Such inclusionary frameworks often involved more states than function would have suggested, but the broader groupings were favored.

East Asia was never seen as a group separate from others. The singular exception to this was the proposal by Malaysian Prime Minister Mahathir bin Mohamad for an East Asian Economic Grouping. This, like the Asian Monetary Fund more recently, was put aside in the face of U.S. objection and the doubt of some fellow Asians. At the subregional level, ASEAN united the nations of Southeast Asia. There was, however, little comparable cooperation among countries in Northeast Asia. A priori, cooperation was poor between Northeast Asia and ASEAN, and therefore in East Asia.

It is against this context that some have begun in this new millennium to speak of a "new" regionalism. This new regionalism is yet indefinite in longer-term purpose. Nor is its grouping definite. But there are fresh and different initiatives afloat. There is a general sense of East Asia as something that is broader than ASEAN and narrower than Asia Pacific. The ASEAN + 3 formula has taken a central place in this discussion, and pragmatic, step-by-step consultation and cooperation has begun in different sectors. But there is no clear overarching vision. Moreover, Asia has no strong history of unity and accepted commonality, whether in polity, culture, language, or religion. The antecedents of East Asian regionalism have been brief and contested.

Why then East Asia now? Several factors are at play. The first and most obvious is the economic crisis. Interdependence has come to be recognized, and the need for cooperation has, as such, grown. Regionalism, in this view, is a process for handling globalization. The crisis also generated frustration with APEC and the ARF for their lack of ready response, and the urge to find a better alternative. A related factor is Asian dissatisfaction with the IMF, the primary institution that responded to the crisis, which has led to complaints over the lack of Asian representation in global institutions. Another, and perhaps underlying, factor is Asia-U.S. relations. A final factor worth mentioning, although less significant, is the convening of the Asia-Europe Meeting (ASEM). This grouping brought together East Asians and their European counterparts in an inter-cultural dialogue between two regions. In this sense, ASEM is built upon the supposition that East Asia has some unity or identity.

But there are limits currently to any East Asian unity. The first major factor is the importance of the United States to the region as a whole and to individual countries in particular—in terms of both security and economics. The second factor is China-Japan relations, which are troubled by history and suspicion, notwithstanding the high levels of Japanese investment in China. Japan's amnesia about its role in World War II affects its ties to

Simon S. C. Tay

South Korea and ASEAN as well. ASEAN has chosen to stress a pragmatic and forward-looking emphasis on trade, investment, and other aspects of the relationship. To a far lesser extent, South Korea under President Kim Dae Jung also took steps toward a more normal reconciliation.

Japan's role in the region is further complicated by its own decade-long recession and mixed attempts at reform. Until the internal debate in Japan is decided, Japan's ability to contribute strongly to the leadership of the region must be doubted. Conversely, there is the suggestion that smaller and medium-sized countries, such as South Korea and members of ASEAN, may have a greater role to play than their size or strength might normally dictate.

From these observations, several principles for a new East Asian regionalism might be suggested: one, it should be an open and flexible caucus, not an exclusive group or bloc; two, it should emphasize functionality, not political fixity; three, leadership should be by issues, not by great powers; and four, leadership should be by coalitions of the willing.

If these principles are put to good effect, the result in East Asia will be considerably different from the European experience. This is not so much a failure of vision or an anti-European reaction. It is, instead, a recognition of existing realities in the politics and relationships among Asian states and a wish to take the initiative despite those realities. These efforts to bring the states of East Asia closer together will of course impact the other states of Pacific Asia which are left outside the nascent East Asian grouping of ASEAN + 3, like Australia and New Zealand. This need not be negative provided that the principles of flexibility, function, and openness are followed. In this way, East Asia can be part of the engine that drives processes in Pacific Asia and the wider Asia Pacific that includes the United States.

CROSS-CUTTING ISSUES AND THE X FACTOR

Looking at the diverse topics surveyed by the chapters in this book, a number of cross-cutting issues and concerns emerge about the region as a whole:

1. The growing gap between less and more developed countries in terms of their development;
2. The weakness of many national governments and systems of governance in responding appropriately to new regional trends and concerns;

3. The increasing competition between China and other economies, especially less developed economies, for trade and foreign direct investment;

4. The lack of integration and political coordination to deal with the increasing economic integration of the region, particularly in terms of trade and investment and in the movement of human talent across borders;

5. The region's continuing reliance on the United States for security and economic development;

6. The lack of shared understanding and leadership among countries; and

7. The weakness of institutions in dealing with regional issues and taking advantage of regional opportunities.

Pacific Asia, as such, seems less a region than a neighborhood of disparate countries, linked by little more than geography and problems. There is insufficient political vision and will in the region for the region. Nation-building concerns remain foremost, which is understandable, but this same focus contributes to neglect of the wider vista.

In many ways, national concerns should be paramount. We must put our own houses in order first.

However, the regional dimensions of assistance and cooperation can prove vital even on that level, and even as the challenges are large and overwhelming for some.

The years since the financial crisis have been intense. What happened was not simply a blip on the chart of growth. We cannot go back to what was before and resume operations as if the crisis had never occurred. Some things will not be the same again.

This debate about recovery is often made in terms of capital letters. In the crisis, we hoped for a V-shaped recovery. We feared the U shape, with its broader, and longer, low point. Even worse would have been an L-shaped pattern in which the region went down and never got up again. Looking at the economic indicators and the relatively short duration of the crisis, the V-shaped recovery seems to have been the kindly outcome for many in the region. But facing the continuing and new factors of uncertainty, we could add other capital letters. One of these is "W." Market fluctuations, W-shaped, which are often the response to external impacts, continue in Asia. Far too much depends on the United States, not enough on Pacific Asia itself, and as the United States responds to a sluggish economy and the imperative following 9-11 to combat terrorism, more fluctuations and turbulence must be anticipated.

Yet, we can take the analogy a letter further: to X. The letter X may be seen, in the context of Pacific Asia surveys, to represent the greater diversity and complexity that now exists among different countries, sectors, and enterprises. Some are headed downward and will stay down. Others may go down and then up. Still others will go up and keep going up. Globalization is proceeding apace and has not stopped for the Asian recovery. X is the current pattern not only because we are emerging from a crisis, but because we are entering a much more competitive global marketplace.

In this regard, there is unlikely to be an Asian miracle in which all or nearly all prosper. There are going to be winners, true. But, with globalization and more competition than ever, there will also be losers.

Winners and losers will, however, share the same societies and region. How we adjust and how we accommodate one another in a world of stark differences will be a challenge. For countries—which have not the legal protections of companies—cooperation is therefore critical. It is the essence of international relations. In ASEAN, member states range from the rich like Brunei and Singapore to some of the poorest countries in the world, like Laos. In East Asia, the distance between Tokyo and Pyongyang is as great. The Pacific Asian region and any framework that seeks to connect these states must address these contrasts.

The contrasts are not merely in gross domestic product, they are in the mindset—and in the underlying factors of technology, experience with globalization and marketplaces, and the ability and willingness to provide governance that is acceptable, accountable, and correct.

East Asia, Pacific Asia, and Asia Pacific

The early, easy predictions of an Asia Pacific community and an Asian century seem now to belong to history. Looking ahead through the present uncertainties, we see a future fraught with difficulty. Yet, sketching regional futures for Pacific Asia is a risk that we must take.

Unless we actively seek out such longer-term views, we will be unable to raise our heads above the immediate exigencies and tasks. We may lose out on opportunities to link the immediate and shorter-term concerns to themes and processes that can help shape the medium and longer term. The future decades should not simply be the sum total of days, months, and years. Emerging trends can and should provide cardinal points for analysis and planning for the future. And in our particular case, by taking proactive steps, we recognize and strengthen this new sense of a region.

It is true that challenges to cooperation in the region are being magnified in the world of starker differences and global competition. But this only emphasizes the need for greater institutionalization of East Asia and the Pacific countries of Australia and New Zealand. This may not square with the idea of the Asia Pacific as a single community on both sides of the ocean, but this is not intended as a rejection of that vision. A change in conception is necessary if Asian and Pacific countries are to be full partners in Asia Pacific.

In this, one of the prerequisites for an Asia Pacific future is to have a Pacific Asia future, with a greater institutionalization in East Asia and, in certain modalities, with the Pacific countries of Australia and New Zealand. This suggestion draws from recent trends and developments. It also draws from recent initiatives with minilateral and bilateral arrangements that cut across established regional and subregional arrangements.

Asia Pacific is, in this view, no longer a singular, driving frame of reference, but one that can and must accommodate regional, subregional, and bilateral arrangements. While this departs from views of Asia Pacific as a single community, as APEC has held out, there is no suggestion that institutionalism and regionalism in East Asia and Pacific Asia should displace the wider Asia Pacific ideal. Rather, it holds out the possibility of synergy, where smaller groupings and arrangements assist the broader, overarching Asia Pacific reference point as parts of a variable geometry in the region.

Notes

1. Paul Krugman's article in *Foreign Affairs* in the mid-1990s was perhaps the first well-known question mark over Asia. Krugman's doubts, however, centered on the lack of increases from productivity as measured by total factor production (TFP) and wrote off the growth as stemming from Soviet-style infusion of resources and capital. It neither identified the trigger to the crisis nor the underlying factors, such as cronyism, corruption, and nepotism.
2. The kind assistance of Lim Tai Wei, researcher at the Singapore Institute of International Affairs, in providing a first summary of the draft chapters in this volume is gratefully acknowledged.

2

A Vision of Demographic Changes in Pacific Asia

Yu Xuejun

Population is among the development issues that will be of global concern in the twenty-first century. The demographic changes in the Pacific Asian region—which in this chapter includes the ten member countries of the Association of Southeast Asian Nations (ASEAN), China, Japan, South Korea, Australia, and New Zealand—will have a crucial impact on global socioeconomic development, because not only of its large share of the world population, but also its rapidly changing population size, structure, and distribution associated with modernization and globalization. In the past decades, the population of this region has undergone substantial change in growth and structure; large parts have been successful in the reduction of fertility and mortality. Several countries have undergone this demographic transition, accompanied by population aging, while in many others both fertility and mortality rates remain high. Levels of urbanization and growth of the urban population also vary across these countries.

The diversity of the population situation in different countries has sparked a variety of population-related problems in the new century. This chapter aims to provide a vision of demographic changes over the next two decades by examining the trends of population growth, population migration, and population aging in the region.

POPULATION GROWTH

Population and health policies, and through them public sector health and family planning programs, have had a major influence in the shaping of the region's demographic transformation (Asian Development Bank

1997). In sharp contrast with the earlier fertility decline in Europe, which was a "natural" process driven by socioeconomic development without governmental intervention, in Pacific Asia governments played a leadership role through population policy, particularly population and family planning programs—although the importance of policies and programs was by no means the same throughout the region. Meanwhile, rapid economic growth and an improvement in health, particularly the decline in infant and child mortality, helped to promote and reinforce the desire for smaller families.

Thanks to socioeconomic development and the success of family planning programs in the region, fertility, as measured by the total fertility rate (TFR), has declined substantially over the past several decades. The overall figures for the region in 2000 hide the differences among countries, however. TFRs vary considerably: from 1.3 births per woman in Japan and 1.5 births per woman in Singapore to 5.0 births per woman in Cambodia and Laos. In China, the 2000 total fertility rate was 1.80, a drop from 5.81 in 1970 (see table 1).

In 2000, the population of the world reached 6.1 billion; in Pacific Asia, the population was more than 2 billion, or about one-third. The region includes China, with the world's largest population at 1.27 billion, as well as Japan and Indonesia, each with a population that exceeds 100 million.

Table 1. Selected Demographic Indicators in Pacific Asia, 2001

	Annual Growth Rate (%)	Crude Birth Rate (%)	Crude Death Rate (%)	Total Fertility Rate (%)	Life Expectancy at Birth	
					Males	Females
China	0.8	14.9	7.0	1.8	69	73
Japan	0.2	9.4	7.8	1.3	77	84
South Korea	0.8		5.3	1.5	71	78
Brunei	2.3	22.3	2.8	2.7	74	76
Cambodia	2.5	35.9	10.7	5.0	54	59
Indonesia	1.3	20.8	7.2	2.4	65	69
Laos	2.3	36.5	13.1	5.0	53	55
Malaysia	2.0	24.4	4.4	3.1	70	75
Myanmar	1.3	24.2	11.7	3.0	60	59
Philippines	1.9	26.7	5.3	3.3	68	72
Singapore	3.2	12.8	4.5	1.5	76	80
Thailand	1.0	16.1	6.0	1.8	71	76
Vietnam	1.3	20.2	6.6	2.4	66	71
Australia	1.2	13.3	6.8	1.8	76	82
New Zealand	0.8	14.6	6.9	1.9	74	80

Source: UNESCAP (2001).

Yu Xuejun

By the year 2020, the population of another two countries will surpass 100 million—the Philippines and Vietnam (see table 2).

Table 2. Population Size and Growth Rate in Pacific Asia, 1990–2020

	Population (100,000)				Average Annual Rate of Growth		
	1990	2000	2010*	2020*	1990–2000	2000–2010*	2010–2020*
China	1,155,305	1,277,558	1,372,920	1,454,462	1.0	0.7	0.5
Japan	123,537	126,724	127,315	123,893	0.3	0.0	-0.3
South Korea	42,869	46,844	49,976	51,893	0.9	0.6	0.4
Brunei	257	328	384	436	2.4	1.6	1.2
Cambodia	8,652	11,168	13,250	15,545	2.6	1.7	1.6
Indonesia	182,812	212,107	238,012	262,291	1.5	1.2	1.0
Laos	4,152	5,433	6,965	8,757	2.7	2.5	2.3
Malaysia	17,845	22,244	25,919	29,254	2.2	1.5	1.2
Myanmar	45,520	45,611	50,903	55,960	1.2	1.1	0.9
Philippines	60,687	75,967	90,544	102,404	2.2	1.8	1.2
Singapore	3,016	3,567	3,885	4,091	1.7	0.9	0.5
Thailand	55,595	61,399	66,511	70,975	1.0	0.8	0.6
Vietnam	66,689	79,832	90,764	102,532	1.8	1.3	1.2
Australia	16,888	18,886	20,615	22,321	1.1	0.9	0.8
New Zealand	3,360	3,862	4,207	4,540	1.4	0.9	0.8

Source: United Nations (1999a).
* UN forecast figures.

Population size will continue to grow in the next twenty years as the TFR of some countries is higher than the replacement level (2.1 births per woman). Even in countries with low fertility, the population will continue to grow mainly because of population momentum rather than a high fertility rate. According to projections by the United Nations, the population of the region in the year 2020 will be more than 2.30 billion, a growth of about 300 million people from the current level. In this period, only Japan's population growth will turn negative, but the growth rate of all countries is expected to decline rapidly.

For countries at very different stages of demographic transition—from high to low levels of fertility and mortality—policies have needed to address population issues differently. Given the varying situations of growth, three kinds of policies were adopted. The low birth rates in Japan and Singapore have resulted in population aging and labor shortages, and the governments have introduced pro-natalist policies to encourage couples to have more children. In contrast, with high fertility levels in Cambodia, Indonesia, Laos, Malaysia, the Philippines, and Vietnam, policies have implemented national family planning programs to control births. China, South Korea, Brunei, Myanmar, Thailand, Australia, and New Zealand are satisfied with their fertility levels, and their governments are making efforts to stabilize the current birth rates.

The successful demographic transition in this region is, of course, associated with the stunning economic and social changes that have occurred during the same period. There were big rises in real incomes and massive reductions in poverty levels as the region's economies shifted away from nearly total reliance on agriculture to emphasis on modern, urban-based industries. Big social changes occurred alongside spectacular economic growth. These have included, in particular, the spread of basic education and the rise in literacy levels. At the same time, it is hardly an exaggeration to say that the region's demographic transformation has made a significant contribution to what can be called the Asian miracle (Leete and Alam 1999).

Although the demographic transition in some countries has been accomplished, in others it is still underway. The bonus of the demographic changes cannot be taken for granted. The financial and economic crisis of 1997 had the impact of interrupting and reversing economic growth and social development throughout the region. But among countries, the effects differed sharply. They were most marked in Indonesia, which suffered the most dramatic economic collapse, and in Thailand. Elsewhere, reflecting the interdependence of countries in the global economy, even countries not directly affected by the crisis experienced indirect effects through, for example, loss of trade and investment. As economic downturns tend to affect the social sectors disproportionately, the declining exchange rates and substantial reductions in government budgets saw a curtailment of reproductive health programs, including family planning programs, and setbacks in efforts to address problems in the quality of care (United Nations and Australia National University 1998). In sum, the crisis exposed the vulnerability of the social sectors. Population problems persist in several parts of Asia, and strengthening the provision of basic social services, particularly for poor countries, remains a challenge.

INTERNAL AND INTERNATIONAL MIGRATION

The pattern of changes in population mobility has been correlated with demographic as well as other transitions associated with modernization. The issue of domestic and international migration has been widely recognized as a vital element in the development process, both influencing and being influenced by development. For many countries and regions, international migration is also a component influencing population growth and socioeconomic programs. Consequently, issues related to international migration have been in the international agenda for many years.

Migration is an outcome of economic and political change. Economic growth creates disparities in wealth among countries and among areas within countries. These disparities stimulate movement from places of limited opportunity to areas with greater opportunity. Other migration flows, such as refugee movements between countries or movements of displaced persons within countries, result from political conflict. The emergence of substantial income differentials provides an incentive for relocation to a particular area, within or without a country. This is reinforced by demographic transitions, which affect population growth and age distribution and thereby, other factors remaining the same, per capita income and unemployment rates.

Internal Migration and Urbanization

Although international migration gets the most attention in this region, migration within countries constitutes the majority of movement. Generally speaking, the characteristics of internal migration as concerns this chapter can be stated thus: internal migration in countries in Pacific Asia is increasing; the mainstream of internal migration is from rural to urban areas; temporary migration is increasing; and migration flows include a significant proportion of young females.

Internal migration facilitates the process of economic and social development because it contributes to urban growth, provides much of the workforce for industrial expansion, and increasingly permits women to participate in development. In the region, net rural-to-urban migration accounts for roughly half the urban population growth, with the remainder deriving from natural increase and the reclassification of rural areas to urban areas as they become more densely settled.

In several countries, the migration rates of females are growing faster than those of males. Females predominate in all internal migration in the Philippines, South Korea, and Thailand (especially Bangkok). Women migrate as the result of a decision taken autonomously, by themselves or by the family, as their status in the family is usually enhanced by their becoming wage earners.

Rural-to-urban migration has consequences for the development of both rural and urban areas because of the particular characteristics of the migrants. They are usually younger and better educated. Most move in order to seek employment. As such, they constitute a valuable addition to the labor force in the cities. However, to the extent that rural-to-urban migrants are better educated and more ambitious than those who do not move, the pattern becomes a drain on useful human resources in rural areas and has detrimental effects on rural development.

Although the proportion of urban population in the region is lower than the world average, both urbanization—the percentage of the population living in urban areas—and urban growth—expansion of both population and land area—have been accelerating over the last three decades. In less developed countries, the urban population will continue to grow more rapidly than in developed countries where urban growth is already slowing down. In the next twenty years, there will be a large share of population added to the urban areas. China alone will account for the rural-to-urban movement of over 300 million people.

At the regional level, and assuming only negligible reclassification, the growing significance of population mobility can be seen in the marked increase in rural-to-urban migration as a component of urban growth over the past decades. Studies show that migration can help to alleviate rural poverty. Authorities need to bear this benefit in mind when they attempt to introduce policies that might act to restrict population mobility. Policies that accept the wider mobility of the population are likely to accord with policies that enhance the well-being of greater numbers of people (Skeldon 1997).

Currently, more than 50 percent of the population in the region lives in rural areas. Table 3 shows that the level of urbanization ranges from a low of 16 percent in Cambodia to a full 100 percent in Singapore. On the whole, the growth of the urban population will remain high, and urban society will expand. In the next two decades, it is expected that more than half of the region's population will be urban citizens.

This movement, however, will vary from one part of the region to the other. Levels of urbanization cannot be expected to increase significantly in Japan, South Korea, Singapore, Australia, and New Zealand; levels there are equivalent to those of most industrialized countries in the world where stabilization is observed to occur above the level of 70 percent. For other countries in this region, the concentration of populations in urban areas will be an integral part of development. The natural growth of populations generally remains moderate to high, and urban growth will be fueled by both migration and natural increase, as well as by the reclassification of rural areas to urban centers.

Table 3. Urban Population

	Urban Population in 2001 (%)	Annual Growth Rate (%)	Projected Urban Population in 2025 (%)
China	33	2.4	47
Japan	79	0.3	84
South Korea	82	1.5	90
Brunei	73	2.6	81
Cambodia	16	4.3	29
Indonesia	42	3.8	61
Laos	24	4.9	39
Malaysia	58	3.0	71
Myanmar	28	2.8	43
Philippines	59	3.3	72
Singapore	100	3.2	100
Thailand	22	2.6	36
Vietnam	24	3.6	30
Australia	85	1.0	88
New Zealand	86	1.1	89

Source: UNESCAP (2001).

The Growth of Mega-Cities

The rapid growth of mega-cities and their management will be a major challenge around the world, and particularly in this region, in the coming years. In the twenty-first century, half the world population will be living in an urban environment for the first time in history. New waves of techno-economic paradigms are replacing old production systems and reshaping metropolitan centers in both industrialized and developing countries. A major challenge for the international community is, therefore, to develop an informed response to such unprecedented population, economic, and technological changes in the management of urban settlements.

Mega-cities are a recent addition to the world population scene. They are popularly associated with a wide range of environmental, social, and economic problems and are seen by planners and city dwellers alike as providing the context for a poor quality of life (Bose 1992). Rapid development will place huge burdens on the infrastructure, resources, and environment of these cities. The negative consequences of such rapid urban growth and over-urbanization have been observed in areas surrounding cities as well as within cities. The mega-changes to the Pacific Asian urban system, however, are yet to come. The United Nations predicts large increases to the already bulging populations. In 1975, only five cities worldwide had ten million or more inhabitants, of which three were in developing countries. By 2015, the number will increase to twenty-three, of which all but four will be in developing countries (see table 4).

Table 4. Cities with Populations of 10 Million or More (in millions)

2000		2015	
Tokyo	26.4	Tokyo	26.4
Mexico City	18.1	Bombay	26.1
Bombay	18.1	Lagos	23.2
São Paulo	17.8	Dhaka	21.1
Shanghai	17.0	São Paulo	20.4
New York	16.6	Karachi	19.2
Lagos	13.4	Mexico City	19.2
Los Angeles	13.1	Shanghai	19.1
Calcutta	12.9	New York	17.4
Buenos Aires	12.6	Jakarta	17.3
Dhaka	12.3	Calcutta	17.3
Karachi	11.8	Delhi	16.8
Delhi	11.7	Metro Manila	14.8
Jakarta	11.0	Los Angeles	14.1
Osaka	11.0	Buenos Aires	14.1
Metro Manila	10.9	Cairo	13.8
Beijing	10.8	Istanbul	12.5
Rio de Janeiro	10.6	Beijing	12.3
Cairo	10.6	Rio de Janeiro	11.9
		Osaka	11.0
		Tianjin	10.7
		Hyderabad	10.5
		Bangkok	10.1

Source: United Nations (2000).

In Pacific Asia, rapid growth of the urban population has resulted in the formation of mega-cities, defined by the United Nations as cities with eight million or more people (United Nations 1991). In 1950, there were only two cities, London and New York, with more than eight million people. Ten years later these two cities were joined by Tokyo and Shanghai, and ten years after that, an additional six cities, namely Mexico City, Buenos Aires, Los Angeles, Paris, Beijing, and São Paulo, had reached that threshold. The number of mega-cities has continued to increase since that time. Pacific Asia contains the largest number of mega-cities of any geographical region.

High population growth rates have fueled the growth of large urban areas and contributed to a distinctive demographic structure of mega-cities. This structure is characterized by a young population, with a high proportion of females of reproductive age. The impact of population change on the growth of large cities cannot be divorced from economic issues.

Yu Xuejun

The emergence of mega-cities is partly an outcome of paths of economic development being pursued around the world. These patterns of economic growth have made an impact on the pace of population growth and on the spatial distribution of the population.

Although population growth rates have fallen throughout much of the developing world, especially in East Asia and Southeast Asia, the effects of past high rates of population growth have resulted in an age structure that contributes to high rates of migration. Other changes, including lowered fertility and older age at marriage, are associated with high rates of female migration into the large cities of the region. The result is that mega-cities, even with their lower rates of fertility compared with rural areas, have an age-gender structure conducive to population growth.

When the mega-cities' share of the urban population around the world is examined, the differences between developed and developing countries are very clear. Among the mega-cities in developed countries, it is rarely that one sees one with more than 20 percent of the national urban population, but in developing countries, many mega-cities exceed this figure. Bangkok contains over half of the urban population of Thailand.

The great achievements in curbing population growth in many Pacific Asian countries is already being felt in reduced pressure of population on the growth of urban centers—and in particular the growth of mega-cities. That the effect is not as pronounced as might be expected, given the rapid decline in fertility, can be explained by the demographic sources of growth of urban centers. Urban growth is primarily a result of natural increase and migration. As both these processes are most strongly affected by the number of young adults, especially females, in the population, a reduction in fertility requires at least a generation before it has significant impact on urban growth. Only now are some developing countries starting to see reductions in the numbers of young adults. It is among these that the probability of migration is highest, particularly to large urban centers. It is also among these that family formation begins. The migration of young females to urban places sets up the potential for two forms of growth. The first is that associated with migration; the second is the contribution of migrants to natural increase.

In the long term, reductions in population growth can be expected to have a beneficial effect on mega-cities by reducing the pace of growth. Efforts to reduce fertility can therefore be justified on these grounds and as regards more traditional concerns for welfare and the economy. In the more immediate term, while the effects of past levels of high fertility continue to be experienced, efforts need to be made to make contraceptive services available to female migrants. As levels of urbanization increase, the main source of growth of mega-cities will be through natural increase, a significant proportion of which will result from the fertility of female migrants from rural areas; it makes sense that they should constitute a target group for the delivery of contraceptive services.

Mega-cities will get larger as improvements in communication and transport infrastructure allow primate cities—that is, cities twice as large as any other in the country—to transform large areas of rural hinterland into suburbs. Even with a stationary population, countries with relatively low levels of urbanization can expect to experience increased urbanization and attendant increases in the size of urban centers. With the impetus for increased centralization of economic activities in many developing countries, this will also mean the growth of mega-cities. Reductions in population growth will make it easier for governments to accommodate the increasing numbers of people in these large cities and ultimately will result in mega-cities of a smaller size.

The rapid growth of cities in developing countries in the region presents a dilemma. Cities historically have been centers of industry and commerce and magnets for millions of people. Today, however, the sheer size of cities and the rapid, continuing influx of urban migrants cast doubt on the ability of cities to provide improved standards of living. Cities in Pacific Asia are centers of both hope and despair: while being engines of economic and social development they are also congested centers of poverty and environmental deterioration.

While there is no evidence that a threshold population size exists beyond which cities generate more negative than positive effects for their countries, in many cities the rapid pace of population growth and the enormous size of the population have overwhelmed the capacity of municipal authorities to respond. Overpopulation in the cities of developing countries has strained the ability of government to meet people's basic needs for shelter, water, food, health, and education.

Still, people keep moving to cities. For all their problems, big cities in developing countries continue to be centers of economic activity, offering more potential than most rural areas can. If cities are not able to cope with the influx, however, poverty and hopelessness could become widespread, leading to rising discontent and civil unrest.

Yu Xuejun

International Migration

With the rapid demographic changes, the major concern in Pacific Asia has shifted from fertility to population movement, particularly the movement from one country to another, that is, international migration. It is an issue that is likely to be the subject of intense political debate and have a profound impact on societies and economies throughout the region (Skeldon 1992).

The causes of international migration are, generally, the disparities in development among countries in the region and beyond, and the relationship between development and fertility decline. Numerically, the most important migration flows are toward the most developed regions, although not necessarily from the least developed regions. All the most developed areas, both in and outside the region, have undergone the demographic transition to low levels of fertility. All are concerned about the present and future growth of their labor forces, and, hence, there is a growing demand for labor from outside the region and increasingly from within. This is the principal force behind international migration in Asia Pacific, a force that, once started, tends to take on a momentum of its own, with migration leading to further migration as family ties build.

Hugo (1996) has observed a labor market in the region based on transfers of labor among countries, partially as neighboring countries have very different demographic structures. China, the Philippines, and Vietnam are major sources of out-migrants. Although both Malaysia and Thailand still export labor, mainly to Singapore and the economies of Northeast Asia, they have also emerged as significant destinations for migration as their demand for cheap labor has outstripped local supply. It is estimated that there are more than one million foreign laborers in Malaysia, the majority coming from Indonesia, and also over one million in Thailand, the majority coming from Myanmar; the more highly skilled workers come from India, Pakistan, and the Philippines (Chalamwong 1996). Many of the unskilled workers out-migrating are illegal, with no protection against abuse or the non-payment of wages.

Other countries are magnets of net in-migration. Japan, South Korea, Singapore, Australia, and New Zealand are facing declining labor forces and need to add working-age populations by accepting migrants from neighboring countries and areas. Much of this movement to the developed economies of the region, while legal initially, has become illegal, as many have overstayed their visas. The admission of large numbers of migrants who are culturally distinct has had profound social, political, and economic implications for the host countries.

Within the region, it is important to distinguish between legal and illegal migration, long-term and contract-labor migration, as well as labor migration and refugee movements. Much of the long-term migration is of migrants leaving for settlement in countries such as Australia and New Zealand. These migration streams have included large numbers of migrants from developing economies such as Malaysia and the Philippines, most of whom are legal, migrating not only for labor, but also for business and study. Substantial numbers of students also study outside the region. However, it is labor migrants on short-term contracts and undocumented migrants who constitute the main flows (Guest 1999).

Historically, in the latter part of the twentieth century, contract-labor migration involving the region was to oil-rich countries such as Saudi Arabia and Kuwait (Huguet 1995). But the destination has since shifted to the rapidly developing economies of East Asia and Southeast Asia, such as Brunei, Japan, and Singapore. The countries that have relied most heavily on the export of contract labor—Indonesia, Malaysia, the Philippines, and Thailand—experienced rapid economic growth during the 1980s and 1990s. It was assumed that they were well on the way to a migration "turnabout," where they would begin to import labor instead, as was evidenced by the large flows of undocumented migrants into Malaysia and Thailand during the 1990s. However, in the wake of the 1997 economic crisis there have been calls for the forced repatriation of undocumented migrants and government initiatives to increase the number of contract migrants going overseas (Skeldon 1999).

It is undocumented migrants who most concern the countries that import labor. Their numbers are difficult to assess. Martin (1996) notes that, although the number of undocumented workers in East Asian economies such as Japan and South Korea is high, it is dwarfed by the number in Malaysia and Thailand. In 1997, approximately one million undocumented foreign workers, mostly Indonesians, were estimated to be in Malaysia. The estimate for Thailand is approximately one million as well, with most coming from Myanmar.

Over the last half-century, Asia Pacific has been the site of large involuntary migrations. Some have comprised refugees, with host governments going to great lengths to limit interaction between these people and the local population. The flows of migrants from Vietnam in the 1970s and 1980s and from Cambodia during the 1980s represent such refugee movements, although they undoubtedly included some who were migrating solely for economic reasons. Other large-scale displacements, such as of Laotians to Thailand, and of Burmese and members of ethnic minorities to Thailand from Myanmar, often combine features of both labor migration and refugee movements.

In general, males dominate international migration flows in the region, but there are exceptions. The migration of contract labor from Indonesia and the Philippines includes as many or more women than men. The women work mainly as domestic servants, and a large number of Philippine women also go abroad as "entertainers." The emergence of East Asia and Southeast Asia as migrant destinations has also contributed to increasing the proportion of female workers. The development of these migration networks will help to reduce the risks of migration and can be expected to contribute further to female international migration (Gulati 1993; Guest 1999).

International migration and the management of labor migration are now acknowledged as one of the central issues facing governments and nongovernmental organizations worldwide. The International Labour Organization (ILO) indicates some five million to seven million migrant workers and their dependents outside their countries of origin across the continent of Asia, and another eight million to nine million in the Middle East, the majority from Asia (International Labour Organization 2002).

The issue of cross-border migration affects not only lower-value workers but also higher-value skilled workers and professionals. In the more industrialized countries, shortages in skills to sustain the rapid growth of the new knowledge-based industries have led doors to open wide to professional immigrants, but across Asia there are legal and social obstacles to the freer movement of skilled workers. For example, Japan is facing a shortage of information and communications technology (ICT) workers but legal and social constraints block their entry. In comparison, Singapore is pursuing a U.S.-style policy to allow, and even encourage, skilled foreigners to work and settle in the country.

Patterns of migration are creating new economic and social relations in Pacific Asia, and these patterns form an integral part of the process of globalization. The migration systems are reinforcing and redefining trade and political linkages, which will have consequences reaching far into the twenty-first century. While policies designed to foster economic and social relations are encouraged, often through the efforts of regional bodies, migration policies typically go the other way, restricting the movement of migrants.

A Vision of Demographic Changes

An increasing number of governments have recognized the need to establish, modernize, or improve their legislation, policies, practices, and administrative mechanisms to address migration issues, particularly labor migration. However, in many cases, migration policies clash with the interests of the increasing economic and political integration of the region. Accordingly, increasing political and social tensions between countries of emigration and host countries have been observed in the region.

The current migrations within Pacific Asia are largely the product of forces beyond the control of any single government. They are part of the processes of globalization. A slowing of economic growth and economic restructuring will have an impact on international migration. But the increasing political, trade, and aid ties among countries will contribute to higher levels of migrant flows, and economic interdependence within the region will lead to an increased level of international migration.

THE AGING OF POPULATIONS

With rapidly changing population dynamics underway, problems related to the aging of populations are now emerging. Because the majority of the world's older persons (defined as aged sixty or over) live in Asia, these problems are, with reason, attracting greater policy attention.

The two phenomena of declining fertility and the consequent aging of populations are likely to be the most significant demographic developments in Asia during the past half century and the half century to come. Their implications for social and economic life are far-reaching and profound. But while the two phenomena are inextricably linked, with the reduction in birth rates driving the aging of the population, government planners and policy makers typically view them quite differently. Most countries in Asia have not only welcomed lower fertility but actively encouraged it through family planning programs and other such measures. In contrast, population aging and the increase in the number of older persons have been viewed unfavorably, mainly because they are perceived as burdens requiring economic support and health care, hence a "crisis" to be averted (World Bank 1994).

No country in Pacific Asia is likely to escape the substantial aging of its population sometime during this century. A transition from high to low levels of fertility is the main demographic cause of population aging, and it is inconceivable that any country can indefinitely maintain high fertility in the context of modern low mortality levels. To do so would lead to continuing levels of population growth that would be unsustainable. Indeed, fertility is either currently falling or has already reached low levels in most countries in the region. Nevertheless, among these countries there is marked diversity in the trend of fertility and, to a lesser extent, mortality. Thus, there will also be considerable diversity in the timing, and perhaps level, of population aging. By 2050, China, Japan, South Korea, Singapore, and Thailand are anticipated to have between 30 percent and 40 percent of their populations aged sixty or over. Cambodia and Laos will have reached only half those levels (United Nations 1999b).

In contrast, it is a universal demographic inevitability that the absolute numbers of older persons will grow, even where aging may be relatively slow in occurring. In many respects, it is this numerical growth that is of prime importance for social and economic programs in the short and intermediate terms.

As planners and policy makers focus their attention on the aging of populations, they might also study the changing social and demographic characteristics of the old-age group. Not only are such changes traceable in the past but, based on the principle of cohort succession, projecting the changing composition of the elderly in the future is a rather straightforward exercise. These projections make clear that the elderly of the coming decades will be quite different from their counterparts in the last decades of the twentieth century. For example, the elderly of the not-too-distant future will be more literate, better educated, more likely to have urban experiences, and to have fewer living adult children than the elderly of the current generation. These changes in composition have important implications for the demands the elderly will pose for health care and formal and informal support, independent of just their increasing numbers.

But the numbers of elderly people in the population alone should make governments realize that aging issues cannot be discounted as matters of small importance. Rapid economic development, with concomitant social and structural changes that the majority of the countries have been experiencing in the last few decades, strongly indicates that the long-time tradition of family care for the elderly can no longer be assumed. Governments need now to adopt a proactive attitude toward population aging, to view the welfare of their older citizens as equally important as that of other members of society, as well as to facilitate and strengthen family support.

To some extent, reduced fertility, which is the major determinant of population aging, also reduces the ability of the family to care for older persons.

Bearing fewer children means fewer potential sources of economic support for parents as they age. The increasing levels of migration, from changing economic structures, will tend only to exacerbate this situation.

Resolutions, Policy Implications, and Suggestions

Thanks to socioeconomic development and the success of family planning programs over the past three decades, fertility in countries of Pacific Asia has declined rapidly. But holding down population growth does not mean an end to the population problem. On the contrary, in the new century population issues will become more complicated. The population will not only continue to grow, but will also age and move. Problems concern not only the size of the population, but also its structure and distribution. In response to these demographic problems, governments in this region must strengthen their cooperation and coordination.

Promoting Public Policy on Population and Health

It is clear that population policies need to address issues differently since countries are at very different stages of the demographic transition from high to low fertility and mortality. While some countries make efforts to reduce population growth, others will need to adjust the functions of their population and family planning programs and address issues of health, particularly as the pattern of causes of death has come to resemble that of Western societies, with diseases of the circulatory system and various forms of cancer now dominant. Moreover, the rapid spread of the HIV/AIDS pandemic in many parts of the region will, if it continues unabated, make it difficult to maintain increases in average survival. As elsewhere in the world, the containment of HIV/AIDS requires urgent action by governments and nongovernmental organizations to provide an appropriate range of education and services to prevent further transmission.

Developing Internal and International Migration Policy

The next two decades will see an overall shift in the region toward more urban societies. The policy requirements related to migration will vary from one part of the region to another, and it is important that these should be formulated according to specific needs and capabilities so that they fit the particular pattern of urbanization and migration in each region.

The mobility of the region's populations is increasing as large numbers have moved from rural to urban areas, particularly in the demographic giants China and Indonesia. Policy makers will have to address issues brought on by these migrations. The patterns and impact will vary from country to country, but across the region urbanization and migration are certain to have profound social, economic, and ultimately political consequences. A clear trend is the growth of mega-cities, requiring urban planning by governments on a size and complexity never before seen.

International migration, while providing economic benefits for migrants as well as out- and in-migrating countries, has seen heightened tension among migrant and non-migrant groups. There is, furthermore, concern about the relationship between cross-border movements and the spread of disease, particularly HIV/AIDS. As intraregional migration is often associated with processes of globalization, which integrate the economies of countries, there is a need to seek regional solutions to these problems.

Meeting the Challenges of Population Aging

It is clear that, in the face of significantly changing demographic scenarios, the long-term development planning of countries in Pacific Asia must address the need for increased social support services, such as health care, housing and educational facilities, and the labor force. Following the Vienna International Plan of Action on Ageing, which was endorsed by the United Nations in 1982, the developmental impact of aging on society must be recognized, complementing the conventional approach to aging as just a humanitarian or "welfare" concern. A shift toward a population with a high proportion of old people, a declining work force, a deterioration in the health of the elderly, particularly among those aged eighty and over, and a need for income support calls for adjustments in national expenditures and allocations, investment and consumption patterns, labor, and employment.

Bibliography

Asian Development Bank. 1997. *Emerging Asia: Changes and Challenges.* Manila: Asia Development Bank.

Bose, Ashish. 1992. "Metropolitan growth and urbanization, and their implications." Paper presented at the Fourth Asian and Pacific Population Conference, Bali, Indonesia, 19–27 August.

Chalamwong, Yongyuth. 1996. "Thailand." Paper presented at the meeting on International Migration and the Labor Market in Asia: National Policies and Cooperation, Tokyo, Japan, February.

Guest, Philip. 1999. "Mobility Transitions within a Global System: Migration in the ESCAP Region." *Asia-Pacific Population Journal* 14(4): 57–72.

Gulati, Leela. 1993. *Women Migrant Workers in Asia: A Review.* New Delhi: United Nations Development Programme/International Labour Organization.

Hugo, Graeme. 1996. "Counter urbanization." In P. W. Newton and M. Ball, eds. *Population Shift: Mobility and Change in Australia.* Canberra: Australian Government Publishing Service.

Huguet, Jerrold. 1995. "Data on international migration in Asia: 1990–1994." *Asian and Pacific Migration Journal* 4(4): 521–529.

International Labour Organization. 2002. "Migrant Activities in Asia" (June). <http://www.ilo.org/public/english/protection/ migrant/projects/asia.htm> (8 November 2003).

Knodel, John. 1999. "The Demography of Asian Ageing: Past Accomplishments and Future Challenges." *Asia-Pacific Population Journal* 14(4): 39–56.

Leete, Richard, and Iqbal Alam. 1999. "Asia's Demographic Miracle: 50 Years of Unprecedented Change." *Asia-Pacific Population Journal* 14(4): 9–20.

Martin, Philip. 1996. "Leading issues in Asian labor migration." Paper presented at the Conference on Dynamics of Labor Migration in Asia, Nihon University, Tokyo, Japan, February.

Skeldon, Ronald. 1992. "International migration within and from the East and Southeast Asian region: A review essay." *Asian and Pacific Migration Journal* 1(1): 19–63.

———. 1997. "Rural-to-urban migration and its implications for poverty alleviation." *Asia-Pacific Population Journal* 12(1): 3–16.

———. 1999. "Migration in Asia after the Economic Crisis: Patterns and issues." *Asia-Pacific Population Journal* 14(3): 3–24.

Yu Xuejun

UNESCAP. 2001. *2001 ESCAP Population Data Sheet.* Bangkok: UNESCAP, Population and Rural and Urban Development Division.

United Nations. 1991. *World Urbanization Prospects, 1990.* New York: United Nations.

————. 1999a. *World Population Prospects: The 1998 Revision. Volume I: Comprehensive Tables.* New York: United Nations, Department of International Economic and Social Affairs.

————. 1999b. *World Population Prospects: The 1998 Revision, Volume II: Sex and Age.* New York: United Nations, Department of International Economic and Social Affairs.

————. 2000. *World Urbanization Prospects: The 1999 Revision.* New York: United Nations Population Division.

United Nations and Australian National University. 1998. *Southeast Asian Populations in Crisis: Challenges to the Implementation of the ICPD Programme of Action.* New York: United Nations Population Fund.

World Bank. 1994. *Averting the Old Age Crisis: Policies to Protect the Old and Promote Growth.* Oxford: Oxford University Press.

3

Toward the Formation of an East Asian Regional Arrangement

Okamoto Yumiko

After three decades of high, sustainable growth, East Asia became a major pole of the world economy. The 1997 Asian financial crisis, however, had a profound impact on the region. A force of divergence rather than convergence set in. While some countries escaped the crisis or emerged from it swiftly, others were slow in their recovery. But the crisis also contributed to a sense of East Asia as a community and advanced the idea of East Asia–wide economic cooperation. In a new international environment, the challenge for East Asia today is how to promote and institutionalize regionwide integration of and cooperation on trade and investment (Bergsten 2000).

New Patterns of Development in East Asia after the 1997 Crisis

A Third Pole of the World Economy

East Asia enjoyed miraculously high, sustained economic growth between 1965 and 1990. The region grew faster than all other regions of the world (World Bank 1993, 1). Most of the growth was generated by eight countries: Japan; the newly industrialized economies (NIEs) of Hong Kong, South Korea, Singapore, and Taiwan; and the newly industrializing economies of Indonesia, Malaysia, and Thailand.

In the decade of the nineties, excluding the year 1998, East Asia grew at an annual rate of over 6 percent (Asian Development Bank [ADB] 2001, 5). Compare this with growth rates in Latin America (3.4 percent) and sub-Saharan Africa (2.4 percent). This remarkable growth was attributable to the dynamism of China as well as the above-mentioned economies (but not Japan). China grew at an average annual rate of more than 10 percent, and up until the crisis, member countries of the Association of Southeast Asian Nations (ASEAN) grew at about 7 percent. The overall favorable economic performance led to substantial improvement in living conditions in the region.

The 1997 crisis hit East Asia sharply, particularly South Korea, Indonesia, Malaysia, and Thailand. These countries experienced one of the most severe economic contractions in history since World War II. In 1998, gross domestic product growth rates were -6.7 percent for South Korea, -13.1 percent for Indonesia, -7.4 percent for Malaysia, and -10.8 percent for Thailand. With the exception of Indonesia, however, these countries showed a V-shape recovery in 1999. In 2000, the recovery continued, due partly to domestic monetary and fiscal stimuli and partly to a favorable external environment (International Monetary Fund 2000).

Further, despite the sharp reversal of private foreign capital in general, foreign direct investment (FDI) continued to flow into the region. FDI has greater permanence than other types of foreign capital and is, therefore, more important for long-term development. In 1999, the region still attracted around 45 percent of all FDI flows to the world's developing countries (ADB 2001, 2). These figures seem to indicate that East Asia continues to stand as a major pole of the world economy, along with North America and Western Europe, in the twenty-first century.

The Emergence of China as a Major Economic Force

East Asia still holds high growth potential, but the balance of economic might among countries may be shifting. Throughout the 1990s, China performed dynamically and emerged as a global industrial power (ASEAN-China 2001). Its average real GDP grew as much as 10.1 percent. Its exports grew threefold, making China the seventh largest exporter in the world. At the same time, among developing countries, China was the recipient of the largest FDI inflows.

The 1997 Asian crisis, which disrupted many economies in East Asia, especially ASEAN members, does not seem to have affected China as severely. Between 1997 and 2000, the Chinese economy continued to grow at about 7 percent to 8 percent annually. China's growth over the next decade is projected to be around 7 percent annually (ASEAN-China 2001, 13). This is in contrast to ASEAN nations, where growth has fallen since the crisis and prospects have declined.

In the twenty-first century, China will be an important factor in the development of many East Asian economies. In particular, the entry of China into the World Trade Organization (WTO) in 2002 will have a significant impact on East Asia, as well as other countries, through the expansion of world trade. It is China, however, that will be the big winner (Walmsley and Hertel 2001, 1021).

According to a study by the Development Research Center in China, using a computable general equilibrium (CGE) model, tariff reductions by China would alone increase China's average annual growth rate by a full percentage point (ASEAN-China 2001, 18). Exports would expand 24 percent, imports 18 percent. However, because of a shift away from selective to comprehensive market liberalization—which will produce a sharp increase in imports and a temporary surge in unemployment—China will have to face new challenges. Since the introduction of its Reform and Open Door Policy in 1979, the country has been gradually acquiring the capability to cope with economic changes, and thus it seems likely that China will overcome the challenges without great difficulty.

The entry of China into the WTO will provide opportunities and challenges for other East Asian countries as well. Certainly, trade liberalization in China will bring an expansion of trade to East Asia, but it will also afford East Asia the diversification of its export markets. The benefit of this is a security derived from no longer relying on a single market, namely, the United States. The dangers of such exposure became clear when the U.S. high-technology sector collapsed in 2001, leading, in East Asia, to a sharp decline in exports and GDP growth.

As regards ASEAN nations, China's accession to the WTO will likely see an expansion of ASEAN exports of electronics and agricultural or natural-based products to China (ASEAN-China 2001, 19). There are similarities in the industrial structures of China and many ASEAN countries, and although they may compete in areas of labor-intensive manufacturing, such as textiles and apparel, they are increasingly complementary, particularly in such areas as trade in computers/machinery and electrical equipment.

But challenges for ASEAN nations remain. The real competition between ASEAN and China lies in the markets to which they both export, in particular the industrialized markets of the United States, the European Union, and Japan. These countries are the major export markets. In 2000, the United States represented 19.5 percent of the exports of the original six ASEAN members (Indonesia, Malaysia, the Philippines, Singapore, Thailand, and Brunei); the EU represented 14.4 percent, and Japan 13.5 percent. China, on the other hand, made up only 3.6 percent of ASEAN's exports.

The large share borne by the three industrialized markets is no different in the case of China's exports. Based on data of various years from the International Monetary Fund, the United States made up 20.9 percent of China's exports, the EU 15.5 percent, and Japan 16.7 percent. ASEAN represented but 6.1 percent. It seems clear that with so much at stake, the competition between ASEAN and China is likely to intensify.

ASEAN can expect further competition from China for available FDI, as both have been its recipients rather than investors in each other's markets. Despite the sharp drop in FDI flows to ASEAN nations since the financial crisis, FDI continued its flow into China, although between 1997 and 1999 its absolute value declined from US$44 billion to US$39 billion (ADB 2001).

Convergence or Divergence?

Another feature to emerge since the financial crisis is the divergence of performance among East Asian countries. Although several countries hit by the crisis showed a V-shaped recovery, the degree of recovery varies from country to country (Alburo 2001, 45).

Table 1, which notes GDP growth rates of East Asian countries in the years before and after the crisis, documents how recovery differed among them. In South Korea, Malaysia, and Singapore, recovery was quick and strong. In Thailand, Indonesia, and the Philippines, it has been much less robust.

Although Indonesia was not the first country to be hit by the crisis, the contraction of its economy in 1998 was the most severe of any East Asian country. Indonesia's recovery has, furthermore, been slow, compared with that of many East Asian countries. For the Philippines, which may not have been hit directly by the crisis, conditions deteriorated sharply after the crisis; the economy started to record positive growth rates after 1999, but the vibrancy observed in the mid-1990s has not yet returned. The differences that are observable in the performance of East Asian nations seem to be attributable to the strength or weakness of the underlying fundamentals of individual economies (Alburo 2001, 41–45). The crisis may have done some damage to the fundamentals, although not across all countries nor to the same degree.

Table 1. Growth Rates of East Asian Countries in the 1990s

	Per capita GNI* (US$), 2000	1991–1996 (Average, %)	1997 (%)	1998 (%)	1999 (%)	2000 (%)
Cambodia	260	6.0	3.7	1.5	6.9	5.4
China	840	11.6	8.8	7.8	7.1	8.0
Hong Kong	25,950	5.2	4.9	-5.3	3.1	10.4
Indonesia	570	7.2	4.7	-13.1	0.8	4.8
South Korea	8,910	2.3	5.0	-6.7	10.9	8.8
Laos	290	6.5	6.9	4.0	7.3	5.7
Malaysia	3,380	9.6	7.3	-7.4	5.8	8.5
Myanmar	NA.	5.9	5.7	5.8	10.9	6.2
Philippines	1,040	2.8	5.2	-0.6	3.4	4.0
Singapore	24,740	8.9	-0.4	9.3	5.8	9.9
Thailand	2,010	8.0	-0.4	-10.2	3.3	4.4
Vietnam	390	8.4	8.2	5.8	5.0	6.6

Source: International Monetary Fund (2001); World Bank (2002).
* GNI: gross national income.
Note: Data for Brunei not available.

Figure 1. FDI Flows into China and ASEAN Countries (in millions US$)

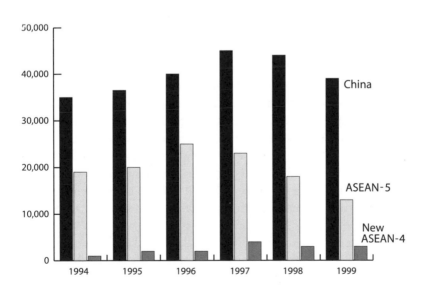

Source: ADB (2001).
Note: ASEAN-5 includes Indonesia, Malaysia, the Philippines, Singapore, and Thailand; data for Brunei, also an original member of ASEAN, are not available.

Okamoto Yumiko

For example, China and new ASEAN members Vietnam, Cambodia, and Laos were not hit directly by the crisis (statistics for Myanmar are not available). Therefore, they did not experience any output contraction as did other ASEAN economies. However, the economic dynamism that the new ASEAN countries demonstrated before the crisis has not yet returned. As figure 1 shows, the flow of FDI into new ASEAN countries is not only small in comparison with that into China and the original ASEAN members (data for Brunei not available, however), but it has also declined since the crisis, mainly because FDI flowing from the original ASEAN members decreased substantially. New ASEAN members are considered by many to have joined the ASEAN free trade area (AFTA) partly to attract FDI. This intention has not seen full realization yet.

In sum, to bring back a force of convergence and to integrate new ASEAN members with the rest of the region will be the big challenges for East Asia in the twenty-first century.

RISING ENTHUSIASM TOWARD REGIONAL ECONOMIC INTEGRATION AND COOPERATION

Emergence of Financial Cooperation in East Asia

Another impact the 1997 financial crisis is a new enthusiasm for economic integration and cooperation in East Asia (Scollay and Gilbert 2001). Unlike the situation with the EU, however, regional financial cooperation has preceded trade and investment cooperation. In 2000, the finance ministers of ASEAN + 3 (China, Japan, and South Korea) met in Chiang Mai, Thailand, and concluded the Chiang Mai Initiative (CMI), which represented the first significant step in official financial cooperation for the entire region (Chaipravat 2001, 990).

By this agreement, the ASEAN Swap Arrangement (ASA), one of the main components of the CMI, was enlarged to US$1 billion in November 2000. Then, with respect to the network of bilateral swap arrangements (BSAs) and repurchase agreements, substantial agreements have been reached between South Korea and Japan, Malaysia and Japan, and Thailand and Japan. ASEAN countries, China, Japan, and South Korea will continue to work toward establishing a network of bilateral swap and repurchase agreement facilities (Kim and Wang 2001, xlviii).

The reason for this regional financial cooperation is largely understood to be the dissatisfaction of many East Asian countries with the International

Monetary Fund during the financial crisis. While this may or may not be true, more important is the realization of these countries that self-help and self-support mechanisms are to their mutual benefit and should be strengthened. First of all, many small and medium-sized economies in the region were, by themselves, unable to cope with speculative attacks on their currencies (Kim and Wang 2001, xlvi). Second, international organizations had been spreading their resources thin and their facilities are far from complete (Chaipravat 2001, 990–991).

Thus, an intermediary or regional financial arrangement, which would step in as a suitable lender of last resort, was considered as a way to cope with the volatility of capital flows and the fluctuations of international currencies in East Asia.

Proliferation of Bilateral and Subregional Trade Agreements

From Financial to Trade and Investment Cooperation

To be sure, the currency swap scheme is, alone, too meager to prevent future financial crises. Nonetheless, the advancement of regional financial cooperation is important in shaping the future direction of regional economic cooperation. It has helped to revive the idea of an East Asian Economic Group (EAEG) by holding the ASEAN + 3 summit. The formation of such a group had been proposed by Malaysian Prime Minister Mahathir Mohammed in the early 1990s, but the idea, under a different name, was never put into practice due to strong opposition by the United States. And it gave rise to "a new technique of organization which perhaps better reflects the political realities of constructing economic cooperation in the region" (Phongpaichit and Baker 2002).

Trade and investment liberalization in East Asia is currently progressing through a network of bilateral or subregional agreements instead of through a central plan for regional cooperation. On the economic side, as observed above, there are huge income disparities in East Asia, and economic performance post-crisis diverged more than converged. The wider the divergence, the less consensus building and cooperation among countries. Therefore, promoting liberalization through bilateral or subregional agreements has the advantage of being more flexible and suitable to the reality of the region, though it is still debatable whether such liberalization actually improves welfare.

Okamoto Yumiko

Spread of Bilateral and Subregional Agreements

Free trade agreements (FTAs) appear increasingly to be regarded by policy makers as effective instruments for achieving trade liberalization (Rajan, Sen, and Siregar 2001, 7). The new trend in East Asia is the promotion of regional trading initiatives by countries that had before relied mainly on the multilateral system. Japan, one of few countries that had not belonged to a regional trade group, recently reoriented its trade policy. Instead of keeping to multilateral liberalization through the WTO process, Japan began a multilayered approach where multilateral, regional, and bilateral cooperation was all advanced (Toyoda 2001, 4).

As a first step, the Japan-Singapore Economic Agreement for a New Age Partnership was concluded in January 2002. The agreement will be a "new-age FTA," which not only includes the removal of traditional tariff and non-tariff barriers, but also seeks to promote investment and agreement on rules and standards (Yamazawa 2001, 47). In other words, Japan has acted to reorient its trade policy as well as to promote deeper bilateral cooperation. Currently, Japan is considering other FTAs—with South Korea, Mexico, and Chile.

South Korea has engaged in a similar shift in trade policy and, like Japan, has begun to use the FTA as a practical policy apparatus. South Korea is currently conducting negotiations with Chile and examining the feasibility of agreements with major economies such as Japan, the United States, and China. According to Sohn and Yoon (2001, 23), the successful formation of a Korea-Chile FTA will be of particular importance for South Korea's trade policy, as potential agreements will depend very much on the first case. One of the main obstacles in pursing the agreement with Chile is the response of sensitive sectors such as agriculture. As Yamazawa (2001, 44) points out, a strong impediment to forming an FTA does not come from abroad but from domestic vested interest groups.

In the late 1990s, Singapore likewise started to pursue a track to liberalization through the regional route, although Singapore has long been a proponent of global trade liberalization and has adopted a free trade and investment policy (Rajan, Sen, and Siregar 2001, 3). It has expressed a strong desire to enter into FTAs with the United States and Japan, as well as with other countries outside Southeast Asia but within the Asia-Pacific Economic Cooperation (APEC) region—including South Korea, Australia, Mexico, Canada, and Chile. Singapore advocates the view that new FTAs might be "building blocks" for achieving free trade objectives in Pacific Asia (Scollay and Gilbert 2001, 14).

Although China in the 1990s was too occupied with joining the WTO to plan FTAs, it has finally taken steps to join in the FTA boom. In November 2000, Premier Zhu Rongji suggested an FTA between China and ASEAN, and an ASEAN-China Expert Group on Economic Cooperation was formed to study the possibility.

In October 2001, while the expert group proposed establishment of a WTO-consistent ASEAN-China FTA within ten years, along with economic cooperation in other areas (ASEAN-China 2001), it was a surprise that ASEAN even agreed to start talks on the matter with China, given their competitive industrial structure. What seems to have persuaded ASEAN was the opening of the agricultural sector in China and the flexibility accorded new members of ASEAN (Terada 2002).

An ASEAN-China FTA may have a broad impact on the advancement of regional economic integration in East Asia. First, China's desire to establish an agreement with ASEAN led Japan to explore a similar relationship. In January 2002, Japanese Prime Minister Koizumi Jun'ichiro visited ASEAN countries to propose the Japan-ASEAN Comprehensive Economic Partnerships. Second, it might represent a big step toward economic integration in East Asia, serving as a foundation for an East Asian Free Trade Area that encompasses ASEAN, China, Japan, and South Korea.

Factors behind the Emergence of Bilateral and Subregional Trade Agreements

The Bogor Declaration, concluded at the second summit of APEC in Bogor, Indonesia, in 1994, adopted the goal of trade liberalization for developed countries by 2010, and for developing countries by 2020. Between 1994 and 1997, however, East Asia saw very little movement toward subregional trade agreements. Since the end of 1998, attitudes within the region have changed suddenly and dramatically.

One reason, common to all countries, is the fact that regionalization was beginning to shape a new world order. In the period 1948–1994, the General Agreement on Tariffs and Trade (GATT) received 124 notifications of regional trade agreements (RTAs), but since the creation of the WTO in 1995, there have been notifications of over one hundred additional arrangements covering trade in goods or services (World Trade Organization 2001). In Europe, the European Union will likely expand and end up including more countries from central and eastern Europe. And by

2005, the Free Trade Area of the Americas (FTAA) will also be established, involving thirty-four countries. Free trade agreements are increasingly being regarded as a realistic approach to achieving global liberalization (Yamazawa 2001, 5).

In the case of Japan and South Korea, two other factors may account for the reorientation of trade policy. First is concern over possible isolation in light of developments in Europe and the western hemisphere (Scollay and Gilbert 2001, 8; Dobson 2001, 1009). Second is a new form of *gaiatsu*, or foreign pressure, to stimulate needed domestic reforms (Dobson 2001, 1009). In the past, multilateral trade liberalization and the government of the United States represented two sources of foreign pressure that facilitated painful but necessary domestic reforms in the two countries. Japan in particular, with its power eroding over the last decade, needs an effective policy tool to promote structural reforms to regain its economic dynamism and contribute to regional development.

Among ASEAN countries, Singapore has been active in promoting trade and investment liberalization through bilateral arrangements since the late 1990s. Multilateral trade liberalization through the WTO process turned out to be very lengthy and time-consuming, and APEC had grown so large that it was not handling trade and investment liberalization issues effectively. Further, after the financial crisis of 1997, some ASEAN countries slowed down the liberalization process, negotiating exceptions and exclusions for pet projects, specific products, and priority sectors (Phongpaichit and Baker 2002, 5). In the face of such disappointing progress, Singapore started to explore alternative liberalization paths (Rajan, Sen, and Siregar 2001, 3).

In the case of China and ASEAN, regional economic integration and cooperation, including the formation of an FTA, were desirable for three reasons. The first was the proliferation of regional trade agreements on a global scale. Second was the emergence of China itself as an economic force in the world economy. As described above, the economy of China has been dynamic both as an exporter and as an absorber of FDI. In a way, China and many ASEAN countries share the same experience, and the mutual benefit they could derive provided impetus for economic cooperation and integration. The third factor was the Asian financial crisis, which, among other things, made China and ASEAN recognize their economic interdependence (ASEAN-China 2001, 4–6).

A SCHEME FOR MORE EFFECTIVE
EAST ASIAN REGIONAL INTEGRATION AND COOPERATION

Three Possible Scenarios

Whether a regional arrangement is a building block or a stumbling block of the open world trading system is an often-posed questioned these days. However, as Krueger (1999a) concludes, preferential trade agreements (PTAs) are here to stay and the challenge is how to make them compatible with multilateral liberalization.

Regionalization, as noted above, is beginning to shape a new world order in East Asia. This seems to be one of the irreversible evolutions that are taking place in this region. The challenge is, under the new regional environment, what kind of institutions East Asia will construct to enhance economic integration and cooperation in the region, and how best to coordinate its economic relations with the rest of the world (Bergsten 2000).

As Scollay and Gilbert (2001, 18) observes, East Asian trading relationships seem to be at a point from which they could move in several different directions: further proliferation of bilateral or subregional trade arrangements, gradual emergence of an East Asia–wide free trade area, or renewed commitment to APEC.

There is no doubt that the third option—renewed commitment to APEC—would be the best in economic terms because of the nondiscriminatory way that liberalization would be promoted within the region. At the same time, however, it would be the least feasible politically, because APEC has failed to achieve much in the way of concrete results, and Japan and the United States, major players in APEC, no longer consider APEC as an effective policy body for trade liberalization. What is most efficient and desirable economically is least feasible politically.

It does not mean, however, there is no role for APEC in the region. First of all, the main mission of APEC lies not only in liberalization but also in facilitation and cooperation. Therefore, it still could play an important role in promoting cooperation, even as it makes little impact on liberalization. Besides, as the membership of APEC encompasses not only East Asia but also part of the Western Pacific area, it could continue to serve as a consultative forum.

Currently, as indicated above, the most fashionable way to promote trade and investment liberalization in East Asia is through bilateral and subregional trade agreements, the first option. This may continue to be most feasible politically in East Asia for the first decade of the twenty-first century, but economically it would be the least efficient and least desirable. Economic theory suggests that regional integration may be trade-diverting or trade-creating. If the diverting force is stronger than the creating force, regional integration will end up diminishing the welfare of parties to the agreement—and non-parties as well.

Another concern, expressed repeatedly by trade economists, is the proliferation of different rules of origin or provisions (Panagariya 1999; Krueger 1999b). That is, if a country is simultaneously a party to more than one agreement, which agreement takes precedence (Scollay and Gilbert 2001, 17)? Under such circumstances, economies may be fragmented, and trade may be discouraged rather than facilitated.

Considering both economic and political factors, the second option—the gradual emergence of an East Asia–wide free trade area—emerges as most desirable for East Asia in the medium and long term. To form a regionwide FTA in East Asia may take time. Yet, it bears recalling that, after the financial crisis, East Asia saw economic cooperation occur first on the financial side—in tandem with a growing sense of an "East Asian community." Even so, acting upon this option requires the consolidation and gradual shift of bilateral or subregional trade agreements into a regionwide FTA.

Obstacles to Forming an East Asia–wide Free Trade Area

For economic and political reasons, however, forming an East Asia–wide FTA would not be without obstacles. First of all, a huge income disparity in East Asia persists. Ever since Cambodia, Laos, Myanmar, and Vietnam (the CLMV countries) joined ASEAN in the middle to late 1990s, their integration into the association has been a real economic issue. For the new members, social and infrastructure development are of far greater concern than industrial and trade liberalization, which has priority for the original members (Thongpakde 2001, 69). Special attention within ASEAN would need to be paid to these disparate interests if a shift to a regionwide FTA is to be made.

Weakened prospects for economic growth for ASEAN countries in the wake of the crisis could constitute another economic obstacle. Although no ASEAN country was unaffected by the crisis, their responses varied widely. Regardless of the magnitude of the immediate economic hit, Indonesia and the Philippines have been slow in their recovery. Unless both countries, especially Indonesia, return to their previous growth track, regionwide integration will not proceed easily.

There are, as well, political difficulties to the formation of an East Asia–wide free trade area as long as the area includes Japan, South Korea, and China (Kim 2002). A strong sense of nationalism can be found in Northeast Asia, where distrust persists due to unresolved history. World War II may not, in a true sense, be over. In addition, the strong vested interests of the agricultural sector in Japan and South Korea might create a formidable barrier to any regionwide trade liberalization.

However, the recent agreement between China and ASEAN on working toward the establishment of a free trade area within ten years seems to have brought about a so-called domino effect (Baldwin 1999). Japan was swift in following China's lead. After signing the Japan-Singapore Economic Agreement for a New Age Partnership, Japan proposed the Initiative for Japan-ASEAN Comprehensive Economic Partnership in January 2002. The Japan-ASEAN agreement is intended to strengthen the economic relationship, extending it beyond trade and investment to science and technology, human resources development, and tourism. The goal of the partnership was stated to be the creation of an East Asian community.

Despite the various political and economic barriers to trade and investment liberalization, in 2002 a gradual shift toward the formation of a regionwide free trade area seems to have begun.

Policy Decisions

The formation of a free trade area necessitates certain policy decisions: (1) the countries that would be parties to the agreement, (2) the policy stance of the agreement vis-à-vis the outside world, (3) the depth of integration, and (4) the breadth of the agreement (World Bank 2000).

Parties to the Agreement

Currently, the idea of an East Asian community is that of ASEAN + 3, but membership of the community might be extended as well to Australia and New Zealand. That is the official stance of the Japanese government, as indicated by Prime Minister Koizumi in a January 2002 speech, and ASEAN has initiated a study of that possibility. One obstacle to the inclusion of Australia and New Zealand, however, is the strong opposition by

Okamoto Yumiko

Malaysian Prime Minister Mahathir, who has exercised veto power over their membership in a broader East Asian economic or political grouping (Scollay and Gilbert 2001, 56).

Policy Stance vis-à-vis the Outside World

There are three options: Members of the East Asia–wide free trade area could act as one in their trade policy as regards the rest of the world, as in the case of a customs union; members could set up their own individual trade policy as regards the rest of the world, as in the case of a free trade area; or members could adopt an open regionalism, as in the case of APEC. Given the importance of extra-regional trade and investment relationships for many of the member countries, the principle of open regionalism would seem preferable. Although the definition of open regionalism is always contentious, here it is defined as a process of regional cooperation in which economic barriers are removed not only against member countries but also against nonmember countries. In fact, open regionalism can be fully achieved if the member countries continue to work for global liberalization under the WTO process as well.

As is shown in table 2, in a comparison of three free trade areas, the intraregional share of exports in East Asia has been the lowest. After a peak in the mid-1990s, this share declined with the dramatic fall in economic activity that accompanied the outbreak of the Asian financial crisis. This is in sharp contrast to NAFTA where intraregional trade increased from 48 percent to 56 percent in the latter 1990s. Intraregional trade in the EU has remained at about 62 percent. There is a huge potential for increase in East Asian intraregional trade, as China grows more rapidly than the rest of the world and as Japan opens up more toward the region. Even so, the major export markets of East Asia can be expected to lie outside the region at least for the first decade of the twenty-first century. For economic reasons, therefore, this makes a strong case for the principle of open regionalism, which is also desirable to ensure that RTAs are building blocks rather than stumbling blocks in the global trading system.

The Depth of Integration

A Japan-Singapore FTA or a Singapore-New Zealand FTA can be regarded as a new-age FTA, as it contains not only a contract to abolish traditional tariffs and non-tariff barriers, but also proposals to promote far-ranging

Table 2. Intraregional Export Shares (%)

Year	East Asia	NAFTA	EU
1994	42.1	48.0	61.9
1995	44.0	46.2	62.4
1996	45.1	47.6	61.4
1997	44.1	49.1	61.7
1998	37.8	51.7	65.5
1999	39.2	54.6	61.8
2000	41.9	55.7	62.1

Source: IMF (various years).

cooperation on such issues as investment agreements, standards certification, and intellectual rights. These initiatives exceed the provisions of the WTO. They are expected to serve as a model for future regionwide integration, to create a larger and more harmonized market in East Asia, and to promote deeper integration over the long term.

Such integration would bring greater benefit in many areas since gains from competition and economies of scale could be realized (World Bank 2000, 9). However, for individual countries, this also involves some loss of sovereignty—that is, in terms of domestic policy independence—and greater political commitment. The implication is that, especially for developing countries, deeper integration may not always be good, as their own development priorities may be surrendered to regional interests and these countries may face a formidable political opposition from domestic vested interests. Due consideration and flexibility in terms of scope and timetable, therefore, are warranted for developing countries, should deeper integration be pursued.

The Breadth of Agreement

After merchandise trade, investment and services are the two most prominent issues if the scope of integration is to be broadened. Other issues include labor mobility, fiscal harmonization, and monetary union. However, as the World Bank (2000, 89–90) cautions, extending the scope too broadly may detract from the economic benefits of integration. This is especially the case in East Asia where the gap between the highest and the lowest income level is huge.

What could be more relevant in the region is a comprehensive approach to trade and investment liberalization along with trade facilitation and cooperation. As is often the case, the implementation of trade facilitation measures, such as the simplification of customs procedures, is just as effective as trade liberalization in smoothing out the flow of goods across borders. Besides, unless cooperation in areas such as human resource development, information technology, and science and technology is provided to developing countries, integrating East Asia into one economic unit might not be feasible.

CONCLUSION

The high sustainable growth of the past three decades has made East Asia one of the most vital areas of growth in the world. During this period, economic interdependence deepened through market-led integration in the region, and trade and investment liberalization under the global trading system brought dynamic growth. The result today is that East Asia stands as a third major pole supporting the world economy, alongside North America and Europe.

In the wake of the Asian financial crisis, however, a pattern of divergence rather than convergence seems to have set in among countries in the region. On one hand, we witness the V-shaped recovery of South Korea, Singapore, Hong Kong, and Malaysia, and we observe the emergence of China as a global economic force in the twenty-first century. On the other hand, Indonesia and the Philippines have yet to return to their previous growth track, and it appears that the crisis has eroded, especially as regards Indonesia, the economy's underlying fundamentals. In addition, the weakened growth prospects of the original six ASEAN members have slowed down the integration of the CLMV countries into the association.

But another outcome of the financial crisis has been the creation of a sense of an East Asian community. To strengthen support mechanisms and to prevent such crises in the future, countries in the region were quick in advancing financial regional cooperation. Unlike in Europe, financial cooperation in East Asia preceded trade and investment cooperation. Amid rising global enthusiasm toward a regional approach to trade and investment liberalization, the new East Asian challenge is to revitalize struggling ASEAN countries and to institutionalize a regionwide economic integration process.

Currently, in East Asia, bilateral and subregional trade agreements are in fashion. Although they are most feasible politically, they may be least desirable economically. Therefore, the gradual shift from a bilateral or subregional to a regionwide trade agreement is something that East Asia needs to work on. Although formidable economic and political barriers to economic integration still exist, a domino theory of regionalism seems to be moving the process forward. A proposal for enhancing economic cooperation between China and ASEAN, including the formation of an FTA, has led Japan to propose a similar notion for an East Asian community.

Four policy decisions need to be made before the formation of a regional integration agreement can be realized. With respect to membership, the existing ASEAN + 3 seems a good place to begin. However, for larger economic benefit, it would be desirable to include Australia and New Zealand as core members.

Given substantial extra-regional trade, East Asia's adherence to open regionalism is both economically desirable and politically feasible since retaliation from nonmember countries would be unlikely. With the huge income gaps that exist in countries in the region, a softer, more flexible form of regional arrangement is also desirable. Acting too hastily may cause a regional integration scheme to fail. Due consideration needs to be paid to the needs of developing countries.

Finally, to generate a force of convergence once again and to deepen regional integration, a broader East Asian regional arrangement might be preferable. In other words, liberalization together with facilitation and cooperation would have a greater chance of effectively integrating East Asian economies into a regional and global entity.

BIBLIOGRAPHY

Alburo, F. 2001. "Competitiveness and Sustainable Growth in ASEAN." In Mya Than, ed. *ASEAN beyond the Regional Crisis.* Singapore: Institute of Southeast Asian Studies.

ASEAN-China Expert Group on Economic Cooperation. 2001. "Forging Closer ASEAN-China Economic Relations in the Twenty-First Century." Report submitted by the ASEAN-China Expert Group on Economic Cooperation, October. <http://www.asean.or.id/4979htm> (October 2001).

Asian Development Bank. 2001. *Key Indicators 2001.* Oxford: Oxford University Press.

Baldwin, R. E. 1999. "A Domino Theory of Regionalism." In J. Bhagwati, P.

Krishna, and A. Panagariya, eds. *Trading Blocs: Alternative Approaches to Analyzing Preferential Trade Agreements*. Cambridge, Mass.: MIT Press.

Bergsten, F. 2000. "The New Asian Challenge." Working paper 00-4. Washington, D.C.: Institute of International Economics.

Chaipravat, O. 2001. "Towards a Regional Financing Arrangement in East Asia." *The World Economy* 24(8): 989–994.

Dobson, W. 2001. "Deeper Integration in East Asia: Regional Institutions and the International Economic System." *The World Economy* 24(8): 995–1018.

International Monetary Fund. Various years. *Direction of Trade Statistics Yearbook*. Washington, D.C.: International Monetary Fund.

———. 2001. *International Financial Statistics 2001*. Washington, D.C.: International Monetary Fund.

———. 2000. *World Economic Outlook October 2000: Focus on Transition Economies*. Washington, D.C.: International Monetary Fund.

Kim Yoon Hyung, and Wang Yunjong, eds. 2001. *Regional Financial Arrangements in East Asia*. Seoul: Korea Institute for International Economic Policy.

Kim Young-Ho. 2002. "Towards a New Framework of Regional Integration in East Asia." Paper presented at the symposium Co-Design for a New East Asia after the Crisis, Nagoya, Japan, 7 February.

Krueger, A. 1999a. "Are Preferential Trading Arrangements Trade-Liberalizing or Protectionist?" *Journal of Economic Perspectives* 13(4): 105–124.

———. 1999b. "The Developing Countries and the Next Round of Multilateral Trade Negotiations." *The World Economy* 22(7): 909–932.

Panagariya, A. 1999. "The Regionalism Debate: An Overview." *The World Economy* 22(4): 477–511.

Phongpaichit, P., and C. Baker. 2002. "Experience and Prospects of Financial Cooperation in ASEAN." Paper presented at the symposium Co-Design for a New East Asia after the Crisis, Nagoya, Japan, 7 February.

Rajan, R. S., R. Sen, and R. Siregar. 2001. *Singapore and Free Trade Agreements: Economic Relations with Japan and the United States*. Singapore: Institute of Southeast Asian Studies.

Scollay, R., and J. P. Gilbert. 2001. *New Regional Trading Arrangements in the Asia Pacific?* Washington, D.C.: Institute for International Economics.

Sohn Chan-Hyun and Yoon Jinna. 2001. "Korea's FTA Policy: Current Status and Future Prospects." Discussion paper 01-01. Seoul: Korea Institute for International Economic Policy.

Terada T. 2002. "Higashi-ajia togo he Nicchu kyoryoku" (Japan-China cooperation toward East Asian regional integration). *Nihon Keizai Shimbun* 18 February, morning edition.

Thongpakde, N. 2001. "ASEAN Free Trade Area: Progress and Challenges." In Mya Than, ed. *ASEAN beyond the Regional Crisis*. Singapore: Institute of Southeast Asian Studies.

Toyoda M. 2001. "WTO, APEC and RTA: Has Japan's Trade Policy Changed?" Paper presented at the International Conference on Trade and Monetary Systems in the Asia-Pacific Region, Kobe University, Kobe, 3–4 February.

Walmsley, T. L., and T. W. Hertel. 2001. "China's Accession to the WTO: Timing Is Everything." *The World Economy* 24(8): 1019–1049.

World Bank. 1993. *The East Asian Miracle: Economic Growth and Public Policy*. Oxford: Oxford University Press.

———. 2000. *Trade Blocs*. Oxford: Oxford University Press.

———. 2002. *World Development Report 2002*. Oxford: Oxford University Press.

World Trade Organization. 2001. "Regionalism: Facts and figures." <www.wto.org/english/tratop_c/region_e/regfac_c.htm> (October 2001).

Yamazawa I. 2001. "Assessing a Japan-Korea Free-Trade Agreement." *The Developing Economies* 39(1): 3–48.

4

Digital Dreams and Divergent Regimes: The Impact of ICT on Pacific Asia

JAMUS JEROME LIM and YAP CHING WI

The information and communications technology (ICT) revolution, which began in the early 1990s, has swept the world, Pacific Asia included. From Hanoi to Hong Kong, it is hard to find an average person unaware of the pervasiveness of cell phones, computers, and the Internet. Indeed, the popular press acknowledges a "new economy"—one marked by rapid increases in productivity and growth with minimal inflationary pressure—due to ICT. Computers have progressed so quickly that many things once the domain of governments, corporations, and wealthy individuals are now available to the man on the street. This rapid pace of change has sent policy makers and academics scrambling to distill the myriad impacts of ICT.

To be sure, recent developments—such as a global recession led by the United States, Japan, and Germany, the world's three largest economies—have led many to reconsider the strength of the ICT revolution. The voices of naysayers have rung loud recently, but the new economy is likely to be sustained, even though the revolution would now seem more akin to a glacial diffusion rather than a volcanic redefinition.

This chapter addresses the manifold impacts of ICT on the economics, politics, and societies of Pacific Asia. The dearth of research in the political and social areas as regards ICT necessitates a focus on these two concerns. As such, the chapter seeks redress for topics that have what has commonly been accepted as secondary in mainstream discussions.

* The authors wish to thank participants of the APAP Cebu conference, in particular, Chia Siow Yue and Simon Tay, for invaluable input.

Digital Dreams and Divergent Regimes

The ICT Revolution in Pacific Asia[1]

The impact of ICT on the region is varied and complex. However, it is hypothesized that in the wake of the Asian financial crisis, the growth of ICT in some countries will be more pronounced than in others. Given limited resources, countries that are less developed will likely scale back ICT investment in order to realign priorities, whereas industrialized countries that have already established an ICT landscape will take the opportunity to forge ahead.

This divergence has been further expedited by the global slump in electronics goods. Countries that have yet to engage in the production of ICT-related goods will proceed with caution, allowing countries with ICT production facilities in place to use this time of lower export demand (hence prices) to upgrade their infrastructure. The discussion will proceed by segregating the countries into several admittedly artificial groups: the newly industrializied economies (NIEs), comprising Hong Kong, South Korea, Singapore, and Taiwan; the developing countries, comprising Indonesia, Malaysia, the Philippines, Thailand, and Brunei; and the transition economies, comprising the CLMV countries of Cambodia, Laos, Myanmar, and Vietnam. Japan and the nations of Australia and New Zealand in Oceania, as industrialized nations, and China, as potentially the largest market in Asia, are treated separately.[2]

ICT Infrastructure as Building Blocks for the Information Revolution

Telecommunications infrastructure refers to the penetration level of telephones (teledensity), both fixed-line and mobile, and the extent to which the provision of Internet service is available to an area. In terms of the information technology (IT) infrastructure, the benchmark applied is the extent of personal computer (PC) usage in the population.[3] The importance of an adequate telecommunications infrastructure cannot be overemphasized: the infrastructure forms the prerequisite backbone for many other forms of ICT, and in the absence of a proper network, advanced ICT such as the Internet cannot be deployed.

In general, the telecommunications infrastructures in Pacific Asia range from moderately developed to highly developed. Japan and Oceania display very mature levels of telecommunications infrastructure, although such development in the NIEs is on a par with, and in some cases exceeds, these levels. With notable exceptions, the economies of the developing countries have less developed infrastructures. The teledensity of China is difficult to evaluate, as major cities such as Beijing and Shanghai possess developed infrastructures, while rural areas are very poorly connected. As regards diffusion of personal computers, this difference among nations is magnified; in some there are computers for every other person, while in others computers are virtually absent.

The NIEs all display a high level of telephone penetration. For 1999, the teledensity in Hong Kong is highest, exceeding 57 lines per 100 people; South Korea is the lowest, at slightly more than 44 lines per 100 people. Nonetheless, as a group, fixed-line density is very high, averaging about 51 lines per 100 people. This high teledensity is reflected in mobile cellular telephone subscriber figures, with NIEs averaging about 52 lines per 100 people (International Telecommunications Union [ITU] 2000). Most of these economies have implemented, or are in the process of implementing, advanced digital technology such as ADSL and ISDN.

In the main, telecommunications firms tend to operate in a competitive environment, although there are few dominant players; more often than not, they are the former state monopoly providers. For example, in Taiwan, Chung Hwa Telecom Co., Ltd., is dominant, and in South Korea, the Korea Telecommunications Authority is the leading provider. PC penetration in these economies is also high, the group average being about 48 PCs per 100 people. For Singapore, the economy with the highest rate of diffusion (61 per 100), a study in 2000 estimated that 23 percent of homes had more than one PC (Dawson 2001).

Development of telecommunications infrastructure in Japan and Oceania has modest but very respectable rates, with about half the population in each having access to fixed lines, although mobile access is less pronounced (cellular teledensity is 45 per 100 in Japan, but averages only 25 per 100 in Oceania) (ITU 2000). Telecommunications technology in these countries is advanced, especially in urban centers such as Tokyo, Sydney, and Auckland. In terms of telecom providers, all three nations have an oligopolistic market structure; for example, Nippon Telegraph and Telephone (NTT) is the major provider in Japan, Telstra in Australia. PC penetration in these countries, averaging about 20 per 100 head of population, is inferior to that of telecommunications penetration.

In the developing economies of Indonesia, Malaysia, the Philippines, Thailand, and Brunei, teledensity for fixed lines is low. The average is slightly more than 9 lines per 100 people, although variation among the countries is wide: Brunei, with the highest teledensity, has almost 25 lines per 100 people, whilst Indonesia, with the lowest, has only 3 lines per 100 people. Similarly, China has a low teledensity of 9 per 100 people (ITU 2000). However, as indicated above, urban areas display very different statistics, as, for example, is the case in major Chinese cities where teledensity is estimated to be as high as 28 per 100.

Mobile communications are still in the nascent stages in the developing economies, with many countries having densities below 5 per 100; Malaysia and Brunei have slightly higher ratios (ITU 2000).

Communications technology varies widely among developing countries as well. Malaysia introduced T1 and ISDN in 1996 (National Trade Data Bank and Economic Bulletin Board 1996), whereas the Philippines only decided to build a new multi-service switching backbone network in late 1999 (Cisco Systems 1999). China is rapidly catching up in introducing new technology, and has recently begun to expand its ADSL, ISDN, and broadband projects (Gesteland 1999). In most of these nations, former state telecommunications providers remain the dominant players. For example, China Telecom maintains 95 percent of the Chinese market, and in Indonesia, PT Telekom has exclusive rights for the provision of telecommunications services through 2010.

For PC penetration, rates hover between 6 percent in Malaysia and slightly less than 1 percent in Indonesia. In China, the raw figures for PC diffusion are low, but access to PCs is higher mainly because of the workplace (37 percent) and Internet cafes (11 percent), although, notably, the majority (78 percent) of all individuals with access is below the age of thirty (China Internet Network Information Centre 2000).

Teledensity in the CLMV transition economies tends to be extremely low. Vietnam is an exception (at 2.6 fixed and 0.2 mobile telephones per 100 people), while the others have very poor line densities and antiquated technology (the average for the entire group is about 1 fixed and 0.2 mobile telephones per 100). Telephone access, if available at all, usually has to be put in place through the government. The situation is similarly dismal for PC penetration, with PCs little more than entirely absent (with, again, Vietnam the exception).

James Jerome Lim *and* Yap Ching Wi

Internet and E-Commerce Activity: Key Measures of ICT Diffusion

The status of electronic commerce displays wide variation across countries, not least because standardized measures of e-commerce activity do not exist. Increasingly, e-commerce activity has centered on Internet-based commercial exchange. Valuations of e-commerce activity can vary widely as a result of the application of different methodologies (Buckley and Montes 2001), however, so it is important that emphasis be placed less on raw figures than on the overall picture in terms of ordinal rankings.

Overall, Internet and e-commerce activity in Pacific Asia ranges from nonexistent to extensive. For many nations, Internet activity has been a recent phenomenon, although growth has been exponential in many cases. Where Internet access is available, most countries enjoy a liberalized Internet Service Provider (ISP) market, with multiple gateways to the Internet. Although Japan is the undisputed leader in number of Internet hosts,[4] China and Taiwan are rapidly catching up. E-commerce activity, however, is high only in Japan and, its potential notwithstanding, remains a small part of the economies of the region.

Japan's number of hosts—6,081,390 as of May 2001 (Netsizer 2001)—clearly dwarfs that of China and Taiwan, while the average of the world's three dominant countries is slightly more than 30 million. Japan is second only to the United States (78,484,100 hosts), and is followed by Canada (5,602,150 hosts). Unfortunately, telephone and Internet access fees are high in Japan, a reflection of the high cost of living. Japanese e-commerce spending levels of US$27.3 billion account for 70 percent of all Asian e-commerce (eMarketer 2001). Business-to-business (B2B) tends to dominate online e-commerce transactions, a trend that is not uncommon, even in industrialized countries. Australia and New Zealand average about 1.1 million hosts (Netsizer 2001), and rates tend to be affordable; in New Zealand, unlimited access by Xtra, the market leader, costs approximately US$10 a month.

Following close behind, the NIEs average about 787,000 hosts. Taiwan has the most, at slightly more than 1.5 million, ranking eighth in the world; Singapore has the fewest, at 276,000 (Netsizer 2001). Given vastly different populations, more pertinent would be the Internet penetration rate: by this measure, Singapore and Hong Kong have the highest at 48 percent, with South Korea at 35 percent and Taiwan at 29 percent (Nua Internet Surveys 2000). Due to freely competitive ISP markets in the NIEs, the cost of access is affordable. Taiwan experienced a broadband price war in 2000, and monthly charges for ADSL fell drastically, with monthly access on HiNet, the largest ISP, now only US$18. E-commerce in the NIEs involves both Internet-based e-commerce as well as the proprietary electronic data interchange (EDI) networks. Singapore has the TradeNet EDI system, which facilitates electronic B2B transactions (Teo and Lim 1998). In general, B2B features more prominently than business-to-consumer (B2C) in the region, although market size for both in the NIEs is still relatively small; contrast South Korea's market size of US$47.3 million with Japan's far larger US$27.3 billion market.

Among the group of developing economies, the number of Internet hosts is small. Thailand has about 67,600 hosts, and the Philippines has about half as many at 34,400 (Netsizer 2001). E-commerce activity in this group is nascent, although rapidly growing. In 2001, revenue from e-commerce averaged—with the exception of Brunei, for which figures were not available—about US$1.1 billion. Malaysia enjoyed e-commerce revenue totaling US$2.6 billion in 2000, more than twice the group average (Stat-USA 2001), while revenue in Indonesia, with the slowest rate of e-commerce growth, was generally negligible.

In China, as of 2001, there were approximately 126,600 Internet hosts (Netsizer 2001). Access charges tend toward prohibitive, despite the purported competitive environment in the ISP market (with sixteen ISPs). For example, ChinaNet charges US$73 for forty hours of access per month, an amount greater than the monthly average wage of US$60. The e-commerce scene is still in the early stages, having begun only in 1997.

The CLMV transition economies have largely been left behind by the Internet revolution. Only Vietnam has any notable Internet presence. Still, with access charges of US$20 per month, when per capita annual income is US$50, and poor service by the state-owned, government-managed Vietnam Datacommunication Company, this is little comfort.

Nuts and Bolts: Hardware and Software Production in Pacific Asia

Hardware production refers to the production of ICT goods, which includes components such as integrated circuits (ICs) and memory chips, electronic equipment such as cellular telephones and personal digital assistants (PDAs), and accessories and peripherals such as printers, scanners, and modems. Software production generally involves the production of applications (both generic and proprietary), together with systems development, database programming, and Web/multimedia content design and development.

The NIEs, together with some developing countries (in particular, Malaysia and the Philippines), are major world manufacturers and exporters of ICT hardware. Each economy tends to maintain its own area of specialization. Taiwan has very strong notebook PC, motherboard, scanner, and casing industries. In 2000, Taiwan accounted for 79 percent of world production of motherboards; and in semiconductor equipment, the Taiwanese market was estimated at US$9.78 billion, second only to that of the United States. Similarly, in 2000, Singapore held a comparative advantage in hard disk drives, South Korea in memory chips, and Hong Kong in semiconductors and integrated circuits (Low 2000). Although hardware has been the traditional strength of the NIEs, there is a growing awareness of the importance of software. Efforts at expanding the industry have seen strong results. In 2000, South Korea was projected to have a US$9.3 billion software industry, up from US$6.6 billion in 1999 and US$5.7 billion in 1998 (Hong 2001). Although at a somewhat slower pace, the other NIEs are also developing software capabilities.

Among developing economies, only the Philippines and Malaysia have significant export bases in hardware and software. In 1998, exports of electronics from the Philippines were valued at US$18.55 billion, from Malaysia at US$12.9 billion. The Philippines, exploiting a proficiency in English and an ability in programming, provided a boost to the country's software industry; in 2000, exports of software were targeted at US$300 million (National Information Technology Council 1997). Software development in Thailand has also grown recently, with exports reaching US$204 million in 1999. Other developing countries have meager ICT goods and services sectors. The transition economies have little or no hardware production to speak of, although the situation is rapidly changing in Vietnam ("Vietnam Stakes" 2001).

The industrialized economies have largely moved toward consumption, as opposed to production, of ICT hardware. Japan, however, remains a market leader in high-technology electronics and innovation. Australia and New Zealand, with their strong research-oriented universities, have also been involved in software and technology development, although niches exist in hardware production. One example is KRONE, an Australian firm providing high-speed data connectivity solutions.

In sum, hardware production in Pacific Asia is strong on the whole, albeit in different products and components. Software production is clearly increasing, although only Japan and the Philippines have established significant bases. Hence, the pattern for hardware and software production mirrors that of ICT infrastructure and Internet and e-commerce activity in the region: that is, with Japan, the NIEs, Malaysia, and Thailand having clear production capacities, and the other economies having little or none.

ICT Labor Markets: The Human Resources Paradigm

On the supply side, the ICT labor market is influenced first by literacy rate, especially in the English language, coupled with secondary education in mathematics and science, and higher education in technical and computer-related areas. Beyond educational preparation, the demand-side strength of markets for ICT manpower is critical. A profile of ICT professionals in terms of various indicators—nature of job, salary level, educational attainment, and years of experience—together with general employment statistics, will provide a fuller picture of the ICT labor market.

In some ways, ICT manpower in China and in Japan represents two ends of the spectrum. China's literacy level of 80 percent falls far short of Japan's almost 99 percent. With advanced research and development (R&D) capabilities, Japanese ICT workers are also engaged in production activities that are higher in the value chain compared to the overwhelming majority of ICT workers in China, who are engaged in low-skilled, labor-intensive assembly and production. With a large percentage of Japanese ICT professionals drawing annual incomes of between US$44,000 and US$87,000, the remuneration of Chinese workers is clearly eclipsed. It is important to keep in mind, however, the far larger base of human resources that China has; for example, an estimated 872,000 Chinese workers are involved in producing ICT connectors, cable assemblies, and backplanes alone (Fleck Research 2000).

With the high literacy rate that is characteristic of the group, the NIEs have rapidly adapted to fill the increasing demand for a high-technology, ICT-trained workforce. The literacy rate, generally based on individuals aged 15 and over with reading and writing ability, is in excess of 90 percent. Most citizens have a working knowledge of the English language, with English taught widely in schools (South Korea, Taiwan), used as the primary medium of instruction (Singapore), or widely used in government and business (Hong Kong). Furthermore, most have an admirable proportion of their population with a tertiary-level education; Taiwan, for example, has a 31 percent college-graduate ratio and has produced roughly twenty thousand technology professionals every year since 1996. Remuneration tends to be on the high side—a reflection of the increasing shift away from low-skilled ICT goods production toward high-skilled ICT services. In South Korea, the average monthly wage for the telecommunications sector in 1998 was 2,104,646 won (US$1,800) (Korea Information Society Development Institute 1998), compared to the industrial average of 1,426,797 won (US$1,190) in 2000 (National Statistical Office of Korea 2000).

These four countries do not experience significant "brain drain" problems. In fact, South Korea and Taiwan are enjoying a reverse brain drain, and Hong Kong and Singapore are net importers of ICT talent. With respect to the ICT workforce, the economies of Oceania approximate the situation in the NIEs, although the market for ICT manpower in Australia and New Zealand is somewhat smaller. For example, about 235,000 Australians, 2.7 percent of the workforce, are employed in ICT-producing industries. These jobs are higher paying than most: A$51,243 (US$28,950) per annum, compared to the average of A$29,409 (US$16,615) in 1998–1999 (Houghton 2001).

In the developing economies of Pacific Asia, the workforce trend displays a lower level of literacy—the average for the group of five countries was 88.8 percent (a mean somewhat inflated by the Philippines' 94.6 percent)—although levels are appreciable nonetheless. English skills tend to be weaker, however, than in the NIEs. With the exception of the Philippines and Malaysia, ICT professionals are few. Contrast Malaysia's estimated 50,000 software professionals (0.6 percent of the workforce) to Thailand's estimated shortfall of 150,000; or the Philippines' 357 computer schools, colleges, and training centers (National Information Technology Council 1997) to the ICT training facilities in Brunei, which are limited primarily to universities. Due to generally lower labor costs, compensation for ICT professionals is relatively low; for example, 78.3 percent of ICT labor in Indonesia is paid under US$5,000 annually (South East Asia Regional Computer Confederation 2001). The brain drain problem is especially acute in this group, notably in the Philippines and Thailand, as skilled workers often migrate to either the United States or nearby Singapore and Japan to earn higher wages.[5]

The situation in the group of transition economies is generally poor. That is, effective literacy rates are approximately 30 percent—with the exception of Vietnam, with 93.7 percent—and in 1997 the average for public expenditures on education was 2.3 percent of gross domestic product (World Bank 2000a). Even for Vietnam, the most ICT-advanced economy of the group, translating science and technology education into ICT and economic development has been a struggle, primarily due to weak ICT infrastructural support (Levinson 2000). This is aggravated by the poor quality of training that ICT graduates often receive (*Saigon Economic Times* 3 August 2000). As in the case of developing countries, there is a brain drain problem as well, although the incomplete integration of the transition economies into ASEAN has limited employment and education prospects.

Nature or Nurture? Getting the ICT Environment Right

The environment for ICT growth is dependent on, although not confined to, government policy on ICT development—in particular, national information infrastructure (NII) building programs and national innovation systems (NIS). Other important aspects include the regulatory environment, especially in the telecommunications industry, as discussed above, and the legal environment. Discussion of each country's ICT policies would in itself be a voluminous task (Chia and Lim 2002), and so the focus here will be on general trends for the respective groups from which distinctions in approach and philosophy may be drawn.

The NIEs, together with Japan and Oceania, tend to exhibit a pro-activity in formulating a coherent strategy for ICT development. In terms of R&D and science and technology policy, South Korea has emphasized a large-firm internalization model through its *chaebol* conglomerates, Taiwan a model based on a network of small and medium enterprise–led innovation, and Singapore a model that leverages foreign direct investment through multinational corporations (Wong 1999). Even the Hong Kong administration, once the paragon of laissez-faire capitalism, has yielded to interventionist government policy and begun investment efforts in R&D.[6] Similarly, the NIEs also have targeted national information infrastructure building plans. For example, Hong Kong has drawn up the Digital 21 IT strategy, and Singapore has the ICT 21 master plan. Japan has a Global Information Infrastructure plan that aims to implement a nationwide optical fiber network by 2010. The legal and regulatory environments for the NIEs also tend to be pro-business, with adequate respect for and enforcement of intellectual property (IP) rights, resulting in an average piracy level of 54 percent in 2000 (International Planning and Research Corporation [IPRC] 2001)—a decent rate, but certainly short of Western standards that average 30 percent. In this area, the industrialized nations have been the most successful. For example, Japan has managed to reduce its piracy levels dramatically from 55 percent in 1995 to 37 percent in 2000 (IPRC 2001); recent amendments to the Patent, Trademark and Copyright Laws have also served to reestablish Japan's commitment to an ICT-friendly legal framework.

The developing countries, although latecomers to creating a positive ICT environment, have made large strides, and many countries already have blueprints for NII programs. The Philippines introduced its first National Information Technology Plan in 1994, and in 1996 Malaysia embarked on its ambitious Vision 2020 plan—together with its Multimedia Super Corridor—to transform its economy into a knowledge-rich one. NIS efforts, however, tend to be more muted in the group, owing principally to smaller ratios of researchers, scientists, and engineers, a stronger focus on ICT infrastructure development, and the absence of a comparative advantage in R&D. Furthermore, higher levels of piracy (averaging 74 percent, not including Brunei) undermine incentives for software development (IPRC 2001), although steps taken since 1995 have led to greater conformity of IP laws to international standards. Still, enforcement in these countries tends to be weak.

The Chinese government has also engaged in several major ICT initiatives, many of which are patterned after those adopted by the NIEs and the more ICT-advanced developing countries.[7] Although well-developed IP laws are in place, enforcement has been extremely poor, with conflicts arising from issues as diverse as cyber-squatting to software counterfeiting. Reducing the piracy rate from the present 94 percent (IPRC 2001) may prove to be a more complex problem than might first appear.[8] This situation deteriorates dramatically for the transition economies, where there is generally no NIS policy, or even where one might exist, it is a resolution with little detailed, concrete measures. Piracy is rampant—in Vietnam it is 97 percent (IPRC 2001)—and although national R&D centers exist, they often carry the baggage of the socialist system.[9]

THE MULTI-FACETED INFLUENCES OF ICT

The ICT revolution has challenged traditional thinking in economics and, to a lesser extent, political and social theory. It is therefore useful to review the central theories and concepts that have arisen in the study of the information and knowledge-based economy, of which ICT is the key driver. To a limited degree, some of these issues have been empirically tested, at both country and industry level, although conclusions have been far from concrete. These issues include challenges that arise from technological advancement, the economics of networks and information, the impact on social development, the digital divide, the changing dynamic between government and people, and the effect of ICT on culture and values.

On Technological Advancements and Productivity Paradoxes

Conventional economic theory has long trumpeted the importance of technological advancement as a source of economic growth. Earlier studies have generally treated technology as an exogenous force. Although elegant in concept, the persistence of disparities in growth among countries over time has meant that this view of the world is increasingly at odds with empirical evidence about the response of economies to technological change. Moreover, treating technology shocks as a "black box" effectively isolated the contribution of technology as a key driver of growth. In order to reconcile these contradictions, and to afford more insight into the central role of technology, a new growth theory model was formulated on the endogeneity of technological progress, mainly through process innovation or human capital augmentation, in the process of growth. Endogenous growth theory has also led to the justification of government intervention in the provision of technology, given its nature as a public good (Solow 1956; Romer 1986; and Grossman and Helpman 1991).

A primary motivator for investment in ICT has been the positive effects of increases in total factor productivity that ICT engenders—in particular, the beneficial effects of ICT on the productivity of labor and capital. However, despite the large investment in ICT from the 1970s through the mid-1990s, there was little perceptible gain in terms of productivity—a phenomenon that subsequently came to be known as the Solow "productivity paradox" (1987).

However, from the mid-1990s onward, a series of papers established positive returns to ICT in the United States (Brynjolfsson and Hitt 1996; Oliner and Sichel 2000), in European countries such as Finland (Niininen 2001), in the Organisation for Economic Co-operation and Develpment (Calderón 2001; Schreyer 2000), and even in NIEs such as South Korea (Jeong, Oh, and Shin 2001) and Singapore (Wong 2000). The record for developing countries, however, was less promising (Dewan and Kraemer 2000), although the feeling was that realized gains were only a matter of time. Studies rushed to explain the paradox, with the most persuasive hypotheses as follows: first, that technological advances require a period of diffusion before productivity is influenced, resulting in the lag; second, that the productivity benefits of ICT has been limited to gains in the ICT manufacturing industry itself, not the wider economy; and third, that measurement issues cloud the true contribution of ICT to productivity (Triplett 1999).

Recent thinking, however, has increasingly called into question the assumption of returns on investment in ICT. In a sharp response to the turbulence of high-technology markets in 2000–2001, voices in the business community (Madrick 2001), academics (Gordon 1999; Krugman 1997), and even consumers ("The U.S. Productivity Puzzle" 2001) have been critical of the sustainability of the alleged gains in productivity. More importantly, these critiques may lead to concerns that countries that have embraced the technology revolution may find themselves caught in a host of excessive and inappropriate ICT investments. Indeed, these concerns are exacerbated by the nature of general purpose technologies, which are characterized by their pervasiveness and complementarity with production.

As illustrated by Helpman and Trajtenberg (1998a, 1998b), Helpman (1998), Chung (2000), and Beaudry and Green (2001), the introduction of a major new technology into an economy generates a cycle consisting of two distinct phases. The first—aptly called a time to sow—involves the diversion of resources into developing complementary inputs that utilize this new technology. Consequently, output and productivity fall, as they are channeled toward this task. When the time to reap arrives in the second phase, enough complementary inputs will have been developed, and it becomes worthwhile to harness the advantages of manufacturing using this new technology. As a result, output, wages, and profits rise. Extensions of this case to an open economy (Chung 2000) show that when an industrialized country (the North) engages in the first phase of the cycle, developing nations (the South) will enjoy a temporary boom. This ends in the second phase, when the North completes its R&D processes and reasserts its lost competitiveness.[10]

Translating theory to reality, it is possible to envision that the period between the 1980s and first half of the 1990s—the period of the productivity paradox—was possibly the gestation period for ICT in the industrialized economies. From the mid-1990s onwards, the productivity surge in both the United States as well as the European Union suggests the maturation of these industrialized nations into the second phase. This implies two things. First, that the Asian miracle, fueled by the electronics boom, may well be at an ebb. This is a serious outcome, implying an urgent need for economies to leverage the ICT revolution to propel themselves to the status of an industrialized nation, as well as to pursue R&D and science and technology programs. Second, that countries left behind will find the catch-up game far more difficult to play. This suggests that the developing countries and the transition economies, lagging in the information economy, will need, rapidly and actively, to engage in ICT diffusion and R&D if they are to bridge the technological chasm, or risk being left even further behind.

The Economics of Networks and Information

A major problem that afflicts economic systems is the presence of incomplete, or asymmetric, information. Asymmetric information occurs at a microeconomic level in both consumer and producer markets (Akerlof 1970; Rees 1989), as well as at a macroeconomic level between economies engaged in cross-border transactions. The promise of ICT has been its unique ability to enhance informational flows, thereby correcting deficiencies in information that might lead to inefficiencies or failures in the market mechanism. Reinforcing this are the benefits that accrue through network externalities, which are the economic gains that arise when users of a particular technology attain a critical mass.[11] Therefore, network externalities and the elimination of asymmetric information form two pillars that give rise to an entirely new field in economics: the study of networks and information. This field, in turn, has led to a reexamination of traditional modes of business associated with electronic commerce and weightless goods (Choi, Whinston, and Stahl 1997; and Shapiro and Varian 1998).

The economics of e-commerce can be broken down into three major areas. First, due to low marginal costs of production and distribution coupled with high initial fixed costs, production and value chains are changed, requiring businesses to develop new models of pricing and distribution. Second, weightless goods tend to yield increasing returns both in scale and scope due to production efficiencies and product complementarity. Third, e-commerce exerts influences on market structure, generally by promoting competition and market creation through mediums such as online auctions and electronic exchanges. The stiffer competition is likely to create incentives for firms to differentiate their products in order to maintain profits, as well as to limit their ability to extract consumer surplus through exercising price discrimination. On balance, therefore, e-commerce is expected to lead to improved production processes and greater consumer sovereignty.

Possibly the most practical application of e-commerce is in the establishment of electronic marketplaces. These include older electronic exchanges such as proprietary electronic data interchange networks, as well as Internet-based B2B, B2C, and consumer-to-consumer (C2C) portals. Regional examples include SESAMi (a B2B portal established in Singapore and now with offices in Hong Kong, China, and South Korea), Amazon.co.jp (the Japanese arm of the B2C bookseller), and InterAuct! (a C2C auction site in Singapore). Although such e-markets are unlikely to displace the more traditional methods of exchange completely, especially in the B2C and C2C areas, there is some evidence that businesses are increasingly seeking to conduct their transactions online due to significant cost savings (Lucking-Reiley and Spulber 2001). This has also meant that ICT has expedited and advanced cross-border trade and investment flows (Okamoto in this volume).

In Pacific Asian economies, this means challenges to both consumers and producers: consumers require a change in their current mindset regarding buying and selling electronically, whilst producers must work to ensure the security and privacy of online transactions. Although e-commerce has not led to the overnight removal of the middleman, the complete revamping of businesses, or the end of the shopping experience (so prized in Asia), it will, in time, nonetheless become integrated into business practices and personal lifestyles. Governments have a role to play by expediting the spread of e-commerce through actively integrating ICT into their online procurement procedures (business-to-government, known as B2G) and their provision of public services (government-to-consumer, known as G2C). Indeed, countries such as Singapore and Thailand have been active in the spread of e-government (Infocommunication Development Authority of Singapore 2000; National Information Technology Committee 2000). The Chinese market will also be important, due to its sheer size and the large amounts of capital inflows that are entering the country from both industrialized nations and regional economies such as Taiwan and Singapore.

The weightless economy is comprised of four components (Quah 2000): information and communications technology, thus including the Internet and telecommunications; intellectual assets broadly construed—not only patents, but also copyrights, trademarks, music, video entertainment, advertising, images, industrial trade secrets, financial consulting services, health and medical consulting, education, and so on; electronic libraries and databases; and biotechnology: carbon-based libraries and databases.

These components of the knowledge economy are characterized by several economic relationships. First, due to the negligible marginal costs of production and distribution, there is infinite potential for expansion, and the resulting economic efficiency would imply the free dissemination of knowledge. However, in opposition to this is the absence of any prior incentive to produce knowledge in the event that compensation is nil. Second, in contrast to the standard model for knowledge and growth, the weightless economy reduces the effective distance between the consumers and producers of knowledge, fostering a positive consumer feedback that drives growth. Third, sources of growth led by knowledge include the use of human capital (Grossman and Helpman 1991; Levinson 2000), an institutional framework that supports R&D (Porter 1990), and even population growth (Beaudry and Green 2001).[12]

These factors pose challenges to Pacific Asia. In order to develop human capital, manpower policy must evolve rapidly. Levinson (2000) has argued that education, together with technology—in particular, training and exposure to ICT—is necessary to equip human capital for the ICT revolution, and that education is possibly the most valuable intervention. With the exception of Japan, the NIEs, and Oceania, nations in Pacific Asia need to upgrade their levels of math and science education coupled with higher utilization of computers. The coupling is important. For example, Vietnam, which ranks high in the quality of its education, is ranked poorly in terms of overall competitiveness by the Global Competitiveness Report (Porter et al. 2000) precisely due to its low level of computer use. Here, ICT provides the very solution to the problem: computer-assisted and Internet-based learning would open the doors of opportunity to a wider segment of the populace than ever before.

In transition economies and, to a lesser extent, developing Asian countries, rigidities that impede inflows of skilled manpower remain in the labor markets and, if progress on the ICT front is to be made, will have to be removed. In particular, policies that promote foreign talent recruitment and local talent retention need to be pursued. These policies, together with productivity gains from ICT, should then lead to improvement in employment performance.

Institutional reform in Pacific Asia poses something of an enigma, not least because of the so-called unholy trinity of corruption, cronyism, and nepotism, which, with the possible exception of Singapore, permeates society, both public and private (Political and Economic Risk Consultancy 2001). The resounding lesson of the Asian financial crisis is the importance of good corporate governance and a sound institutional environment; with the introduction of ICT, such emphasis assumes greater importance. With proper institutions in place, ICT can expedite the dissemination of public policy, and the free flow of information ensures that distortions arising from both market and government failure are less likely to occur. With regard to R&D, these would include a national innovation system that coordinates science and technology policy, oversees R&D bodies, and pools national technological resources, a sound legal and regulatory framework, adequate ICT infrastructure, and developed financial bodies that provide venture capital financing.

For physical infrastructure, the approach would depend on the stage of development of the country. Obviously, there is a logical progression to the task: if telephone penetration rates are dismal, discussing digital broadband networks makes no sense. The transition economies of Cambodia, Laos, and Myanmar will certainly need to upgrade their ICT infrastructure. Similarly, in the absence of reliable electricity provision, fast computers add little to productivity. Here, technologically backward countries possess a potentially distinct edge, as the absence of legacy systems affords opportunity to leapfrog over countries that must address systems in place. Nonphysical infrastructure will benefit from deregulation in the ICT sectors, laws that explicitly recognize electronic transactions and protect intellectual property, and caution in the taxation of e-commerce and ICT.

Although focus on the supply side of the ICT equation is clearly an important driver of ICT development, Quah (2001) convincingly argues that the source of growth in the future will be demand-driven. In this respect, therefore, Pacific Asia has the greatest potential for growth and leadership, as evidenced by the widespread use of high-technology products in most major cities. Indeed, Japan could be the model for the region, with its global leadership in the adoption of wireless communication technology and advanced consumer electronics.

Disenfranchisement of Small States? Global Governance and Security Concerns[13]

The globalization process poses external challenges to sovereign states, especially small states, including those of Pacific Asia. These are best summarized as challenges to governance and security. The varying—even haphazard—efforts at global governance have led to different degrees of social and economic exclusion. In order to avoid such exclusion or marginalization, governments in the region have negotiated with institutions—such as the International Telecommunications Union (ITU) and the International Consortium for Assigned Names and Numbers (ICANN)—that establish regulations and standards in the globalized network economy. In the wake of allegations of systematic unfairness in ICANN's Universal Domain Name Dispute Resolution Policy (Geist 2001), it is important that these smaller voices be heard, as these organizations can powerfully influence ICT investment flows, protect individual privacy, and ensure information security.

A possible way forward would be to get the regional house in order. Through ASEAN + 3 (member countries of the Association of Southeast Asian Nations plus Japan, China, and South Korea) agreements, a common regional standard for e-commerce and intellectual property can be meted out. The importance of this cannot be overemphasized as the departure of regional standards, particularly by the transition economies, from international norms has been soundly criticized by Western governments and even within regional forums. Australia and New Zealand might play a valuable role here, aiding in the establishment and maintenance of these standards, given their position as more mature democracies with a tradition of respect for intellectual property and the rule of law.

Digital Gaps within and among Asian Countries—ICT in a Country Framework

ICT is embraced by many developing countries in Pacific Asia as a means to economic growth and state governance; Malaysia's Vision 2020 offers one such example. In this regard, ICT is seen as both a technology and a discourse for national development. Accordingly, scholars such as Andrew Webster, informed by Thomas Kuhn's *The Structure of Scientific Revolutions* (1962), have stressed the linkages between technology and society. As science and technology affect and are affected by economics, politics, and culture, the production of technology is a common good that must be integrated with social development and equal access (Sapp 2001).

Digital divides, which exist among as well as within countries, take different permutations. Common factors used to measure the divides include fixed teledensity, mobile teledensity, personal computer density, Internet host density, secure server density, and e-commerce usage density (Fazio et al. 2000). Inter-country gaps may be wide, and they tend to be harder to address than intra-country gaps. Among countries, the divide is mitigated by production networks (Borrus, Ernst, and Haggard, eds. 2000), the free flow of trade in ICT goods and services, and the e-ASEAN agreement.[14] Future efforts might wish to explore the possibility of a sustainable regional innovation system.

The framework for analyzing the impact of ICT and the digital divide is more productive if considered at the country level. Often, intra-country divides mirror income, rural-urban, racial, gender, educational, and generational gaps (World Bank 2000b). Disadvantaged groups within a country suffer from a combination of exclusions, making it harder for them to access and benefit from social and economic resources such as ICT. As observed by Touré (2001), the disparity is more in countries with large rural areas such as Malaysia, whose rural population makes up 43 percent of total population. Internet penetration in the capital, Kuala Lumpur, however, is thirty-five times greater than in the entire state of Kelantan. Around 25 percent of households in eastern Malaysia have no electricity, while in peninsular Malaysia coverage is 100 percent.

In China's major urban centers, Internet users represent the elites. This minority tends to be young, educated, wealthy, single, and male (Hachigian 2001a). However, even as only 3.4 percent of the population is rural, the absolute numbers are staggering, at about 34 million in 1999 (United Nations Development Programme [UNDP] 2001).

In Nepal, of the wealthiest quintile of households, only 11 percent has access to a phone. In comparison, only 0.5 percent of households in the next quintile have access to a phone. Further, the ratio of private phone access in urban to rural regions is 1-to-100 (World Bank 2000b).

Wong P. K. (2001) cautions that the market forces in the Pacific Asia ICT market are fragmenting the region into many small markets divided by language, culture, technical standards, lack of legal institutions, and other barriers. ICT by its interconnected nature spans countries, and in a globalized world the gap between developing and industrialized countries has grown larger. For example, in 1998 the six least industrialized Asia

Pacific countries had an average level of ICT adoption about one-tenth the levels achieved by the five most industrialized Asia Pacific countries. The statistics for Internet hosts and secure commerce hosts are much worse, at 3 percent and 2 percent (Wong P. K. 2001). One-fifth of adults in industrialized economies, compared to less than 1 percent of adults in developing countries, uses the Internet. The number of Internet users in Singapore is the same as that in the whole of Indonesia, which has fifty times Singapore's population (Touré 2001). Given these disparities, Wong P. K. suggests that nations establish policy that promotes regional cooperation and cross-border transactions at the same time that they focus on in-country ICT development.

It is therefore an absolute necessity that countries, as they face a growing disparity with their neighbors, address the social welfare of their citizens. Embedded in ICT is its potential as a social leveler, as it affords small and medium-sized enterprises access to markets and gives individuals access to information once the preserve of the upper class. In this changed environment, policy should be aimed at the public as well as private sector. For example, enhancing learning and educational opportunities through electronic delivery methods could be implemented through accrediting private providers that use ICT and the Internet as an instructional tool (as has been experimented with in Singapore), or by funding the use of ICT in public universities (most common among the NIEs, although now widespread in the region save for the transition economies). Other policies should target improving access to ICT, as, for example, through the use of telecenters, as discussed below.

It should be noted, however, that there is dissent with regard to how the information highway should be paved. Baker (2001, 1–2) argues as follows:

> A disservice is done in reducing the apparent inequities in the diffusion of the technologies to a simple socio-economic concern. Rather than a one-dimensional "digital divide", more accurately there is a policy problem related to the use and deployments [*sic*] of ICTs with multiple geographic, social, economic and organisational components. . . . Further, ICTs present policymakers with an array of complex issues that extend beyond purely technological concerns. . . . Rather than answering the question of how should public sector functions respond to the changes made possible by diffusion of ICTs, a more critical step seems to be to accurately gauge the nature of the issue rather than jump in and lay "digital pavement".

The country profiles above highlight the complexity of ICT development in Pacific Asia. The political-social-economic context of each country has got to be fundamental to any consideration of what the impact of ICT will be.

Processes and Factors Affecting ICT Diffusion in Pacific Asia

Within the discourse of ICT as technology, ICT is also innovation. It is an idea, a practice, or an object that is perceived as new. Generally, as Rogers (1995) points out, in any population adopters of innovation fall into five categories (table 1).

Table 1: Adopters of Innovation

	Characteristics
Innovators (2.5%)	Venturesome, cosmopolitan, have networks with other innovators, have financial resources, understand complex technical matters, cope with uncertainty
Early Adopters (13.5%)	More locally oriented than innovators, influential opinion leaders, respected by society
Early Majority (34%)	Interact frequently with peers, seldom hold positions of opinion leadership, interconnected to the system's interpersonal networks, require long period of deliberation before making an adoption decision
Late Majority (34%)	Adopt on basis of economic/social necessity due to effects of diffusion, skeptical and cautious, with relatively scarce resources
Laggards (16%)	Most localized, with past as point of reference, suspicious of change, with few resources

Source: Rogers (1995).

For each category of adopter, the rate of adoption of ICT is based on several factors, but primary among them are the compatibility of the idea of ICT with existing values, past experiences, and needs of potential adopters, and the visibility of the results of the innovation to others (Rogers 1995). In both cases, the role of opinion leaders and the mass media is vital in creating a widespread culture of acceptance and information transmission.

The "late majority" and the "laggards," which make up half the population, are the focus groups to promoters of ICT as economic and social development. The late majority can be induced to adopt ICT via training in work skills or the linking of ICT to economic gain. Laggards represent a more challenging category, as, in the face of globalization and a mobile workforce, it is this group that tends to be excluded. Hence, attention and resources need to be channeled to this group.

Bazaar and Boalch (1997), in its study of thirty developing countries, identifies five factors necessary for ICT rollout and Internet use: national/ organizational needs and/or new opportunities; technology; people/skills; capital resources; and management of technology adoption and diffusion. The most important component affecting the diffusion process, according to Bazaar and Boalch, is the underlying telecommunications infrastructure within a country as well as its capacity for international links; this is key to the technology component. Other factors include policies and regulations regarding telecommunications and Internet services; the level of economic development of the country; cultural factors—such as value systems, personal beliefs concerning technology, and attitudes toward information sharing—which are significant in the degree of adoption and integration into the global community; and language.

The work of Bazaar and Boalch, in addition to that of Wong P. K. (2001), Touré (2001), and Rodríguez and Wilson (2000), helps to explain why ICT diffusion within a country and across the region is inconsistent, resulting in gaps among countries and within countries. Moreover, it is apparent that Pacific Asia's global leadership in ICT production, has not, with the possible exception of the NIEs, seen diffusion into society or the economy. There needs to be a shift in emphasis, therefore, toward adoption and utilization of technology as a medium for economic growth and development. This has been evident in major cities, but governmental policy could help to break down the rural-urban divide.

Social Development and ICT Diffusion—A Central Role for the State?

One implication of the above studies is the need for strong leadership and concerted efforts at the national level to promote ICT. If not taken up, a worst-case scenario could be that of a "fourth world," as suggested by Castells (1998), characterized by the social exclusion of people or economies that are of no use to the dominant interests in "informational capitalism." They offer little or no contribution as either producers or consumers, and they are the uneducated, functionally illiterate, sick or intellectually challenged, and chronically poor. Unless changes are made, for example, one candidate for the fourth world would be the Philippines, where the 2000 People Power II revolution seems not to have benefited the marginalized sectors of society in whose name the revolution was staged. With only 2 percent of the population having access to the Internet, Philippine civil society understands that ICT must focus on the "touchstone issues on which moral victories are translated," such as agrarian and electoral reforms (Sicam 2001).

In his understanding of the impact of ICT on the entire range of population, Midgley (1995) draws heavily on the social development approach, which gauges improvement in the quality of life through the integration of social welfare and economic development. This framework exemplified the optimism among developmental workers who viewed the globalized economy as providing opportunities for developing countries to integrate their social development with economic growth (Midgley 2001). However, as cautioned by Castells (1998), this requires political will, international cooperation, and investment from the business sector to reduce marginalization of countries or parts of countries. Rodríguez and Wilson (2000), for example, finds that most developing countries do not associate economic growth with ICT.

Castell's definition of social development (1998, 2) sums up best the values and approaches needed:

> Social development today is determined by the ability to establish a synergistic interaction between technological innovation and human values, leading to a new set of organizations and institutions that create positive feedback loops between productivity, flexibility, solidarity, safety, participation and accountability, in a new model of development that could be socially and environmentally sustainable.

China's recent US$2.5 million pilot ICT project with the United Nations Development Programme (UNDP) to reduce poverty in rural areas provides a case in point. To improve the livelihood of families and to develop longer-term ICT-related businesses in rural areas, ICT centers will supply information on market prices, agricultural technologies, and new methods for sustainable farming. The initiative aims to facilitate communication between communities and administrative units on public services, regulations, and policies, thereby promoting transparency and participation (UNDP 2001).

In order to reach equitable social and economic goals, a centralized ICT diffusion system where the state takes the lead would be an effective first step. Government, according to Touré (2001), could be a user of ICT in its administration and planning, demonstrating how computerization and a computer-literate civil service makes for greater efficiency, transparency, and cost savings. Government could be a creator of content for ICT, providing locally relevant applications. Finally, government could be a promoter of ICT, promulgating legislation, building infrastructure, and liberalizing markets.

Singapore is a good example.[15] The primary advantage of a centralized diffusion system is that the state finances and coordinates R&D and communications infrastructure building. On the other hand, the state also carries out centralized decision making, which leaves people as passive adopters (Rogers 1995). Hence, Baker (2001) advocates a decentralized, bottom-up approach in developing public sector ICT, so that the focus can be localized and the technological skills can be leveraged to address community issues. The disadvantage of this approach, however, is that local communities, which may lack technical expertise, may fail to use ICT effectively and that unpopular innovations go by the board.

Ideal might be for the state to adopt both the centralized and decentralized systems for different population profiles. The development of rural ICT diffusion would seem best centralized, while a decentralized system of development would suit an urban population, especially if already Internet-savvy. The danger, of course, of increased political input in the diffusion of ICT is that political economic issues come to play. Well-connected political elites as well as special interest groups, such as the ICT business lobby, which can be sizable in some nations, might exert a disproportionate degree of influence on government policy, particularly in countries where the political players adopt a more myopic stance in policy making. Moreover, when the issue of political liberalization is added to the goals of social development, the situation becomes more complex.

Changing the Government-People Dynamics

ICT is seen as a political liberalizer by scholars such as Rodríguez and Wilson (2000) and Tiihonen (2001), who argue for low levels of government distortion and greater room for democratic rights and civil liberties. While this is the general discourse adopted by developmental workers, some strong states in the region, such as Singapore (Rodan 1998)[16] and China (Kalathil and Boas 2001)[17] have used ICT to continue their political hold.

Even so, it is important to note that in some ways ICT has revolutionized the dynamics between government and people. Essentially, ICT has helped in the empowerment of civil society by providing tools to communicate and organize. This has taken place locally, nationally, and globally. Information might be gathered and exchanged globally, with planning done locally to suit specific contexts. The interconnectivity and real-time organization afforded by ICT is a powerful force, leading to new rules of engagement between the government and people.

Such engagement has been seen globally, where the Internet and mobile phones were tools in the protests of meetings of the World Trade Organization (Canadian Security Intelligence Service 2000). On the national level, examples include the ouster of Philippine President Joseph Estrada (Sicam 2001) and the Falun Gong's April 1999 protest in Beijing (Kalathil and Boas 2001).

In China, the Internet has come to be used as a political tool, with people relying on it as a primary source of information. According to a study by the Chinese Academy of Social Sciences, more than 70 percent of respondents viewed the Internet as a forum for the expression of political views. Indeed, there is evidence of empowerment in China's civil society, with the country's few advocacy groups plugging into the network of activists that thrives on the World Wide Web. In addition, niche or marginalized interests, such as the gay community, are able to band together with Web pages and discussion groups (Hachigian 2001c).

While Internet terrorism, such as the hacking of companies during the 1999 London "J18" demonstration (Canadian Security Intelligence Service 2000) against capitalism and international corporations, represents an extreme aspect of ICT, the Internet has been the venue for exciting and constructive movements. Communities linked on the Web have ranged from "A Civilization of the Mind in Cyberspace," as outlined in "A Declaration of the Independence of Cyberspace" (Barlow 1996), to Singapore's gay community finding more security and space (Ng 1999). On the development front, aid agencies are integrating technology with local culture in popular entertainment projects such as Meena (http://www.unicef.org/meena), which helps to educate rural populations in South Asia in gender and child rights. In Pacific Asia, the Western Australian state government has introduced a Website for feedback from the populace.

But ICT has also introduced a range of privacy issues, especially in the wake of the terrorist attacks in the United States on September 11, 2001. Face-recognition technology, realized by advances in ICT, has been used in London's Heathrow airport to help identify potential terrorists. The extension of this to other criminals and then on to private individuals is a fine line that raises the specter of Big Brother and fears of Orwell's *1984*.

At the same time, however, political control continues to erode as technology is able to sidestep government-imposed barriers. Already the Internet firewalls erected by China and Singapore have been riddled with holes, with a variety of anonymizer software and Websites offering encryption of electronic trails, which allow one to evade obstacles to a blacklisted site. It would seem only a matter of time before these firewalls are dropped due to their ineffectiveness.

ICT has been the facilitator for these changes in mindset and culture. And this may be the most significant impact ICT has had on dynamics between government and people—opening up resources for risk takers and innovators of civil society.

Erosion of National Cultures and Values and the Evolution of a Globalized Culture

ICT can also be seen as a tool for both expressed and experienced culture that does not exist in isolation from the social system (Carolan 2001). Citing Turner (1990), Carolan explains that we are now at a "liminal moment" of history, where we stand among the positions assigned and arrayed by law, custom, convention, and ceremony. Hence, ICT as an instrument of communication provides channels for different groups of people, who previously would not interact, to connect with each other. This can be seen in the new social ties and the ready exchange of knowledge among the taste publics identified by Gans (1974)—high culture, upper-middle culture, lower-middle culture, low culture, and quasi-folk culture. Technology has provided the flexibility and the mediation for individuals to transcend categories and routine.

Shamsul (2000, 2) observes that the formation of ICT culture is one of "fragmengration." The culture thrives on fragmentation, cross-cultural permutation, and integration, and rationalization of various resources. In the face of these dynamics, the contest between national and global culture has become a great concern to national governments.

Beyond urban lifestyle fads fueled by MTV, certain postmodern cultural traits such as the ability to relate to and accept multiple truths and realities, are now associated with Internet users. Indeed, in China, Internet users, who tend to be more educated and wealthy, have been found to be more open-minded (Hachigian 2001b). And while the young twenty-something Filipinos, known as Generation Text,[18] taking part in the People Power II revolution are "insistent, hardworking, strong and patriotic," they are also, notably, "free, fun-loving and restless" (Eder 2001).

The cultural impact of ICT can be empowering and liberalizing. The evolution of anti-globalization demonstrations and people's political uprising may see a convincing contest to the hegemonic hold of political and cultural power by the state and other institutional powers that be. In other words, the contest is cultural production, and the prize is ownership of a reality meaningful and beneficial to those in powers. The tension in this clash of culture formation, says Shamsul (2000), is partly due to the state's fear of loss of control over society and of dramatic too-fast-paced social changes. For example, in the Myanmar government's first week-long e-mail campaign in 2000 against Aung San Suu Kyi's National League for Democracy, journalists were sent images of semi-nude NLD leaders (Krebs 2001). In Singapore, Muslim authorities rejected decrees of divorce via a short message service on the mobile phone ("SMS Divorces" 2001). In Thailand, while the Internet spurred the growth of the sex industry, it also gave women the chance to enter chat rooms to find out more about the activities of their unfaithful husbands and to pick up sex tips (Tang 2001).

The pace of cultural production—and the variety of ways it combines with economic goals—is accelerating. For example, Bhutan was connected to the Internet by the UNDP's 1997 Asia-Pacific Development Information Programme (Wong S. L. 2001). Four years later, it announced the launch of its first daily newspaper on the Internet (KnowNet Initiative 2001), with digital advertising. The UNDP's objective for Bhutan to raise its national income with Internet-based activities is now beginning to see results. It could be a model for the transition economies of Pacific Asia to follow.

The Way Forward—Realizing a Mindset Change and Regional Cooperation

With such forces in place, several directions for ICT development have emerged. But given the increasing digital gap within and among countries in Pacific Asia, the framework for development must take into consideration local, national, and regional levels to prevent a scenario of outright winners and losers.

In the region, governments seem to be the leading actors in the development and use of ICT. Even if they cannot finance the building of a broad-based information-communication infrastructure, they would do well to coordinate its long-term plans so as to reduce the exclusion of sectors of the population, such as rural areas and the urban poor. This requires political will.

In the area of social development, ICT diffusion and adoption would be most effective if tied to economic goals and appropriated into the local context. The fostering of human capital via education is crucial so that the younger generation can leapfrog, with their utilization of ICT, the older generation.

Fueled by ICT, a global civil society, sensitive to local concerns, will continue to grow and strengthen. Governments will find it increasingly complex to engage the nonprofit sector, and the local civil society will grow more sophisticated in its advocacy.

The above necessitates the active cooperation of countries in Pacific Asia. In the face of a rapidly evolving globalized ICT culture and economy, this is crucial. Japan's promise in the Okinawa Charter to provide US$15 billion over five years for the narrowing of the digital gap in the region is a positive example of efforts that could be taken in this direction (G7-G8 Secretariat 2000). Similarly, the e-ASEAN framework, once it has been established, could easily be extended to the East Asian countries as well as Australia and New Zealand, providing a Pacific Asia–wide ICT infrastructure.

One concept that seems to be reaping some encouraging impact is that of telecenters, either stationary or mobile. The aim of these telecenters, which are strategically located to provide public access to ICT, is to develop human capital, promote local community empowerment, and generate economic revenue. The range of services includes telephone, fax, e-mail, Internet access, and the availability of multimedia hardware and software.

These telecenters also act as community information centers (Oestmann 2001),[19] where children are taught basic computer skills. They provide a venue for farmers to access the latest prices for commodities, cutting out the middleman, which gives them larger returns (Wong S. L. 2001). International agencies such as the UNDP are funding the construction of these centers in both rural and urban areas in developing countries. In India in 1996, there were already 10,200 such telecenters. The project is currently being initiated in Vietnam and the Philippines.

Central to these emerging directions and encouraging initiatives of ICT development is the need for decision makers to adjust their mindsets to incorporate the impact of ICT as a liberalizing and empowering tool for the marginalized. They will need to be open-minded, willing to accept higher risk and uncertainty generated by rapid technological progress, and willing to share resources and control with a larger pool of stakeholders.

Although the importance of ICT should not be overstated given other development priorities, if a policy of active engagement in ICT is adopted by Pacific Asia, the countries of the region, and even the region as a whole, will be better prepared to handle development challenges that might arise, be they related to ICT, biotechnology, or other areas. This stems from the fact that ICT, in its essence, is a facilitator and a tool, and such tools, when harnessed properly, can allow an acceleration of the other economic goals. It is possible that countries without ICT will continue to find niches in the global marketplace, but complete neglect of ICT policy will only make future attempts to introduce ICT into the economy more difficult.

Conclusion

In the final analysis, comprehending the manifold impacts of ICT is a near-impossible task. Attempting to isolate the many different dimensions leads only to more ancillary influences and cross linkages. Hence, the best way forward in any serious analysis is to view the broad impacts associated with ICT and the causes of these impacts.

Any individual impact can be viewed with optimism, neutrality, or pessimism. Similarly, one might adopt several worldviews in interpreting these impacts: technological determinism, contingency, or social determinism. Yet, the overall trend from this study, as alluded to throughout the chapter, is the clear diverging pattern of development in terms of ICT among nations; on the one hand, the NIEs of Hong Kong, South Korea, Singapore, and Taiwan, the developed nations of Japan, Australia, and New Zealand, as well as, most possibly, China appear to have grasped the essence of the information revolution, and have taken steps to push their economies and societies in that direction. The other nations will need to engage in ICT developmental strategies more actively if they wish to keep abreast. More likely than not, however, due to the multiple priorities these economies face, ICT tends to be a lesser objective. This will prevent much of developing Asia and the transition economies from reaping the full benefits of the information economy.

The limitations of the chapter stem from the general intractability of the subject matter. It is, admittedly, incomplete, although as many key impacts as possible have been dealt with, and especially those that have been significant to economies of Pacific Asia. This opens the door to future research into narrower areas of discussion—in particular, the proposal for an ASEAN + 3 supranational innovation system, an analysis of the international relations aspects of ICT, and study of local solutions to the negative social impacts of ICT. Urgent research is also needed to examine how economies, like Malaysia and Thailand, that are poised on the fringes of the ICT revolution, can propel themselves forward in ICT development, and how technologically regressive economies, such as Cambodia, Myanmar, and Laos, can leapfrog the ICT development process—perhaps by using Vietnam as an early model.

It is perhaps useful to end with a caveat and a warning: ICT is, and remains, a small force in the greater scheme of development objectives. Only 1 percent of the world's population owns a computer, and any ICT initiative should keep that statistic foremost in mind. To concentrate exclusively or excessively on ICT development would not only be myopic, but counterproductive. In the light of alternative economic priorities and social agendas, this is a distraction that countries in Pacific Asia can ill afford.

Notes

1. This section draws heavily on previous work discussing the ICT landscape in member countries of the Asia-Pacific Economic Cooperation (APEC) forum (Chia and Lim 2001).
2. A detailed discussion of the position of ICT development in Pacific Asia vis-à-vis other major economic regions of the world is beyond the scope of this chapter. Suffice it to state that Pacific Asia stands in the forefront of ICT production (especially hardware and, to a lesser extent, software), but lags in the areas of ICT diffusion; the NIEs are the exception in this latter respect. The interested reader is referred to Dedrick and Kraemer (1998).
3. Unfortunately, this ignores quality differences in terms of processor speed, graphics adaptor technology, and hard disk size, among other factors. Nonetheless, such specifics are not of foremost importance at the macro level and can safely be aggregated into the PC diffusion statistic.
4. Note that the number of Internet hosts is not necessarily indicative of the depth of Internet penetration in a country. The United States, in particular, has a very large number of hosts, but many U.S.-based commercial hosting sites provide services to users not based in the United States—a testimony

to the borderless nature of Internet service provision.

5. The movement of ICT professionals is a particular example of the more general migration trends in Pacific Asia; it is discussed in detail in the chapter by Yu in this volume.

6. The idea of the Applied Science and Technology Research Institute (ASTRI) was announced in 1998 by the chief executive; in 2000, the Hong Kong ASTRI Company was charged with planning and developing the institute. ASTRI's aims are to support midstream research and development, enhance Hong Kong's technological human resources development, be a focal point for outside R&D personnel wishing to work in Hong Kong, act as a spawning ground for technology entrepreneurs, promote greater application of technology in industry, and provide a venue for industry-university collaboration (Innovation and Technology Commission 2001).

7. The major initiatives are the 836 Project, which funds R&D projects in ICT as well as ICT enterprises, and the Torch Program, which seeks to commercialize discoveries made by the universities and government research institutes. Other initiatives include strategic master plans, high-technology industrial zones, R&D tax incentives, and public funding for venture capital.

8. Chinese culture itself emphasizes the notion of sharing, but there is also high demand for pirated software, an absence of public awareness and education, the lax attitude of software manufacturers, and the underdeveloped local software industry (Ho 1995; Kay and Scott 2000; Wingrove 1995).

9. Specifically, they tend to produce research channeled to support the existing regime and seldom effected for the benefit of the populace. Moreover, there is little interaction between these institutions and private enterprise, in contrast to the role that public research centers and institutions play in the NIEs, Japan, and industrialized economies.

10. The limitation here is that the open-economy model explicitly assumes that, due to comparative advantage, R&D only takes place in the North. Whilst this is an oversimplification of the true state of affairs, the results of the model are likely to hold without loss of generality so long as the North's R&D levels outstrip those of the South. The statistics concur with this finding: as alluded to earlier, relatively little R&D takes place in Asia Pacific outside Japan and the NIEs.

11. For example, consider the case where the fax machine is first employed in Pacific Asia. A single machine in Singapore is of virtually no use,

while two machines, one in Singapore and one in Malaysia, afford instant connectivity between the two nations, and four fax machines, in Singapore, Malaysia, South Korea, and Hong Kong, open up an entirely new permutation of interactions.

12. This may seem somewhat counterintuitive. Beaudry and Green (2001) argue that differences between industrialized nations can be accounted for by population growth differences; specifically, that technological adoption is positively correlated to population growth (due to the possibility of leapfrogging that arises from taking advantage of the abundance of human versus physical capital). Hence, for countries with higher population growth rates, such as Malaysia or Thailand, the possibility of leapfrogging not only exists, but can be exploited.

13. This section confines itself to the international relations aspects of ICT in Pacific Asia. See Tangsupvattana, especially the final section, elsewhere in this volume, for the relationship between the region and international institutions.

14. The e-ASEAN framework set the precedent for regional cooperation in ICT through free trade in ICT goods and services, the establishment of an ASEAN Information Infrastructure (AII), the enactment of e-commerce guidelines, capacity building in ICT, and e-society and e-government initiatives (ASEAN Secretariat 2000a). At the Summit Meeting of the ASEAN + 3 nations in November 2000, agreement was made to extend the initiative to include China, Japan, and South Korea (ASEAN Secretariat 2000b).

15. A multimedia e-citizen Website is planned as a one-stop portal for Singaporeans to access information, public services, and governmental ministries. It is designed according to the life journey, from birth to demise (http://www.ecitizen.gov.sg). Nationwide efforts were carried out to wire households and provide affordable PCs to encourage use of the Internet (Rodan 1998). Concurrently, the government encouraged the attitude of life-long learning to prepare the workforce for the new economy. The most recent effort is a National IT Literacy Programme (http://www.nitlp.com.sg), aimed at equipping all Singaporeans, including senior citizens and homemakers, with basic IT literacy skills such as Internet surfing, e-transactions and Internet Relay Chat (IRC). Courses are affordable and taught in English, Chinese, Tamil, and Malay.

16. Singapore's recent amendment of the Parliamentary Elections Act (Ng 2001) is viewed by some as the shrinking of online political space.

Political parties can campaign in cyberspace given they observe certain rules. It is seen as a response by the state to Singaporeans' increasing use of cyberspace for activism. Such concern may be warranted given Singapore's ICT penetration rate (48 percent), the highest in Asia Pacific. An example of such political activism can be seen at the website of the NGO, The Think Centre.

17. Even as China encourages ICT use, it exercises tight political control over urban Internet users. Still, it allows pockets of relatively free space. The police rarely shut down chat rooms of online university bulletin boards, which carry politically charged criticism against the state. Apparently, there is recognition of the need to give elites a sanctioned place for fairly free speech (Hachigian 2001a).

18. A play on Generation X, Generation Text refers to the penchant of Filipino youths for phone text messaging/short message services, or "texting" in the parlance of the subculture.

19. Oestmann identifies three reasons for telecenters enjoying some financial advantages over industrialized countries. One, in areas where the telecenter is the only basic telecommunications provider, a larger income can be gained. The income can be invested in comparatively cheaper technology such as wireless or satellite technology to build new telecenters and an infrastructure in yet-to-be-reached areas. Two, private developers may benefit from state funding to build telecenters. And three, the low PC penetration of small businesses and households ensures increasing demand for telecenters. So far, telecenters in industrialized countries seem to be able to break even or actually generate income. Development agencies are encouraging private developers to make these telecenters profit-generating in Pacific Asia's developing countries.

Bibliography

Akerlof, G. A. 1970. "The Market for 'Lemons': Quality Uncertainty and the Market Mechanism." *Quarterly Journal of Economics* 84(August): 488–500.

ASEAN Secretariat. 2000a. *e-ASEAN Framework Agreement.* Jakarta: ASEAN Secretariat.

————. 2000b. *Minutes of the ASEAN + 3 (Japan, People's Republic of China, the Republic of Korea) Summit Meeting,* Singapore, November

24. Jakarta: ASEAN Secretariat.

Baker, P. M. A. 2001. "Policy Bridges for the Digital Divide: Assessing the Landscape and Gauging the Dimensions." *First Monday* 6(5). <http://firstmonday.org/issues/issue6_5/baker/index.html> (22 May 2001).

Barlow, J. P. 1996. *A Declaration of the Independence of Cyberspace*. Davos, Switzerland: Electronic Frontier Foundation. <http://www.eff.org/~barlow/Declaration-Final.html> (15 September 2001).

Bazaar, B., and G. Boalch. 1997. "A Preliminary Model of Internet Diffusion within Developing Countries." Southern Cross University, Lismore, NSW, Australia. Photocopy. <http://ausweb.scu.edu.au/proceedings/boalch/paper.html> (24 August 2001).

Beaudry, P., and D. A. Green. 2001. "Population Growth, Technological Adoption and Economic Outcomes: A Theory of Cross-Country Differences for the Information Era." Working paper no. W8149. Cambridge, Mass.: National Bureau of Economic Research.

Borrus, M., D. Ernst, and S. Haggard, eds. 2000. *International Production Networks in Asia: Rivalry or Riches?* London: Routledge.

Brynjolfsson, E., and L. Hitt. 1996. "Paradox Lost? Firm-Level Evidence on the Returns to Information Systems Spending." *Management Science* 42(4): 541–558.

Buckley, P., and S. Montes. 2001. "Electronic Commerce: The Leading Edge of the Digital Economy." In Robert Shapiro, Lee Price, and Jeffrey Mayer, eds. *Digital Economy 2000*. Washington, D.C.: U.S. Department of Commerce, Economics and Statistics Administration.

Calderón, C. 2001. "Productivity in the OECD Countries: A Critical Appraisal of the Evidence." Working paper WP/01/89. Washington, D.C.: International Monetary Fund.

Canadian Security Intelligence Service. 2000. "Anti-Globalization—A Spreading Phenomenon." *Perspectives* (August). <http://www.csis-scrs.gc.ca/eng/miscdocs/200008_e.html> (22 August 2001).

Carolan, B. 2001. "Technology, Schools and the Decentralisation of Culture." *First Monday* 6(8). <http://firstmonday.org/issues/issues6_8/carolan/index.html> (26 August 2001).

Castells, M. 1998. "Information Technology, Globalization and Social Development." Proceedings of the UNRISD Conference on Information Technologies and Social Development, United Nations Research Institute for Social Development, Geneva, 22–23 June. <http://www.unrisd.org/infotech/conferen/castelp1.htm> (15 September 2001).

Chia S. Y., and J. J. Lim. 2001. "The ICT Revolution in APEC: Opportunities and Challenges." Proceedings of the 3rd APEC Roundtable and APIAN Workshop, APEC International Assessment Network, Singapore, 8–9 June.

———, eds. 2002. *Information Technology in Asia: New Development Paradigms.* Singapore: Institute of Southeast Asian Studies.

China Internet Network Information Centre. 2000. *Semi Annual Survey Report on Internet Development in China.* Beijing: CINIC.

Choi S. Y.; A. B. Whinston; and D. Stahl. 1997. *The Economics of Electronic Commerce.* Indianapolis, Indiana: Macmillan Technical.

Chung J. 2000. "Comparative Advantage and General Purpose Technologies." Harvard University, Cambridge, Mass. Photocopy.

Cisco Systems. 1999. "Philippine Long Distance Telephone Company (PLDT) Builds Path to Next-Generation Network Services with Cisco Systems Equipment." Press release, 6 December.

Dawson, S. 2001. "One in Four Homes Has 2 PCs or More." *The Straits Times* (30 August): H11.

Dedrick, J., and K. L. Kraemer. 1998. *Asia's Computer Challenge: Threat or Opportunity for the United States and the World?* New York: Oxford University Press.

Dewan, S., and K. L. Kraemer. 1998. "International Dimensions of the Productivity Paradox." *Communications of the ACM* 41(8): 56–62.

———. 2000. "Information Technology and Productivity: Evidence from Country Level Data." *Management Science* 46(4): 548–562.

Eder, E. P. 2001. "Tinig Ng Generation Txt." *Pinoy Times* (8 February).

eMarketer. 2001. *The eJapan Report.* New York, N.Y.: eMarketer.

Fazio, M., et al. 2000. "Measuring the Digital Divide." Paper presented at the OECD Joint WPTISP/WPIE Workshop (Working Party on Telecommunication and Information Services Policies/Working Party on Information Economy), Dubai, 7 December.

Fleck Research. 2000. "Analysis of Worldwide RF Coax Connectors and RF Coax Cable Assemblies." Research report R-1001/99. Santa Ana, Calif.: Fleck Research.

G7-G8 Secretariat. 2000. Okinawa Charter on the Global Information Society. Okinawa, 23 July. <http://europa.eu.int/comm/external_relations/g7_g8/intro/global_info_society.htm> (12 December 2001).

Gans, H. J. 1974. *Popular Culture and High Culture: An Analysis and Evaluation of Taste.* New York: Basic Books.

Geist, M. 2001. "Fair.com?: An Examination of the Allegations of Systemic Unfairness in the ICANN UDRP." University of Ottawa, Ottawa, Ontario. Photocopy.

Gesteland, L. J. 1999. "China Telecom to Expand ADSL, ISDN and Broad-band Services." *ChinaOnline News* (10 December).

Gordon, R. J. 1999. "Has the 'New Economy' Rendered the Productivity Slowdown Obsolete?" Northwestern University, Evanston, Ills. Pho-tocopy.

Grossman, G. M., and E. Helpman. 1991. *Innovation and Growth in the Global Economy*. Cambridge, Mass.: MIT Press.

Hachigian, N. 2001a. "China and the Net: A Love-Hate Relationship, Part I." *China Online* (5 March).

———. 2001b. "China and the Net: A Love-Hate Relationship, Part II." *China Online* (6 March).

———. 2001c. "China's Future Caught in the Web." *South China Morning Post* (23 July).

Helpman, E., ed. 1998. *General Purpose Technologies and Economic Growth*. Cambridge, Mass.: MIT Press.

Helpman, E., and M. Trajtenberg. 1998a. "A Time to Sow and a Time to Reap: Growth Based on General Purpose Technologies." In E. Helpman, ed. *General Purpose Technologies and Economic Growth*. Cambridge, Mass.: MIT Press.

———. 1998b. "Diffusion of General Purpose Technologies." In E. Helm-pan, ed. *General Purpose Technologies and Economic Growth*. Cam-bridge, Mass.: MIT Press.

Ho K. 1995. "A Study into the Problem of Software Piracy in Hong Kong and China." M.Sc. thesis, London School of Economics.

Hong D. P. 2001. "ICT Sector in the Republic of Korea: Recent Performance and Future Policy Directions." Paper presented at the ADB Capacity Building Workshop on ICT, Singapore, 21–27 February.

Houghton, J. W. 2001. *Australian ICT Trade Update 2001*. Melbourne: Centre for Strategic Economic Studies.

Infocommunication Development Authority of Singapore. 2000. "e-Gov-ernment Action Plan." Singapore: Infocommunication Development Authority.

Innovation and Technology Commission 2001. "Applied Science and Tech-nology Research Institute." Hong Kong: Innovation and Technology Commission. <http://www.info.gov.hk/itc/eng/infrastructure/astri.shtml> (5 September 2001).

International Planning and Research Corporation. 2001. "Sixth Annual BSA Global Software Piracy Study." Washington, D.C.: Business Software

Alliance. <http://www.bsa.org/resources/2001-05-21.55.pdf>.

International Telecommunications Union. 2000. *ITU World Telecommunications Indicators.* Geneva: International Telecommunications Union.

Jeong H. K., Oh J. H., and Shin I. 2001. "The Economic Impact of Information and Communication Technology in Korea." In M. Pohjola, ed. *Information Technology and Economic Development.* Oxford: Oxford University Press.

Kalathil, S., and T. C. Boas. 2001. "The Internet and State Control in Authoritarian Regimes: China, Cuba and the Counterrevolution." Working paper no. 21. Washington, D.C.: Carnegie Endowment for International Peace.

Kay, D. B., and B. Scott. 2000. "Intellectual Property Rights on the World Wide Web, China Update." *Asia Law and Practice IP Profiles 2000.* Jersey, U.K.: Euromoney Publications.

KnowNet Initiative. 2001. "News Clippings on ICT and Knowledge Management." <http://www.cddc.vt.edu/knownet/internetinfo-news.html> (15 September 2001).

Korea Information Society Development Institute. 1998. *Statistical Data.* Kwachun, Kyonggi-do: Korea Information Society Development Institute.

Krebs, V. 2001. "The Impact of the Internet on Myanmar." *First Monday* 6(5). <http://firstmonday.org/issues/issues6_5/krebs/index.html> (6 July 2001).

Krugman, Paul. 1997. "How Fast Can the U.S. Economy Grow?" *Harvard Business Review* (July/August).

Levinson, M. 2000. "Education for Technology or Technology for Education: The Dilemma of the New Economy." *Global Competitiveness Report 2000.* New York: Oxford University Press.

Low L. 2000. *Economics of Information Technology and the Media.* Singapore: World Scientific and Singapore University Press.

Lucking-Reiley, D., and D. F. Spulber. 2001. "Business-to-Business Electronic Commerce." *Journal of Economic Perspectives* 15(1): 55–68.

Madrick, J. 2001. "High Tech and New Economy: Big Idea Deflates." *International Herald Tribune* (11 May).

Malaysia National IT Council. 2000. *Access, Empowerment and Governance in the Information Age.* Kuala Lumpur: National IT Council.

Midgley, J. 1995. *Social Development: The Developmental Approach in Social Welfare.* Thousand Oaks, Calif.: Sage Publications

————. 2001. "Globalisation, Postmodernity and International Social Work." In N. T. Tan and E. Envall, eds. *Social Work Around the World*. Berne, Switzerland: International Federation of Social Work.

National Information Technology Committee. 2000. *e-Thailand Initiative*. Bangkok: National Information Technology Committee Secretariat. <http://www.nitc.go.th/eThailand> (11 July 2001).

National Information Technology Council. 1997. "The Dynamics of the Information Technology Industry in the Philippines." In *IT Action Agenda for the 21st Century*. Manila: National Information Technology Council.

National Statistical Office of Korea. 2000. *Statistical Handbook of Korea 2000*. Seo-Gu, Daejeon: National Statistical Office.

National Trade Data Bank and Economic Bulletin Board. 1996. *International Market Insight*. Kuala Lumpur: National Trade Data Bank and Economic Bulletin Board.

Netsizer. 2001. "Number of Internet Hosts and Internet Users." <http://www.netsizer.com> (23 May 2001).

Ng I. 2001. "Parties Can Now Take Polls Battle to Cyberspace." *The Straits Times* (14 August).

Ng K. K. 1999. *The Rainbow Connection: The Internet and the Singapore Gay Community*. Singapore: KangCuBine Publishing.

Niininen, P. 2001. "Computers and Economic Growth in Finland." In M. Pohjola, ed. *Information Technology and Economic Development*. Oxford: Oxford University Press.

Nua Internet Surveys. 2000. "How Many Online: Asia." <http://www.nua.ie/surveys/how_many_online/asia.html> (23 May 2001).

Oestmann, S. 2001. *Public Access Vehicles in ICT Development: Experiences, Lessons and Trends*. Intelecon Research and Consultancy, Dallas, Texas. Photocopy.

Oliner, S. D., and D. E. Sichel. 2000. "The Resurgence of Growth in the Late 1990s: Is Information Technology the Story?" *Journal of Economic Perspectives* 14(4).

Political and Economic Risk Consultancy. 2001. "The Nagging Problem of Corruption in Asia." *Asian Intelligence*, no. 579 (March).

Porter, M. 1990. *The Competitive Advantage of Nations*. New York: Free Press.

Porter, M., et al. 2000. *World Economic Forum Global Competitiveness Report 2000*. New York: Oxford University Press.

Quah D. 1999. "The Weightless Economy in Economic Development."

Discussion paper no. 417. London: Center for Economic Policy Research.

———. 2000. "The Weightless New Economy." Proceedings of the EVA—Centre for Finnish Business and Policy Studies seminar, Helsinki, 8 September.

———. 2001. "Technology Dissemination and Economic Growth: Lessons for the New Economy." Proceedings of the University of Hong Kong's 90th Anniversary Technology and the Economy Public Lecture Series, Hong Kong, 19 March.

Rees, R. 1989. "Uncertainty, Information and Insurance." In J. D. Hey, ed. *Current Issues in Microeconomics*. Hampshire, U.K.: Macmillan.

Rodan, G. 1998. "The Internet and Political Control in Singapore." *Political Science Quarterly* 113(1).

Rodríguez, F., and E. J. Wilson, III. 2000. "Are Poor Countries Losing the Information Revolution?" Working paper, info Dev.

Rogers, E. 1995. *The Diffusion of Innovations*. 4th ed. New York: Free Press.

Romer, P. M. 1986. "Increasing Returns and Long-Run Growth." *Journal of Political Economy* 94: 163–202.

Sapp, S. G. 2001. "Lectures on Conceptual Approach: Science and Technology." Iowa State University, Ames. Photocopy. <http://www.soc.iastate.edu/soc415/soc415.webster.html> (18 July 2001).

Schreyer, P. 2000. "The Impact of Information and Communication Technology on Output Growth." Working paper 2000/2, OECD STI (Science Technology, and Industry), Paris.

Shamsul, A. B. 2000. "On Preservation of Culture." In National IT Council, ed. *Access, Empowerment and Governance in the Information Age*. Kuala Lumpur: National IT Council.

Shapiro, C., and H. R. Varian. 1998. *Information Rules: A Strategic Guide to the Network Economy*. Boston: Harvard Business School Press.

Sicam, P. P. 2001. "The Role of IT Activism in the Ouster of Estrada." *CyberDyaryo* (8 February).

"SMS Divorces Not Acceptable." 2001. *The Straits Times* (8 August).

South East Asia Regional Computer Confederation. 2001. *Report on the Regional ICT Manpower and Skills Survey, Year 1999—2000*. Singapore: South East Asia Regional Computer Confederation.

Solow, R. 1956. "A Contribution to the Theory of Economic Growth." *Quarterly Journal of Economics* 70: 65–94.

———. 1987. "We'd Better Watch Out." *New York Times Book Review* (12 July): 36.

Stat-USA. 2001. *E-Commerce Market Survey*. Washington, D.C.: U.S. Department of Commerce.

Tang E. 2001. "The Internet Turning into a Web of Vice." *The Sunday Times* (Singapore) 13 May.

Teo, T. S. H., and V. K. G. Lim. 1998. "Leveraging Information Technology to Achieve the IT2000 Vision: The Case Study of an Intelligent Island." *Behavior and Information Technology* 17(2): 113–123.

Tiihonen, P. 2001. "Common Interest and E-things." Proceedings of the International Symposium on Telework and New Forms of Work in the Information Society, Québec City, Québec, 14 May.

Touré, H. I. 2001. "Universal Access to Information and Communication Technology (ICT) in the Asia-Pacific Region." *Connect-World Asia-Pacific Second Quarter 2001*. London: World Infocomms.<http://www.connect-world.com/docs/articles/cwasia2q01/toure_itu_cwasia2q01.asp> (14 September 2001).

Triplett, J. E. 1999. "The Solow Productivity Paradox: What Do Computers Do to Productivity?" *Canadian Journal of Economics* 32(2): 309–334.

Turner, V. 1990. "Liminality and Community." In J. C. Alexander and S. Seidman, eds. *Culture and Society: Contemporary Debates*. Cambridge, UK: Cambridge University Press.

United Nations Development Programme. 2001. "China Harnesses the Internet to Reduce Rural Poverty." *Newsfront* (21 August).

"The U.S. Productivity Puzzle." 2001. *The Economist Global Agenda* (9 August).

"Vietnam Stakes Its High-Tech Claim." 2001. *Asia Times* (15 August). <http://www.atimes.com/se-asia/CH16Ae01.html> (16 August 2001).

Wingrove, N. 1995. "China Traditions Oppose War on IP Piracy." *Research-Technology Management* 38(3).

Wong P. K. 1999. "National Innovation Systems for Rapid Technological Catch-up: An Analytical Framework and a Comparative Analysis for Korea, Taiwan, and Singapore." Proceedings of the DRUID Summer Conference on National Innovation Systems, Industrial Dynamics and Innovation Policy, Danish Research Unit for Industrial Dynamics, Rebild, Denmark, 9–12 June.

———. 2000. "The Productivity Impact of Information Technology in Singapore." Singapore: Centre for Management of Innovation and Technopreneurship. Photocopy.

———. 2001. "ICT Production and Diffusion in Asia: Digital Dividends or Digital Divide?" Singapore: Centre for Management of Innovation and Technopreneurship. Photocopy.

Wong S. L. 2001. "Malaysia: Internet on Wheels." *Choices* September. <http://www.sdnp.undp.org/it4dev/stories/malaysia.html> (15 September 2001).

World Bank. 2000a. *World Development Report 2000*. Washington, D.C.: World Bank.

———. 2000b. "The Networking Revolution—Opportunities and Challenges for Developing Countries." Working paper, *info* Dev.

5

Environmental Change and Transitions to Sustainability in Pacific Asia

Louis Lebel

Development in Pacific Asia has been viewed for several decades as equivalent to macroeconomic growth. The value of this myopic paradigm for the future needs to be challenged and replaced by a regional commitment to sustainability. The pathways that the diverse states and societies in the region opt for or are driven to take will undoubtedly vary, but the shared pursuit of sustainability holds much promise for creating regional futures that are peaceful, just, and prosperous. The immediate and longer-term challenges posed by environmental change and outstanding development problems for sustainability, however, are multiple and interrelated. Much depends on the form and intensity of linkages between places as regional development unfolds, a process filled with huge uncertainties.

The primary focus of this chapter is environmental change and how it has been driven by technological, behavioral, institutional, and political transformations in Pacific Asia. A secondary focus is on how these environmental changes may be, in turn, constraining development. Ultimately, it is the goal here to encourage designers—and dreamers—of alternative futures to pay greater attention to the dependencies of development on the self-organizing, adaptive capacity of complex ecosystems and the societies that use, live, and play within them.

Much of the background material on drivers and trends in this chapter is based on an assessement activity for Southeast Asia supported by the Asia-Pacific Network for Global Environmental Change Research and START. Their contributions and those of the scientists involved are gratefully acknowledged.

Louis Lebel

Drivers of Environmental Change

Industrialization, Consumption Growth, and Integration with Global Markets

Pacific Asia in general—and East Asia in particular—has been a hot spot for both development and environmental change (Lebel and Steffen 1998; Lebel 2002b). Integration into the global economic system has had a profound influence on the development processes in the region (Watanabe 1992), although integration was delayed in the centrally planned and war-affected countries. The rates of economic growth in the region have been faster than in most parts of the world for several decades (Stallings 1995). As a result, much of the region is now more industrialized, diversified, and integrated into the global economy than its counterparts elsewhere (Knight 1998; Rock 1998). After a long tradition of protectionist and inward-looking policies, trade in East Asia today has, in proportional terms, regained the significance it had to economies at the turn of the twentieth century. The volume of commodities, including food and timber—which are directly dependent on maintenance of ecosystems—has increased enormously. East Asia is both the manufacturing belt and kitchen of the world.

Up until the 1997 financial crisis, foreign direct investment had grown very rapidly, accelerating the process of export-oriented industrialization. Thus, between 1970 and 1993, the contribution by industry to the gross domestic product of ASEAN increased from 25 percent to 40 percent, while industrial output increased twenty-five times during the same period. Among East Asian countries, however, the extent of industrialization varies greatly (fig. 1). In Thailand, Indonesia, China, and Malaysia the industrial sector is large and still growing, whereas in Laos, Myanmar, North Korea, East Timor, and Cambodia it is very limited. Japan, South Korea, and Taiwan, on the other hand, have mature industrialized economies. In Singapore the service sector now dominates.

Economies within the region are becoming increasingly interdependent through commodity trade, investment flows, and exchange and division of labor. The integration of China into regional and global markets, through new bilateral trade agreements, could drive this process much further in coming decades. The opportunities are huge and so are the risks and uncertainties. The 1997 Asian financial crisis, for example, was a sharp reminder to states how current development strategies are vulnerable to the vagaries of investment flows (Phongpaichit and Baker 1998; Jomo 1998).

Figure 1. Comparison of National Economies

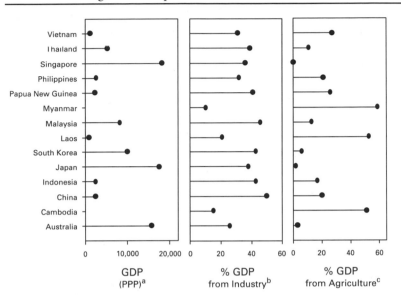

Source: Compiled by author.
(a) Per capita gross domestic product in 1996 (adjusted for purchasing power parity in 1987 U.S. dollars).
(b) Contribution of industrial sector to GDP.
(c) Contribution of agricultural sector to GDP.

As rapid as industrialization has been in Asia Pacific, most of the investment in industrialization of Southeast Asia is still to come (Angel and Rock 2000). A 1994 World Bank study for Indonesia, for example, estimated that as much as 85 percent of the capital stock that would be in place in 2020 was not in place then. Because it is much cheaper to install cleaner and more efficient technologies in new plants than it is to upgrade old ones, this is an opportunity for nations to guide the transformation along more sustainable trajectories. Investment in the industry and energy sectors could be directed toward the use of cleaner technologies to limit the effects of pollutants on local health, regional air quality, and global climate (Forsyth 1999).

There are a number of reasons why the impetus for cleaner production processes, even among the least developed countries in the region, will grow (Angel and Rock 2000). These include an increasing concern about environmental health, awareness of energy and material efficiencies, green consumer markets, international standardization, information and technology flows, and international agreements on the environment (Rock 2002).

Industrialization is not possible without energy. Growth in energy consumption has followed the overall patterns in economic growth. The median average annual growth in per capita energy consumption between 1985 and 1997 for East Asian countries was 8 percent (World Resources Institute 2000). The highest growth was recorded by Thailand with 18 percent per year. Nevertheless, in 1997, per capita energy consumption in Singapore was still more than six times that in Thailand and two hundred times that in Laos, illustrating the huge disparity in levels of consumption. Electricity consumption has increased even faster than overall energy consumption. Thus, between 1986 and 1995 annual electricity consumption increased 24 percent in Indonesia, 22 percent in Thailand, and 19 percent in Malaysia, compared to only 3 percent per year for member countries of the Organisation for Economic Co-operation and Development (OECD) (Forsyth 1999). The industry sector is the largest consumer of energy in most countries, apart from Singapore, where the transport sector dominates, and the less developed nations, such as Laos and Cambodia, where residential use still dominates.

Domestic consumption growth in the newly industrializing economies (NIEs) has received much less attention than export growth from analysts, but is clearly crucial to the future of the region. New hybrid "western-eastern" norms of consumption are being created through expanding advertising budgets in the mass media and even soap operas in which role models preach unconstrained consumption in sets filled with products from program sponsors. Rising wealth is also expanding domestic markets for what were once primarily export commodities.

Cheap energy from fossil fuels has been crucial to regional economic growth. Concerns about energy security in East Asia have been voiced for several decades, but they have been heard anew with the rapid economic growth of China since the nineties, and the re-emergence of U.S. militarism as it seeks to take greater control over oil reserves in South Asia and the Middle East. Although disputes over areas with oil and gas reserves—for example, in the South China Sea—are always present, the likelihood of these leading to major conflicts appears remote (Stares 2000). Of perhaps greater concern is the growing reliance in the region on oil from the Middle East as the era of cheap oil draws to a close.

Urbanization and Demographic Transitions

Urbanization has often accompanied industrialization, because of the need for easy access to labor, markets, and economies of scale, with the result that major polluting industries are either within or near major population centers along the coast. The concentration of large infrastructure projects such as major airports and cargo ports are key features of becoming a world city. On the other hand, development of basic infrastructure, especially for drinking water and sewerage, has often failed to keep up with migrations to cities attracted by private investments in manufacturing and service industries and also by lack of opportunities in rural areas (Forbes 1996; Ness and Low 2000). One outcome has been the urbanization of poverty and the simultaneous fall and rise of living standards in different parts of the same city.

Thus, concern with urbanization has focused on the growth of mega-cities: first Tokyo and Seoul, then Beijing, Shanghai, Bangkok, and Jakarta. As the cores of these cities expand and merge with surrounding satellite towns, administrative and planning boundaries often must be redrawn. Metropolitan Jakarta, known as Jabotabek, for example, consists of seven administrative units, the total population of which was 17.1 million in 1990. When industrial estates have been intentionally sited in rural areas to take advantage of low-cost surplus rural labor, cheap land and natural resources, they have helped create new urban regions out of small agricultural towns. Transformations in a few cities like Tsukuba in Japan or Singapore (Ling 1995) have been strongly "guided." Most urban areas, however, are the result of unregulated market forces, rather than of planning or consultation (Yap and Mohit 1998).

When viewed over historical time frames, demographic changes have been critical for periods both of rapid growth and of stagnation in the economies of East Asia. Fertility and mortality rates continue to fall throughout the region, with the consequence that some countries will face significant changes in age structure and low or negative growth rates of population over the coming decades. An aging population, as already found in Singapore and Japan, will stretch the capacities of states and households to take care of the elderly. Fertility declines and consequent aging population structures have appeared rapidly in the NIEs. In Thailand the impacts on rural towns and agricultural labor are compounded by urbanization and the ravages of AIDS (Jones and Pardthaisong 2000). Exactly what effect these demographic shifts will have on national capacity to maintain economic growth over the next couple of decades will depend on whether the productivity of an aging population can be maintained through, for example, changes in technology and shifts to service-oriented economies (Wallace 1999). The impacts on environmental protection are also complex, and may turn out to be large.

The way urbanization unfolds is critical for regional transitions to sustainability. High-density living helps reduce the energy required for climate control, both cooling and heating, and for mobility, because it makes public mass transit systems economically viable. Improved education, access to information, and opportunities to influence public decision-making could reshape environmental stewardship values.

Intensification, Integration, and Concentration of Natural Resource–Based Industries

Much of the initial capital for industrialization has come from the conversion of land resources, in particular the expansion of export-oriented agriculture and the exploitation of tropical forests for timber (Brookfield and Byron 1990; Than 1998; King 1998). Conversely, remittances sent to rural areas from family members in the city are a critical contribution to the capital needed to introduce new technologies and intensify production methods in agriculture (Rigg 1997).

The intensification and expansion of agriculture for domestic and export markets has resulted in large increases in the application of fertilizer and land cultivated. In Southeast Asia, between 1961 and 1997 land under permanent cultivation approximately doubled. The total consumption of fertilizers increased more than nineteenfold, while the value of trade in pesticides, herbicides, and fungicides increased more than fifteenfold (Food and Agricultural Organization 1998). In addition there have been over time large increases in the intensity of cropping made possible by expansion of irrigation infrastructure. At the same time, prime land and water resources in wider river valleys and deltas are increasingly competing with expanding urban centers.

Changes at the farm level are also reflected in the reorganization of agribusiness. State policies and structural adjustment programs of the multilateral banks have led to greater vertical integration of commodity chains, consolidation of processing and retailing, and, hence, concentration of control (Glover 1999; Goss, Burch, and Rickson 2000). This has occurred even though much of the primary production continues to be based on the efforts of numerous small farm enterprises.

In forestry the emphasis remains on the production of wood and wood products rather than on the sustainable use of forest resources (Lohmann 1996; Thompson and Duggie 1996). Consequently, logging has resulted in deforestation, loss of habitats, and endangered biodiversity. The logging and wood-product industries have been open only to elite business networks with close links to political power (Dauvergne 2001) with the result that many of the benefits of exploitation have not accrued to wider society. The forestry sector also shows parallel trends of intensification and industrialization with logging of native forests, which no longer exist as mature stands, now being replaced by cultivation of tree crops in intensively managed, single species plantations.

In forestry and fisheries, investment from and trade with foreign and transnational companies have been crucial drivers of rapid exploitation, and, arguably, unsustainable industrial practices in the developing countries of Pacific Asia (Dauvergne 1997; Lebel et al. 2002). Roving practices, or sequential exploitation, have been made easier by vertical integration, concentration of control, and weak environmental institutions in the resource-rich developing countries.

Militarization and Insecurity

Security tensions have risen and fallen across Asia Pacific like waves as states untangled themselves from earlier colonial masters, and then realigned during the cold war, braced themselves for the reemergence of China as an economic power, and then held their breath as the United States and its allies launched their "war on terror." Wars and military control have already had a terrible impact on the region's environment and livelihoods. Events since September 11, 2001, have not helped. Tensions between Muslim minorities in southern Thailand and the Philippines and their respective central governments have intensified since the U.S. invasions of Afghanistan and Iraq. Anti-U.S. sentiment remains high among parts of the population in Indonesia. States respond with increased military presence in what is often a vicious cycle of violence that creates greater insecurity. Insecurity, in turn, makes longer-term investments in land, or forest and coastal fisheries management, less likely because investors are aware of the risk that they will not reap the benefits of their efforts. Such processes work against transitions to sustainability. History provides many examples.

Louis Lebel

The military, with its influence on political institutions as well as business, has been a key actor in the exploitation of forests and natural resources. Much of the depletion of forests in Thailand, Laos, Cambodia, and Indonesia from the 1960s to the1990s, for example, can be attributed to military dominance in government and cold war politics. Resource use and development under crony capitalism has proven unsustainable (Pasong and Lebel 2000).

War has also had long-term direct consequences for the environment. During the Vietnam War, the United States dropped thousands of tons of bombs and chemical defoliant on the countryside of Laos and Vietnam. Twenty-five years later, unexploded mines and bombs still represent a threat to farmers (Lovering 2001), but the biggest impact has probably been sanctions and barriers to economic integration. Centrally planned economies like that of Vietnam, after a delayed start, are now among the fastest growing in the region. In more recent times, civil war has created lawless zones where no one has security of access or tenure, leaving forests open for the taking, like on the Thai-Myanmar border (Brunner, Talbott, and Elkin 1998; Earth Rights International 2003). It has also added to human misery, driving people into refugee camps, forced labor, or as illegal immigrants into dangerous and underpaid jobs.

Although conventional international security concerns, and the activities of the military, may seem remote from issues of sustainability, environmental quality, and equity, given images of booming sea-side resorts, productive rice fields, and busy financial capitals in Pacific Asia, it only seems that way. Coercion and violence associated with military strength remain important factors affecting livelihoods and resource management, especially in remoter upland areas and the seas.

Democratization and Decentralization

Democratization and decentralization are often thought of as self-evident progressive trends that have unfolded and helped drive economic and social development in Pacific Asia. The evidence is mixed. Gains are insecure and net progress measured in terms of public involvement, transparency, and accountability remains disappointing. Large infrastructure projects are still frequently decided by political and bureaucratic leaders in consultation with big investors and credit agencies. Public access to assessments, environmental performance information, and details of investing groups remains difficult to obtain. Corruption of public officials, state control over mass media, and poor access to information remain huge barriers to sustainable development in many countries (Phongpaichit and Piriyarangsan 1994; McCargo 2000; Colfer and Resosudarmo 2002).

An important aspect of democratization is the decentralization of power from the central government to local government. Openness and a greater degree of freedom and participation in the public policy process are observable in the region, Myanmar and North Korea being recalcitrant exceptions. Some countries have reformed key political institutions, for example, Thailand with its 1997 constitutional reform, and Indonesia with its post-Suharto decentralization programs. The Asian financial crisis led to sweeping reforms of economic institutions, especially in the financial sector.

Democratization has not been led by the state, but rather is a response to pressure from the rise in number and influence of national and transnational civil society actors (Florini 2000). Environmental, labor, human rights and community development movements and organizations are increasingly challenging standard development and environmental doctrine (Hirsch and Warren 1998; Laungaramsri 2002), while, it could be argued, that much of their population grows apathetic with party politics. These movements are diverse and struggle to remove the shackled perspectives of class (Forsyth 2001). Nevertheless, through the alternative discourses (Dryzek 1999) and arenas they create, the activities of national and transnational civil society are beginning to reshape decision-making over development across Pacific Asia.

CRITICAL ENVIRONMENTAL TRENDS

The interaction of these various drivers has resulted in a number of critical environmental trends across Pacific Asia (fig. 2). The response of local, national, and regional institutions to these trends has been mixed, late rather than timely, but not without hopeful signs (Rock 2002).

Local and Regional Air Quality

Atmospheric emissions have typically increased rapidly in the early phases of industrialization and rapid economic growth. Thus, in Thailand during

Louis Lebel

Figure 2. Drivers and Critical Environmental Trends

DRIVERS

- Urbanization
- Industrialization
- Demographic transitions
- Democratization
- Innovation

- Globalization
- Intensification
- Consumption growth
- Militarization
- Decentralization

CRITICAL ENVIRONMENTAL TRENDS

Land
- Loss of ecological resilience from conversion and simplification of habitats
- Conversion of prime agricultural land for urban and industrial development
- Improvements in agricultural productivity
- Irreversible lossess of biodiversity
- Expansion of conservation and multiple-use management

Air
- Rising number of fixed-emission sources
- Improved emission control technologies and standards
- Recurrent regional episodes of haze from land fires
- Difficulties controlling fine particulates in urban areas
- Rapidly rising aggregate CO_2 emissions
- Long-range transport of pollutants—acid deposition

Water
- Rising demand for water in agriculture and other sectors
- Declines in flows and sediments in dammed rivers
- Improvements in monitoring and treatment of water
- Over-use and contamination of groundwater resources
- Lack of cheap access to clean drinking water for poor
- Degradation of riparian, flood plain, and wetland ecosystems

Seas
- Overharvesting of marine fisheries
- Pollution from land-based activities and ships
- Improvements in fishing technology and monitoring
- Degradation of bottom-dwelling communities from trawling and shipping
- Degradation of coastal ecosystems—mangroves, wetlands and coral reefs

COUPLED SOCIAL TRENDS

- Participation in decision
- Altered vulnerabilities
- Distribution of benefits

- Accountability for actions
- Sharing of involuntary risks
- Maintaining adaptive capacity

Source: Compiled by author.

116

the 1980s, for example, sulfur dioxide emissions from the industrial sector doubled, while nitrogen oxides almost trebled and suspended particulate matter increased almost fourfold (Sachasinh, Phantumvanit, and Tridech 1992). In Malaysia between 1988 and 1995, sulfur dioxide and nitrogen oxides almost doubled, and emissions of particulates increased threefold (Tan and Kwong 1990). Over time most governments have tightened standards, strengthened regulations, and improved monitoring so that the levels of most major pollutants dangerous to human health have decreased. Nitrous oxides and particulate matter have often proved harder to contain. Mobile sources continued to make up around half of the particulate emissions of Bangkok for every year between 1992 and 2000. Clean and efficient public mass transit systems are extremely important for local air quality, but only a few cities in Pacific Asia have effective systems.

The sheer volume of new vehicles, factories, and other polluting activities in the NIEs still poses huge challenges to the regulatory and monitoring capacity of the state. Much needs to be done, for example, to increase energy efficiencies and reduce pollution intensities of industries where a common history of nonenforced regulatory policies (Angel and Rock 2000) has allowed poor practices to accumulate. Scrutiny must also be directed at strategies of relocating polluting industries as these frequently just shift problems onto other populations (Bai 2002).

Much like pollutants from multiple sources, pollutants that are more widely dispersed have proven more difficult to control. In 1990, approximately 18 percent of Asia was affected by acid deposition—that is, deposition exceeding critical loads—with the heaviest concentrations occurring in southeastern China, South Korea, Thailand around Bangkok, and Indonesia in parts of Sumatra near Jakarta. In Vietnam, only 35 percent of the total annual sulfur deposition comes from sources within the country (Arndt and Carmichael 1995); China contributes almost 39 percent and Thailand 19 percent. Projections suggest that in only two to three decades sulfur deposition levels will exceed those observed in the 1970s and 1980s in Europe and North America (Arndt, Carmichael, and Roorda 1996).

Land management practices and conversion policies can also be a major contribution to poor air quality. Smoke from land fires at the end of the dry season creates local air quality problems in many locations in mainland Southeast Asia. In other parts of the wetter tropics, widespread land fires associated with dry phases of the El Niño Southern Oscillation can lead to serious transboundary haze episodes. In the last episode of severe haze around Sumatra and Kalimantan in 1997–1998, many of the fires had been deliberately lit to clear forest and logged land for conversion to oil palm plantations or as part of large-scale new rice cultivation and settlement projects (Murdiyarso et al. 2004; Tomich et al. 1998).

Greenhouse Gas Emissions

During most of the twentieth century, the contribution by East Asia to global greenhouse gas concentrations in the atmosphere was modest. At present, per capita carbon dioxide emissions from industrial, domestic, and transport sectors of developing Asian economies are small compared to those of the industrialized world. Most countries in the region use fossil fuels for the generation of electricity. The main exception is China, which has a large dependence on coal. A few have significant hydropower and geothermal resources. The average annual growth in energy consumption has been around 10 percent. In rural areas, wood is still a major source of energy. Wealthier countries like Japan, Singapore, and South Korea have much higher per capita emissions. The likelihood of further rapid aggregate growth in emissions is high. At the same time, developing countries, especially China, are likely to come under increasing international pressure to minimize emissions growth with economic development. Luckily there are many opportunities to do so in ways that will not hinder economic development but also help improve public health.

The fluxes of carbon associated with changes in land use in Pacific Asia are also globally significant (Canadell 2002). Forestry and agriculture can play a role in sequestering additional carbon, but there are problems of permanency. For example, projects that reforest areas sequester carbon over time, but if the areas are prone to fires—because of social or management practices—then the net benefits may be small (Murdiyarso, Widodo, and Suyamto 2002).

Water Resources

Historically, most societies in Pacific Asia have developed strategies and institutions, sometimes quite sophisticated, to cope with and exploit fluctuations in water supply. Most of the dominant civilizations in deltas and main valleys grew around rice cultivation and the control of irrigation. For the most part, however, these systems were developed in a context where overall demand for water was low to moderate. Thus, most irrigation systems in East Asia are designed for slow continuous water delivery, but really what rice farms need is the capacity to deliver water on demand.

Over time demand has risen greatly, making allocation more complex and contested. Expanding irrigation areas are now frequently in direct competition for water with new urban residential, recreational, and industrial users. In-stream flows must also be managed to meet rising demands for electricity from hydropower. If they can, users respond by also extracting ground water. Water shortages, both real and imagined, become a common topic on policy agendas and a favorite of organizational interests, of, for example, irrigation departments, energy agencies, and engineering construction companies. The call is then for further investments in large-scale water infrastructure—tunnels, diversions, dams, and so on. As for energy, little attention is given to managing and reducing demand, but rather the focus remains on increasing supply. Another call has been to shift from the traditional view of water as a fundamental right to the economic-rationalist view of a commodity that should be paid for and be allocated to the highest value uses. Most major rivers in the region are now dammed for flood control, dry season irrigation, or hydropower. Even so, there are many plans for much more infrastructure including inter-basin transfers. Maintaining flows and flow regimes that would conserve aquatic, riparian, wetland, and coastal marine ecosystems has rarely been a significant priority.

Water Pollution

The amount of water that can actually be used is often reduced from what is available because of pollution. Water pollution problems vary greatly among regions of a country, between cities and rural areas, and among countries depending on the extent of industrialization and effectiveness of government regulations and monitoring.

In the Asian countries that industrialized earliest—notably Japan, South Korea, Taiwan, and Singapore—water quality problems tend to be related to manufacturing industries or human settlements. For the most part, these countries have made substantial progress in improving environmental quality through regulation and incentives for business, but this did not happen before serious water quality problems affecting health were experienced. Today, technology and aid from these countries are important for water management and treatment in other countries in the region.

The same applies to industrial air-borne emissions. It is important that newly industrializing economies guide new investments in industry toward paths that do not worsen already acute water quality problems and other environmental health problems.

The lack of reasonable access to safe drinking water is a constraint on the health and well-being of the region's poor, many of whom, ironically, pay more for their water than the wealthy do. As a result of weak planning and inadequate and late investment in public infrastructure, access to drinking water and sanitation services remain critical environmental problems for the poor in Pacific Asia.

In the transitional and developing economies of East Asia, resource-based industries still account for the majority of water-polluting emissions. This has led to declining water quality in major rivers that discharge their waste into the sea. Recognition of these problems has led to new environmental laws and agencies to control and manage water quality. In Malaysia, for example, concern over pollution of waterways from palm oil and rubber processing led to the Environmental Quality Act of 1974. This, however, did not prevent the Malaysian palm oil–processing industry from being responsible for 63 percent of the country's total water pollution load nearly a decade later (Khalid and Braden 1993). In the period 1978–1984, the Department of Environment introduced progressively more restrictive standards on palm oil effluence, requiring crude palm oil mills to apply for operating licenses every year (Vincent, Rozali, and Khalid 2000). License fees were adjusted according to the quantity of waste discharged. Eventually, as a result of mandatory standards and effluent fees, substantial reductions in bio-oxygen demand were achieved at the same time that industry continued to expand.

Organic pollutants resist natural decomposition processes and accumulate in living tissue. Not only do they persist, but they can be transported long distances as they often lack volatility. These include chemicals used in agricultural pest control, disease-vector control, and industry. Severe restrictions on their use have been enforced in some countries in the region for more than twenty years; in others there are no restrictions at all. In parts of East Asia where export-oriented crops dominate, pollutants from the widespread application of pesticides, fungicides, and herbicides on crops and in plantations can be expected to affect surface water and groundwater (Liwawruangrath et al. 1999; Rattanaphani 1999).

Finally, many water pollution problems that start on land end up being transported by rivers and are discharged into coastal waters where they accumulate. Land-based pollution of regional seas is a common and recurring problem in East Asia, but is especially serious in some highly industrialized areas, for example, around the Yellow Sea, a semi-enclosed body surrounded by China and the Korean peninsula. Oil spills and waste dumping by ships also contribute to marine pollution, especially around major ports and in busy shipping lanes.

Marine Ecosystems and Fisheries

Around the world, major fishing grounds are being overexploited. This is reflected in declining yields per unit effort, as well as shifts to fish of smaller size, and a greater reliance on species further down the food chain. Pacific Asia with its traditionally high levels of fish and seafood consumption, large coastal populations, and relatively small sea areas between countries, has contributed to this global decline, as well as suffered its impacts. It is only massive increases in technology and effort that have enabled fisheries production figures to be maintained. Counter-intuitively, aquaculture because of its dependence on harvesting oceans for fish meal used in feed preparation may be making matters in the ocean worse (Naylor et al. 2000). States in the region have struggled to manage shared fisheries sustainably and have not been able to develop an effective institutional framework (Vanderzwaag and Johnston 1998). Barriers to better regional cooperation on environmental matters appear to be particularly strong in the case of coastal and marine resources (Talaue-McManus 2000) as these are hampered by sovereignty and territorial disputes in the South China Sea. Moreover, long-term development plans for coastal and rural areas are often inconsistent with stated commitments to the protection of biodiversity and sustainable development.

Mangroves and coastal wetlands are under pressure for a variety of reasons, including expansion of urban settlements, exploitation of wood for fuel, agricultural development, and construction of fish and shrimp ponds (Lebel et al. 2002; Chuenpagdee and Pauly 2004). Between 1980 and 1994, most countries in Southeast Asia lost about half their mangrove cover. In Vietnam the conversion of mangroves to shrimp farms, rice paddies, and other uses has increased the vulnerability of coastal communities to sea-level changes and storms (Adger 1999). Rehabilitation of degraded mangrove forests could yield considerable economic benefits, particularly by mitigating storm damage (Tri, Adger, and Kelly 1998). Many other coastal environments are also being impacted by tourism and shipping.

Louis Lebel

Overall, there is little uncertainty about the seriousness of degradation trends in the condition of the marine ecosystems in Pacific Asia. What is less clear is whether calls for more aquaculture, integrated coastal zone management, and ecosystem-based management of fisheries will lead to effective institutional mechanisms that can reverse some of these trends. More gains may depend on altering consumer behavior and the redesign of trade regimes as the fishery industry is built around trade.

Vulnerability to Climate

Floods and droughts have long been part of the way of life for millions in Southeast Asia, but current patterns of infrastructure and architecture fit less and less well with seasonal regimes. In Jakarta and Bangkok, the uncontrolled building of roads and waterways has compounded flooding during the wet season. Ground water extraction exacerbates problems by causing subsidence and salinity intrusions into delta areas.

The pattern of fast-growing cities in low-lying floodplains and coastal areas has increased the vulnerability of human settlements and infrastructure to the natural variability of climate and global environmental change. A rise in sea level or an increased frequency and intensity of storms would have major impacts on these new urban areas. Moreover, the changes to the environment that result from land use, the effect of dams on sediment delivery to oceans, and the channelization of rivers will themselves interact with climate. Such consequences are rarely taken into account in city planning and design. A history of weak implementation of building regulations and codes further increases vulnerability to extreme climatic events in several countries.

On the other hand, increasing wealth, structural shifts away from agriculture-dominated local and regional economies, the growth in insurance services, and increased attention given to risk planning and management suggest that for many sectors and groups in society vulnerabilities to current climate are probably falling. Simple statistics of dollar damage do not contradict such a conclusion because they primarily reflect the much higher value of assets being exposed to risk. Future climate may be a different story. Uncertainty about how precipitation, for example, might change with global warming makes it hard to guess what the future water resources available for rain-fed and irrigated agriculture will be like (Parry et al. 2004). Unfortunately these uncertainties are amplified by further sensitivities of key physical processes. Small changes in mean climatic conditions may be associated with large increases in extreme conditions, affecting the frequencies of droughts and floods. Small changes in rainfall can lead to much bigger changes in run-off. The net economic impacts of climate change on agriculture could be reduced through trade, but much depends on the degree to which different areas are simultaneously affected and whether an affected state or region can buy its way out of trouble. There are also many other interacting factors.

Ecological Resilience and Biodiversity Loss on Land

The intensification and industrialization of agriculture, an ongoing process, has had a profound effect on ecological and social systems in Southeast Asia. Changes in land use and land cover, especially the conversion of forests to agriculture and plantations, are having significant impacts on above- and below-ground biodiversity and biogeochemical cycles (van Noordwijk et al. 1995). The initial impact, which occurs with the clearing of forests, leads to immediate, but short-term alterations to biogeochemical cycles, but depending on the succeeding type and intensity of agricultural use, the cycles change with longer-term effects. Common features of the transformation include shifts from locally consumed to more widely exchanged cash crops, increasing use of fertilizers, pesticides, and herbicides. Irrigation, mechanization, and precision management may also follow. Agriculture has become much more information intensive, both with respect to technologies for testing, monitoring, variety selection and improvement, and also with respect to shifting demands and competition in commodity markets.

The development of agriculture, as an export-oriented sector strongly supported by state and agribusiness, has not eliminated problems of food security for the poor, for example in the uplands and poorer rice-growing regions in the Mekong (Kaosa-ard and Dore 2003). A lack of market development may make things even more difficult. The situation is probably worst in North Korea, which, after floods and droughts in the mid-1990s and loss of special trading privileges with China, has struggled to feed its population. Despite massive international aid, much of it redirected by the government to its military troops, many citizens died of starvation; some sought food or asylum in China, but were promptly returned (Lee 1999).

The main threat to biodiversity has been loss of habitat due to the conversion of native forests to plantations, agriculture, and the development of infrastructure such as dams, roads, and human settlements. Over the past two decades, average annual rates of loss of forest cover have varied between 1 percent and 4 percent among countries in the region, with very little unfragmented or "frontier" forest now remaining. Unsustainable logging practices degrade the remaining forests by damaging soils, spreading weeds, and changing fire disturbance regimes, thus hampering the regeneration of secondary vegetation. Hunting and poaching of wildlife for the medicinal and animal trade also remains a serious threat to large mammals and birds in many areas. Finally, encroachment by agriculture and spread of fires and weeds on forest margins, especially along roads, leads to further degradation of original habitats.

As ecosystems are increasingly simplified by human activities their vulnerability to invasion by alien species increases. The pool of alien species is also likely to increase with globalization of trade and agricultural production. Newly introduced species that establish themselves can cause problems in a number of ways. First, they can act as vectors of disease. Second, as agricultural pests, they can reduce crop yields and be costly to eradicate, an example being the golden apple snail (*Pomacea canliculate*), intentionally introduced from South America to Taiwan rice paddies in the 1980s as a potential food crop, but now a destructive pest of rice ecosystems throughout the Far East and Southeast Asia. Third, they can alter the ecosystem and thus have an impact on whole communities, as, for example, invasive grasses that change fire regimes in forests. Finally, they can lead to loss of biodiversity, when a new species preys upon native species, leading to their extinction. Greater travel and trade increase the opportunities for biological invasion.

Changes to the structure and function of ecosystems are likely to have implications for agricultural and fisheries development, but are generally not yet well documented within Asia Pacific. Evidence from elsewhere in the world, however, suggests that some not-yet-apparent environmental trends may be critical. For example, the fragmentation and loss of forests over wide regions, especially in the lowlands, has probably already resulted in loss of diversity and of natural pollinators and predators critical to agricultural crops. The increasing reliance on a few varieties of a few crops has resulted in the loss of many traditional, local varieties. Retention of knowledge of genetic strains and crop management may be vital in order to combat future disease and pest problems as well as in the development of more sustainable land use. Such losses of ecological resilience may be, in the long run, the most critical environmental trend of all.

THE FUTURE: SCENARIOS

Some features of society, the economy, and the ecological landscape change at relatively slow rates—for example, systems of governance, modes of production, market institutions, trade regimes, soil fertility, and regrowth of forests, mangroves or fisheries stocks. On the other hand, some features change much more rapidly—for example, exchange rates, preferred cash crops in a given area, river discharges, smoke conditions, stock values, commodity prices, and tourism arrivals after terrorism scares. Interactions between drivers, fast and slow, some of which may have thresholds, and the varied human responses to them lead to large uncertainties. Scenarios serve as a helpful tool for exploring futures because they help systematically frame fundamental uncertainties. A scenario is a story that offers a consistent, plausible explanation of how events develop over time. Analyzing these scenarios for sustainability offers opportunities for insight into how society might attempt to influence the directions and decisions it must take.

The following set of four scenarios for Pacific Asia (fig. 3) is informed by the earlier work of the Global Scenarios Group (Gallopin et al. 1997) and my involvement with the Millennium Ecosystem Assessment (Alcamo et al. 2003). More detailed descriptions of a similar set of scenarios can be found in Lebel (2004). The set of scenarios are presented not as a game for the reader to "pick winners," but rather as an illustration of the possibilities for sustainability (and environmental disaster) in a wide range of development trajectories. The key uncertainty these scenarios try to capture is the idea of connectivity, or linkages, between places in the region, and of the region with the rest of the world. These connections include things like investment flows through business networks, commodity trade flows, information exchanges between civil society groups, and formal transboundary agreements on security, trade, and the environment among states. The proposition is that the future of connectivity is highly uncertain and, at the same time, critical for almost every aspect of development and environmental change. In the following pages we explore the opportunities and constraints for transitions to sustainability under various scenarios of regional connectivity.

Figure 3. Scenarios for Pacific Asia

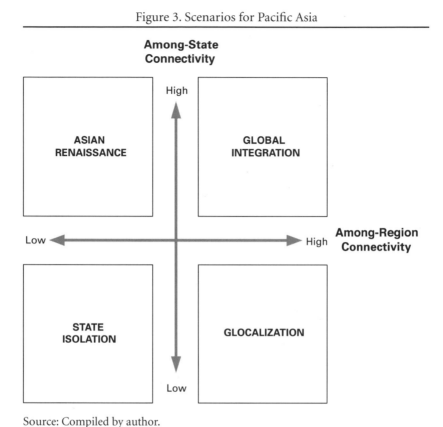

Source: Compiled by author.

Global Integration Scenario

Under this scenario most trends will continue much as they have over the past two decades, but linkages with groups outside the region will begin to take over the current strong regional bias in trade, investment, and cooperation. There is only very modest policy intervention to redirect development toward environmental or social goals. Market mechanisms, especially international trade and investment regimes, designed and controlled by developed country elites, it is believed, will sort problems out as they arise. When they don't various standardization and harmonization procedures driven by large and often vertically integrated corporations are on hand to succeed where states have failed. Ironically, integration will turn out to be exclusionary. Inequities with respect to the sharing of involuntary risks and expected benefits from using ecosystem goods and services will persist. Society under a global integration scenario will neither bridge the digital divide, nor narrow wide gaps in well-being, access to, and control of resources between the rich and poor. Connectivity is very broad and unselective so investments flows, sourcing, labor, and production sites are highly mobile.

The precursors of this scenario are already present in the big cities of Asia. The rich live in private communities complete with guards at the gate and their own recreation, water supply, and garbage collection. The poor, on the other hand, live in slums with little access to freshwater and poor sanitation. The pressure on government to improve services is low because, for the rich and the powerful, these services can be purchased. Air and water quality will improve greatly in places of privilege. Wealthy cities and regions will relocate polluting industries elsewhere. They will also be able to raise standards, monitoring, and screening of food imports. Competition for consumer markets that are growing greener and more health conscious will drive up health benefits, and secondarily, environmental standards, in producing countries and regions. Conservation of biodiversity will essentially be a by-product of nature as a commodity development to serve domestic and international tourism.

The falls in pollution intensities and increases in energy efficiency that arise because of improved technology transfers will be partly offset by aggregate increases in consumption and production. States and business will be like the "Red Queen" in *Alice in Wonderland*: always running to stay in the same place. Nevertheless, overall, conventional air and water pollution problems will be successfully addressed but rapid rates of adoption of new technologies without institutional safeguards will generate many new risks.

New health risks will come with production systems that are highly connected, based on genetically manipulated and uniform organisms, and reared in high-density and high-input systems. Massive outbreaks of disease through infected food chains will, from time to time, kill thousands and perhaps millions of people. The response will be stricter controls, more monitoring, and tighter standards. Management of organic and chemical wastes from such systems will also challenge treatment facilities. As a result of occasional leakages, and "after-the-fact" research on health effects, soils and groundwater resources will become seriously contaminated in several locations.

One of the key features of development under the global integration scenario is that a substantial range of options for regulatory, institutional, and consumer control is conceded to wider, largely external, forces. Rhetorically these are referred to with awe as "free trade" and "the market," but deep down they are concessions of power to others in expectation that the benefits will flow back. In this scenario, therefore, Pacific Asia's future is strongly influenced by decisions made elsewhere. Regional institutions and relations now very important for business will give way first to bilateral and then truly global regimes on trade, investment, currency, and credit markets. This will be accompanied by the rise of global security institutions. Environmental agreements will also go global but corporate interests already well represented by the economic-oriented regimes will not be greatly affected. Some of the improvements in the ICT infrastructure will be co-opted by transnational civil society and used in ways that counter, in part, the dominance of private corporations in decision-making about development. The failure to control greenhouse gas emissions globally, however, will not come as a surprise.

The degree to which the free trade logic is extended to free mobility of labor matters as this could remove some of the social imbalances that the global integration scenario would otherwise reinforce. Labor would migrate to where jobs and best living conditions are. The desire to attract skilled labor that now has a choice would drive competition among cities, regions, and states to make their settings as desirable as possible. Together these processes could become a positive for sustainability by reducing gross inequalities among locations and better matches of production systems with local environmental resources. The threat such mobility would pose to the status quo of power would of course result in a lot of resistance, and presumably, in a cultural and nationalistic rhetoric of resistance.

Either way, global integration would bring several more decades of aggregate growth, especially to China and other newly industrializing and least developed economies. There is no doubt this could greatly reduce poverty, improve health, and lift living standards. The environmental outcomes are highly uncertain, but it is clearly a scenario with risks. If technological and institutional innovations are able to keep apace then transitions to sustainability may still be plausible. The windows of opportunity for such transitions, however, are likely to be few. Development under this scenario creates ecological and social systems lacking resilience. Over time, the direct social and economic costs of the deteriorating environmental quality in an unsustainable version would begin to affect productivity and the populace's attitude toward development. Here the question is, how long it continues and in what state it leaves the critical ecosystems that support life.

The Asian-Renaissance Scenario

This scenario emerges as a reaction to global integration trends and divides Pacific Asia into East and West. In Pacific Asia there is strong resistance to investment and control by corporations or states from outside the region. Rising concerns are voiced by both civil society and political leaders about loss of cultural identity owing to the influx of Western media, values, and consumption patterns. At the same time, they recognize that no nation can go it alone against the economic and military dominance of the United States and the European Union, so they negotiate new regional security and economic institutions that can match the West. Connectivity is high within the region, but more filtered and selective with the outside world.

The Association of Southeast Asian Nations (ASEAN) accordingly becomes the AEAN (Association of East Asian Nations) with the inclusion of Japan, a unified Korea, and China. AEAN breaks off all relations with the World Trade Organization (WTO) and forms as a subsidiary body, the Asian Trade Organization (ATO), which includes mechanisms for protection of indigenous technologies while promoting trade within the region. Because of respect for diversity within the "Asian way," there is no adoption of a single currency, and the institution departs from the model of government developed in the European Union. The AEAN becomes a security framework with shared armed forces for conflict resolution. By the middle of the twenty-first century, the AEAN is as strong economically and militarily as the United States and Europe—in a tri-polar world.

Cultural revival is also reflected in the flowering of Asian arts, literature, religion, and languages, but with a new sense of regionalism, leading to exchanges among cultures. Progressive Islamic and Buddhist religions flourish, while Christianity, because of its association with Westernization, becomes rare. These cultural trends pose some risks for development in that reactionary or conservative values may suppress the innovation upon which further development depends. On the other hand, a great hybridization of traditional, experiential, and scientific knowledge could also take place, stimulating a whole new wave of technological innovation.

Extended family structures reemerge, at least insofar as declining fertility rates allow. Business, operating through family networks, establishes a second-tier welfare system capable of coping with the bulge in aging populations. Over time, Asian countries work toward more balanced but still high-density populations.

Environmental management itself is not given high priority. Nonetheless, as a side effect of the reinvigoration and hybridization of traditional concepts of stewardship and sufficiency through technological innovation, many opportunities arise through which environmental sustainability can be incorporated into (re-)development. On a per-capita basis, societies in Pacific Asia continue to outperform the West in terms of efficiencies of use of space, materials, energy, and water. The first dense eco-cities that are free of private cars arise in Asia. These efficiencies are again and again turned into competitive advantages over other regions.

Complex agro-forestry and multi-species aquaculture become the norm, and traditional varieties of crops begin to reverse trends toward Westernized foodstuffs. As the consumption of meat declines, fish and soybean return as by far the main source of protein in the diet. Markets and local industries around non-tropical timber products flourish under the leadership of Yunnanese entrepreneurs. Western models of conservation in protected areas are rejected outright with the development of an Asia-wide Community Parks network. Property rights are unbundled, providing local communities with legal access to various timber and non-timber products as well as to marine products. Management of these areas is decentralized, but overlapping governance at the regional scale plays an increasingly important role in monitoring transboundary resources and pollution issues.

Within Asia there are already suggestions of this scenario in the rhetoric of political leaders, most entertainingly from a previous Malaysian prime minister, Mahathir bin Mohamad, and his long-term counterpart, Anwar Ibrahim. The emphasis placed on regionalism, it could be argued, is not that different from the past few decades of shared growth.

One risk to the unfolding of the Asian-renaissance scenario is the potential for an assertive China to take control of the regional agenda. However, owing to the Asian-renaissance resurgence in values, China would find itself less united within its borders but strongly connected with its neighbors. Thus a number of provinces become separate nations or at least regain a high degree of autonomy—for example, Yunnan—and have independent representation in regional forums.

In the longer term, the AEAN may become so powerful that it believes its knowledge is what the rest of the world needs to develop. This perspective is encouraged by the now large minorities in most Western cities that maintain cultural connections with Asia. In an ironic reversal, the modernization project begins to be critically seen as "easternization."

The Asian renaissance scenario, depending on the severity of ecological crises and the wisdom of its stewardship, offers several opportunities to take transitions to sustainability seriously, but these pathways are not guaranteed.

Glocalization Scenario

This scenario emphasizes respect for local livelihoods and communities that self-organize. It takes pride in sufficiency rather than wealth accumulation, and production-consumption systems which maintain the regenerating capacity of the ecosystems they depend upon. This yields a more diverse set of locally adaptive circumstances and lifestyles than the two previous scenarios. The scenario does not reject technology, economic growth, or trade, but is much more selective and information intensive in its decision-making. Connectivity is selective with most links local and with only high value, specialized links stretching across wider parts of the globe. This results in very diverse experimentation and adaptation of new technologies in local areas. As a consequence the private sector is dominated by flexible networks of small and medium-sized enterprises with little stable vertical integration or allegiance to a constructed "Asian" regionalism.

Leadership may emerge from the Third World experience, but it will be combined with scientific knowledge of alternative land use, renewable energies, and landscape design. The emphasis will remain on local adaptation, participation, and decision-making. This, in turn, stimulates efforts at developing more efficient multi-scale institutions. Principles of subsidiarity, participation, and precaution are widely upheld in decision-making.

As economic growth ceases to be the all-important goal, overall economic activity slows somewhat, with dramatic reductions in energy consumption and material intensities, but continuing expansion in information flows. Trade is dominated by low-volume, high-value goods. Holiday travel contracts sharply as people find the environment and culture nearer their own homes increasingly interesting, satisfying, and diverse. Population declines, already implied in declining fertility rates, are allowed to run their course and viewed as an opportunity to readjust levels of human activity to well within the renewal capacities of local environments. Sophisticated monitoring systems and cultural norms then work to maintain and reinforce environmental gains made. Environmental quality, in terms of forest cover, biodiversity, and access and availability of key resources, such as freshwater, improve for all. Use of pesticides and nonrenewable agriculture is eliminated. Coastal ecosystems are replanted or recover and under local management regimes near-shore fisheries flourish. Further away from shore many problems in fisheries persist, but overall fishing pressures begin to level-off.

Culture, arts, and creative use of information technologies transform work. People work less and expect more meaningful work. Advertising doesn't disappear, and competition among businesses is still intense, but corporate sensitivity to changed consumer attitudes means transparency, openness, and the certifiable quality of goods and services are the best ways to do business. Labels, for example, contain via electronic tags, substantial information about environmental impacts of the full life cycle of products and services. To enable these changes the international trade organization and multilateral banks are dismantled and reassembled with new systems of rules and procedures of governance that are much more democratic and conducive to sustainable business (Monbiot 2003). The new wave of structural adjustment programs of the "Glocal Development Bank (GDB)" now target the overextended, overconsuming economies, both within the region as well as in Europe and North America.

How could such a scenario get started? What might be the trigger? One possibility is that growing dissatisfaction with the gradual changes in policy that, triggered by a series of environmental disasters such as extreme weather, leads to a crisis in confidence causing a major shift in political discourse and societal goals. As technology and integration among places progress, the same tools become available for redirecting values across the region toward alternative futures. Transnational civil society, therefore, will be a critical source of inspiration for the development of this scenario.

On the whole, technology will continue to grow with increased transfers between rich and poor nations. Sectors that do not require large quantities of material inputs continue to grow. Energy and material use will decline rapidly with improved urban design, efficiency, and reduction in wasteful consumption. Markets become effective at ensuring prices capture what used to be externalities, in part, through better information flows between buyers and sellers.

New forms of polycentric governance will emerge that provide considerable power for communities to manage forest and coastal commons and to make decisions about environmental preservation and uses of biodiversity. Education and health will advance in both poor and richer nations. International structures of governance will attempt to monitor and regulate regional and global environmental change, but for the most part the actions taken at finer levels will dominate decision-making.

Conflict resolution processes at regional and global levels, however, will be developed well enough so that wars and armed confrontation are rare. This final assumption is an important one because if Pacific Asia was to embark along the *glocalization* route, whereas the United States or European Union did not, the region may be open to extraregional military threats. The ultimate result will be significantly reduced spending on militarization of land and space, with the peace dividend available for developing sustainable technologies and institutions.

State Isolation Scenario

Compared to the other three scenarios, this is the most extreme in terms of a reversal of many current trends. Nevertheless, it is plausible given the rising resistance to regional and global economic institution building and the non-trivial probability of regional or global calamities. Under this scenario, most of the filters to connectivity are constructed at the state level. Connectivity within states is high, but connectivity among states is substantially reduced. There are explicit policies to protect domestic industries from foreign competition. Trade is laced with protectionist measures. Transnational corporations are broken-up into much looser consortia of state-constrained organizations. The power of the state increases and overall economic activity slows. Challenges to development are severest in natural resource–poor countries, whereas those that are relatively self-sufficient may continue to perform well, especially if they are also able to build on strong domestic human capacities. Singapore becomes a special district of Malaysia and the two Koreas are reunited, but Indonesia fragments into several independent states, one which now encompasses Irian Jaya and Papua New Guinea.

The shortening of commodity chains now leaves to the consumption drivers the control and stake in the natural resource base within the same national jurisdiction. This creates renewed opportunities for effective local institutions to correct past poor practices. It also reduces the energy and associated greenhouse gas emissions linked to the long-distance transport of raw materials and foodstuffs. Ecologically many of the indicators of sustainability may eventually improve, especially if there has also been a sharp contraction in population concurrent with reduced consumption. On the other hand, many social indicators—health, education, and skills—would be at risk of decline without the benefits of regional and global exchange of information, technologies, and competitive pressures.

This scenario may be thought of as a rather implausible break from the past if it weren't for the fact that most states have pursued such strategies successfully in the past and a number, less successfully, continue to do so (Myanmar, North Korea). This scenario may be more likely to unfold regionally if there was first a serious collapse of the regional economy, for example, as a result of a major war, devastating disease, serious climate change, or calamities. One could then imagine nationalistic rhetoric playing its familiar, frightening, role. Another trigger could be growing resentment from farmers at collapsing agricultural commodity prices, arising for example, under a global integration scenario. A series of election victories by populist agrarian leaders or via less democratic processes, such as pro-rural military dictatorships, could quickly shift regional and global integration policies. It is hard, however, to see how they could be pursued for long given the likely sharp contractions in economies and associated hardships this would produce.

IMPLICATIONS FOR PACIFIC ASIA

The Environment-Development Nexus

For the last several decades, health, education, and other indicators of well-being have greatly improved across Pacific Asia. Economies of the developing countries have grown at dizzying rates, agricultural productivity has risen, and supply of sanitation, electricity, and basic infrastructure has advanced. Mature economies have transformed from manufacturing into service roles, and their societies are among the wealthiest in the world. At the same time, many natural resources have been overexploited or degraded especially in the developing countries of the region which depend on their exports. Cities in the wealthier advanced economies are now cleaner, but the dirty industries that support them have been relocated elsewhere, and the shrimp or salmon they eat are produced on somebody else's coast.

The relationship between poverty, well-being, and environmental degradation is complex because wealth not only facilitates overconsumption but also stimulates technical innovation and knowledge generation, processes that could be made to work for environmental benefit. Conventionally, the poor sectors of society and the poor nations in a region are seen as places of environmental crises and, consequently, where adjustment is needed. This is regardless of whether the poor are seen as victims or villains, but the truth is that the largest adjustments probably need to be made by the rich (Sachs 1999).

Today, society's dependence on goods and services from ecosystems is poorly acknowledged in the models of development and the mix of policies pursued by governments in Pacific Asia. Riparian vegetation is removed and wetlands filled in without considering the bank and flood protection services they provide to cities and agriculture. Forest fragments are turned into evenly grassed parks or parking lots without considering the role native flora and fauna may have for pollination and insect pest control, let alone aesthetic values. Air and water pollution, dusty and hot cities filled with inert concrete surfaces, fail to take advantage of the local climate and atmospheric regulating attributes of vegetation. Delayed and half-hearted policy responses push degraded ecosystems over thresholds from which recovery is impossible or very expensive and slow. The accumulated history of environmental governance failures and neglect is also a constraint on future development opportunities in the region.

The legacy of decades of rapid economic development poses different but large challenges for sustainability transitions under each of the four scenarios. Three attributes of development seem especially critical.

First is the extent to which society recognizes and cultivates the inherent capacities for adaptation that lie within ecosystems and society itself. Each scenario emphasizes different scales of the "catchments" from which solutions can be drawn: global integration effectively drawing on the expertise of much of the world; the Asian renaissance most open to regional contributions, through to the glocalization scenario emphasizing local knowledge and very selective adoption of innovations from elsewhere; and, finally, an isolation scenario that is supremely myopic. Second is the degree to which policies and strategies are viewed as experiments, which need to be monitored and evaluated, especially with respect to thresholds that may push particular ecosystem or social systems into new negative configurations that are costly or impossible to reverse. Third is the quality of governance, from the local through to state and international levels. Key indicators are the degree to which high standards of transparency, accountability, and fairness are reached in decision-making processes, which, in turn, will often depend on providing opportunities for public participation and scrutiny.

Louis Lebel

Prospects for Sustainability Transition

Pacific Asia is diverse. As a geographical whole, there is little that is both shared by and unique to countries in the region. Similarities that do exist, for example in growth of GDP, exports, or trade, have arisen not because of particular national structures of governance or the wisdom of national leaders, but rather as a result of regional processes, especially commodity chains, structural adjustment programs, and corporate networks and their investments. A transition to sustainability in different areas and sectors will not be the same because the starting points and contexts of change vary widely.

The least developed nations in the region face a special set of challenges. First, most of their industries are foreign-owned, and there is little domestic research and development or capital base for the introduction of clean technologies. Second, the resource and technology constraints in these countries make harmonization across Pacific Asia difficult. Without harmonization, the potential for migration of dirty industries increases, especially as political capital and infrastructure constraints in less-developed countries are reduced. On the other hand, many aspects of social, economic, and ecological diversity within the region make a positive contribution to longer-term sustainability at large regional scales. Diversity of methods and approaches to production systems are a continuous source of innovation that can help counteract the boom and bust dynamics of individual commodities. One of the underlying risks of the global integration scenario is that it tends to reduce these internal sources of diversity. On the other hand, the better connectivity outside the region may partly counterbalance this effect. The isolation scenario posts the greatest risk to innovation rates as it assumes that appropriate local solutions to sustainability challenges will be forthcoming.

A transition to sustainability is not just a matter of getting the latest, or even the most environmentally appropriate, technology. It also requires understanding of human behavior, especially as regards institutions, sources of knowledge, markets, and politics. Institutions are important as drivers of, and responses to, environmental change. They guide, constrain, and facilitate human adaptation to challenges from the environment and social system.

In the real world, economic, social, and ecological disturbances and surprises will recur. There is no way to eliminate internal or external shocks. In fact, attempts to keep all disturbances out, even small ones, can lead to a system becoming more brittle to larger shocks. If systems are tightly connected and interdependent, as under the global integration scenario, then the possible outbreaks of diseases and spread of pests, or withdrawal of investments, or discontent with global organization, will spread contagion-like across Asia Pacific and the rest of the world.

Boom-or-bust cycles in the region have generally not been good for the environment. Thus, although some industrial facilities close down, those that continue tend not to allocate resources for pollution control. The environment and sustainability are seen as luxuries. The cumulative consequence of this logic being applied repeatedly as business cycles go boom or bust is probably to reduce the resilience of socio-ecological systems. Without any learning from environmental feedback during periods of economic and ecological crisis, when the signals of inappropriate development strategies are clearest, the potential is great that natural resources will be driven beyond tolerable thresholds—irreversible in result or requiring long periods of time and costly management interventions for recovery.

In Pacific Asia today, regional cooperation and institutional frameworks appear to have largely failed to set the region on a development pathway that keeps open diverse possible transitions to sustainability. While northeast Asia has the excuse of being under-institutionalized, the same cannot be said for Southeast Asia with its history of activities and dialogues under the ASEAN umbrella. Would greater regionalism, as imagined under the Asian renaissance scenario, lead to any improvement? Or would development pathways that reject regionalism, for broader or more local connectivity, fare better?

Regional institutions may be crucial. Firstly, for bringing about necessary social and political changes, because the old models of economic development are embedded in regional cooperation in business, trade, and investment. Secondly, because without them it is unlikely that generalized goals and norms of an even broader group can be sensitive enough to the diverse needs and aspirations of the peoples of Pacific Asia.

CONCLUSION

The prospects for a peaceful, just, and prosperous future for Pacific Asia are real. No other region in the world has been able to maintain such rapid economic growth and improvements in overall welfare and infrastructure for such a prolonged period. At the same time, the natural resource base, the various goods and services of the ecosystem, which much of the region's population still depends directly upon, has been almost ignored in the pursuit of economic growth and integration into regional and global markets. Ecological as well as social challenges resulting from this blind growth may continue to accumulate faster than they are being solved.

The way connectivity unfolds both within Pacific Asia, and between the region and the rest of the world matters a lot. It is also the key uncertainty. Pursuing sustainability as a regional project, while recognizing the diversity of strategies and needs among countries and between richer and poorer nations will go a long way toward making the future more peaceful. Although Asia Pacific may have lost its dream of a renaissance, or an Asian century, maybe this time around the vision for Asia Pacific, built on a better understanding of environmental change and the dependencies of society, can help create new realities in place of the lost dreams from the last century.

Bibliography

Adger, W. N. 1999. "Social Vulnerability to Climate Change and Extremes in Coastal Vietnam." *World Development* 27: 249–269.

Alcamo, J., et al. 2003. *Ecosystems and Human Well-being: A Framework for Assessment.* Washington, D.C.: Island Press.

Angel, D. P., and M. T. Rock, eds. 2000. *Asia's Clean Revolution Industry: Growth and the Environment.* Sheffield, U.K.: Greenleaf.

Arndt, R. L., and G. R. Carmichael. 1995. "Long-Range Transport and Deposition of Sulfur in Asia." *Water, Air and Soil Pollution* 85(4): 2283–2288.

Arndt, R. L., G. R. Carmichael, and J. M. Roorda. 1996. "Seasonal Source-Receptor Relationships in Asia." *Atmospheric Environment* 32(8): 1397–1406.

Bai, X. 2002. "Industrial Relocation in Asia: A Sound Environmental Management Strategy?" *Environment* 44:8-21.

Brookfield, H., and B. Byron. 1990. "Deforestation and Timber Extraction in Borneo and the Malay Peninsula." *Global Environmental Change* 1: 52–56.

Brunner, J., K. Talbott, and C. Elkin. 1998. "Logging Burma's Frontier Forests: Resources and the Regime." Forest Frontiers Initiative, World

Resources Institute. http://www.wri.org/wri/ffi/burma/index.html (February 2002).

Canadell, J. G. 2002. "Land Use Effects on Terrestrial Carbon Sources and Sinks." *Science in China* (Series C) 45 Supplement: 1–9.

Chuenpagdee, R., and D. Pauly. 2004. "Improving the State of Coastal Areas in the Asia-Pacific region." *Coastal Management* 32: 3-15.

Colfer, C. J. P., and I. A. P. Resosudarmo, eds. 2002. *Which Way Forward? People, Forests and Policymaking in Indonesia*. Washington, D.C.: Resources for the Future.

Dauvergne, P. 1997. *Shadows in the Forest: Japan and the Politics of Timber in Southeast Asia*. Cambridge, Mass.: MIT Press.

———. 2001. *Loggers and degradation in the Asia-Pacific: Corporations and Environmental Management*. Cambridge: Cambridge University Press.

Dixon, J. A. 1990. "Renewable Resources, the Environment and Sustained Growth." *ASEAN Economic Bulletin* 7: 159–172.

Dryzek, J. 1999. "Transnational Democracy." *The Journal of Political Philosophy* 7(1):30-51.

Earth Rights International. 2003. *Capitalizing on Conflict: How Logging and Mining Contribute to Environmental Destruction in Burma*. Earth Rights International and the Karen Environmental and Social Action Network.

Florini, A. M., ed. 2000. *The Third Force: The Rise of Transnational Civil Society*. Tokyo: Japan Center for International Exchange.

Food and Agriculture Organization of the United Nations. 1998. *The State of World Fisheries and Aquaculture*. Rome, Italy: Food and Agriculture Organization.

Forbes, D. 1996. *Asian Metropolis: Urbanisation and the Southeast Asian City*. Melbourne: Oxford University Press.

Forsyth, T. 1996. "Science, Myth and Knowledge: Testing Himalayan Environmental Degradation in Thailand." *Geoforum* 27: 375–392.

———. 1999. *International Investment and Climate Change: Energy Technologies for Developing Countries*. London: Earthscan.

———. 2001. "Environmental social movements in Thailand: how important is class?" *Asian Journal of Social Sciences* 29(1): 35-51.

Gallopin, G., et al. 1997. "Branch Points: Global Scenarios and Human Choice." A resource paper of the Global Scenarios Group, Pole Star Series Report No. 7. Stockholm: Stockholm Environment Institute.

Glover, J. 1999. "The Changing Consumer in Asia." Paper, Food and Agribusiness Executive Development Program, Singapore, September.

Goss, J., D. Burch, and R. E. Rickson. 2000. "Agri-food Restructuring and Third World Transnational: Thailand, the CP Group and the Global Shrimp Industry." *World Development* 28: 513–530.

Hirsch, P., and C. Warren, eds. 1998. *The Politics of Environment in Southeast Asia: Resources and Resistance.* London: Routledge.

Jomo, K. S., ed. 1998. *Tigers in Trouble: Financial Governance, Liberalisation and Crises in East Asia.* Bangkok: White Lotus.

Jones, H., and L. Pardthaisong. 2000. "Demographic Interactions and Developmental Implications in the Era of AIDS: Findings from Northern Thailand." *Applied Geography* 20: 255–275.

Kaosa-ard, M., and J. Dore, eds. 2003. *Social Challenges for the Mekong Region.* Chiang Mai: Chiang Mai University.

Khalid, A. R., and J. B. Braden. 1993. "Welfare Effects of Environmental Regulation in an Open Economy: The Case of Malaysian Palm Oil." *Journal of Agricultural Economics* 44: 25–37.

King, V. T., ed. 1998. *Environmental Challenges in South-east Asia.* Surrey, U.K.: Curzon Press.

Knight, M. 1998. "Developing Countries and the Globalization of Financial Markets." *World Development* 26: 1185–1200.

Laungaramsri P. 2002. *Redefining Nature: Karen Ecological Knowledge and the Challenge to the Modern Conservation Paradigm.* Chennai, India: Earthworm Books.

Lebel, L. 2001. "The Industrial Transformation of Southeast Asia." Asia ecoBest 3(3): 5–6.

———. 2002a. "Acid Rain in Northeast Asia." In *Cross-sectoral Partnerships in Enhancing Human Security: Third Intellectual Dialogue on Building Asia's Tomorrow, Bangkok.* Tokyo: Japan Center for International Exchange.

———. 2002b. "Southeast Asia: Economic Globalization as a Forcing Function." In P. Tyson et al., eds. *The Earth System: Global-regional Linkages.* Global Change International Geosphere-Biosphere Programme Series. Heidelberg: Springer Verlag.

———. 2002c. "Synthesis." Report of Chiang Mai Workshop on Sustainability Science: Knowledge, Technology and Institutions for Sustainability Transitions in Asia. Chiang Mai University, Chiang Mai, February.

———. 2004. "Multi-scale Scenarios of Development and Environmental Change in the Mekong Region." USER Working Paper 2004-06 Chiang Mai University. Chiang Mai: Unit for Social and Environmental Research.

Lebel, L., and W. S. Steffen, eds. 1998. *Global Environmental Change and Sustainable Development in Southeast Asia: Science Plan for a SARCS Integrated Study*. Bangkok: Southeast Asian Regional Committee for START.

Lebel, L., et al. 2002. "Industrial Transformation and Shrimp Aquaculture in Thailand and Vietnam: Pathways to Ecological, Social and Economic Sustainability?" *Ambio* 31(4): 311–323.

Lee, S. W. 1999. "Preventing Refugee Crisis: A Challenge to Human Security." *Asian Perspectives* 23: 133–154.

———. 2001. "Environmental Regime-building in Northeast Asia: A Catalyst for Sustainable Regional Cooperation." *Journal of East Asian Studies* 1(2): 31–61.

Ling, O. G., ed. 1995. *Environment and the City: Sharing Singapore's Experience and Future Challenges*. Singapore: Times Academic Press.

Liwawruangrath, S., et al. 1999. "Monitoring of Some Heavy Metals and Organochlorine Pesticide Residues in the Mekong River." In P. Asnachinda and S. Lerthusneem, eds. *Proceedings of the International Conference on Water Resource Management in Intermontane Basins*, Chiang Mai University, Thailand, 2–6 February. Chiang Mai: Water Research Centre, Chiang Mai University.

Lohmann, L. 1996. "Freedom to Plant: Indonesia and Thailand in a Globalizing Pulp and Paper Industry." In M. J. G. Parnwell and R. L. Bryant, eds. *Environmental Change in South-east Asia: People, Politics and Sustainable Development*. London: Routledge.

Lovering, D. 2001. "Taming the Killing Fields of Laos." *Scientific American* 265: 56–61.

McCargo, D. 2000. *Politics and the Press in Thailand: Media Machinations*. London: Routledge.

Monbiot. G. 2003. *The Age of Consent: A Manifesto for a New World Order*. London: Flamingo.

Murdiyarso, D., et al. 2004. "Policy Responses to Complex Environmental Problems: Insights from a Science-Policy Activity on Transboundary Haze from Vegetation Fires in Southeast Asia." *Journal of Agriculture, Ecosystems, and Environment*.

Murdiyarso, D., M. Widodo, and D. Suyamto. 2002. "Fire Risks in Forest Carbon Projects in Indonesia." *Science in China* (Series C) 45 Supplement: 65–74.

Naylor, R. L., R. J. Goldberg, J. H. Primavera, et al. 2000. "Effect of Aquaculture on World Fish Supplies." *Nature* 405:1017-1024.

Louis Lebel

Ness, G. D., and M. M. Low. 2000. Five Cities: Modeling Asian Urban Population-Enviornment Dynamics. Singapore: Oxford University Press.

Parry, M., et al. 2004. "Effects of Climate Change on Global Food Production under SRES Emissions and Socio-economic Scenarios." *Global Environmental Change* 14:53–67.

Pasong, S., and L. Lebel. 2000. "Political Transformation and the Environment in Southeast Asia." *Environment* 42(5): 8–19.

Phongpaichit, P., and S. Piriyarangsan. 1994. *Corruption and Democracy in Thailand*. Chiang Mai: Silkworm Books.

Phongpaichit, P., and C. Baker. 1998. *Thailand's Boom and Bust*. Chiang Mai: Silkworm Books.

Posch, M., et al. 1996. "Integrated Scenarios of Acidification and Climate Change in Asia and Europe." *Global Environmental Change* 6: 375–394.

Rattanaphani, S. 1999. "Monitoring of Some Organochlorine Pesticide Residues in the Ping River." In P. Asnachinda and S. Lerthusnee, eds. *Proceedings of International Conference on Water Resource Management in Intermontane Basins*, Chiang Mai University, Thailand, 2–6 February. Chiang Mai: Water Research Centre, Chiang Mai University.

Rigg, J. 1997. *Southeast Asia: The Human Landscape of Modernization and Development*. London: Routledge.

Rock, M. T. 1998. "A Policy Menu for Cleaner Production." Background paper for the United States–Asia Environmental Partnership, U.S. Agency for International Development, Washington, D.C., July.

———. 2002. *Pollution Control in East Asia: Lessons from Newly Industrializing Economies*. Singapore: Institute of Southeast Asian Studies.

Sachasinh, R., D. Phantumvanit, and S. Tridech. 1992. "Thailand: Challenges and Responses in Environmental Management." Paper presented to the Workshop on Environmental Management in East Asia: Challenges and Responses, OECD Development Centre, Paris, 6–7 August.

Sachs, W. 1999. "Sustainable Development: On the Political Anatomy of an Oxymoron." *Planet Dialectics*. London: Zed Books.

Stallings, B., ed. 1995. *Global Change, Regional Response: The New International Context of Development*. Cambridge: Cambridge University Press.

Stares, P. B., ed. 2000. *Rethinking Energy Security in East Asia*. Tokyo: Japan Center for International Exchange.

Talaue-McManus, L. 2000. "Transboundary Diagnostic Analysis for the South China Sea." East Asian Seas Regional Coordinating Unity (EAS/RCU) Technical Report Series no. 14. United Nations Environment Programme, Bangkok.

Tan, C. Y., and L. Y. Kwong. 1990. "Industrial and Natural Environment Policies on Pollution." Policy Assessment of the Malaysian Industrial Policy Studies and the Industrial Master Plan, United Nations Industrial Development Organization (UNIDO), Vienna.

Than, M. 1998. "Introductory Overview: Development Strategies, Agricultural Policies and Agricultural Development Development in Southeast Asia." *ASEAN Economic Bulletin* 13: 1–12.

Thompson, H., and J. Duggie. 1996. "Political Economy of the Forestry Industry in Indonesia." *Journal of Contemporary Asia* 26: 352–365.

Tomich, T. P., et al. 1998. "Agricultural Development with Rainforest Conservation: Methods for Seeking Best Bet Alternatives to Slash-and-Burn, with Applications to Brazil and Indonesia." *Agricultural Economics* 19: 159–174.

Tri, N. H., W. N. Adger, and P. M. Kelly. 1998. "Natural Resource Management in Mitigating Climate Impacts: Mangrove Restoration in Vietnam." *Global Environmental Change—Human and Policy Dimensions* 8:49-61.

Vanderzwaag, D., and D. M. Johnston. 1998. "Toward the Management of the Gulf of Thailand: Charting the Course of Cooperation." In D. M. Johnston, ed. *SEAPOL Integrated Studies of the Gulf of Thailand.* Bangkok: Southeast Asian Programme in Ocean, Law, Policy and Management (SEAPOL).

van Noordwijk, M., et al. 1995. "Alternatives to Slash-and-Burn in Indonesia." Summary report of Phase 1, International Center for Research in Agroforestry (ICRAF) Southeast Asia, Bogor, Indonesia.

Vincent, J. R., M. A. Rozali, and A. R. Khalid. 2000. "Water Pollution Abatement in Malaysia." In D. P. Angel and M. T. Rock, eds. *Asia's Clean Revolution: Industry, Growth and the Environment.* Sheffield, U.K.: Greenleaf Publishing.

Wallace, P. 1999. *Agequake: Riding the Demographic Rollercoaster Shaking Business, Finance and Our World.* London: Nicholas Brealey Publishing.

Watanabe, T. 1992. *Asia: Its Growth and Agony.* Honolulu: University of Hawaii Press.

World Bank. 1994. *A Review of World Bank Experience in Irrigation.* Report no. 13676. Washington D.C.: World Bank.

World Resources Insitute. 2000. *World Resources Database 2000–2001: People and Ecosystems.* Washington, D.C.: World Resources Institute.

Yap, K. S., and R. S. Mohit. 1998. "Reinventing Local Government for Sustainable Cities in Asia." *Regional Development Dialogue* 19(1): 87–94.

6

Driving the Juggernaut:
From Economic Crisis to Global
Governance in Pacific Asia

AKE TANGSUPVATTANA

This chapter aims to provide a causal analysis of the East Asian economic crisis and, by doing so, to develop a vision of good governance. It is the thesis here that this vision of governance must come to grips not only with the mechanisms of globalization but also with the influence of cultural values, the combination of which produced the crisis.

Although much of the literature on the crisis points to globalization and cultural values as contributing to the crisis, these factors are largely dealt with separately. It is accepted that the state's sovereign power in economic management has been reshaped by globalization, but, ironically, globalization has dialectical and contingent characteristics as well (Giddens 1990, 64; McGrew 1992, 74). While it fosters the global economy at the expense of the state's power in economic management, at the same time it encourages civil society to challenge the state's power. Thus it provides opportunities for civil society to strengthen domestic and international governance.

It is also accepted that even as Asian cultural values helped to create the economic miracle, they played a part in the economic meltdown. While globalization has universal implications, culture is specific to time and place. This specificity is not only regional, it is also national. Leading up to the crisis, these cultural values interacted with the mechanisms of economic globalization within the context of old forms of governance, such as rule by connections and relationships. The interaction proved near-fatal, but the resulting crisis has presented an opportunity to challenge old forms of governance and create new ones.

Not every country in the region was affected by the crisis to the same degree. The impact was felt most in Indonesia, Thailand, South Korea, Malaysia, and the Philippines (a group henceforth referred to as the East

Asia 5), less so in Japan, Taiwan, and Singapore, and even less in the transition economies of Vietnam, China, Cambodia, and Laos. Indeed, China was able to maintain its high level of steady growth. Similarly then, the opportunity to build new forms of governance in the post-crisis period varied from country to country.

In the face of the crisis, the role of global economic and financial institutions (GEFIs)—such as the World Bank, the International Monetary Fund (IMF), the Asian Development Bank (ADB), the United Nations Development Programme (UNDP), and the World Trade Organization (WTO)—was enhanced. Contained in their rescue packages for countries needing assistance were projects of good governance. These projects, together with the dialectical character of globalization, have had the result of strengthening domestic democracy.

To encourage civil society's participation is to resolve some problems of representation and participation in a representative democracy, but at the same time, it creates a cultural struggle for which form of governance will prevail. Again, there are different conditions in each country that produce different levels of domestic governance and domestic democratization. That is to say, conditions such as the degree of the impact of globalization, the prominence of cultural values, and the reliance on assistance from GEFIs can determine the development of good governance.

The GEFIs' program of global governance is not without problems. It aims to further economic liberalism, or what George Soros considers "market fundamentalism," in economic globalization. Yet the political question of who gets what, when, and how, and the ethical issue of reducing poverty and improving equality are left undealt with. Instead, the focus is on technical considerations of private and public management. Because this tends to serve the interests of countries having a dominant role in GEFIs, the inclination runs counter to international or global democracy.

States can still play a role in creating a regionalism that will lead to cosmopolitan democracy and good global governance. A new architecture of international finance can be built through this process. But in order to achieve cosmopolitan democracy and good global governance, it is necessary to enhance the roles of regional and global civil society. True democracy can be created only by the balance of the forces of the state, the corporation, and civil society at national and international levels.

Ake Tangsupvattana

GLOBALIZATION, ECONOMIC GLOBALIZATION, AND ECONOMIC CRISIS

First of all, globalization must be distinguished from economic globalization because the former can have a dual impact on the development of good governance. On the one hand, globalization, as opposed to economic globalization, has dialectical and contingent characteristics that create an opposition on the level of the local community. This increases the role of civil society in challenging the state's power so as to achieve better governance. On the other hand, economic globalization, as a part of globalization, played a part in creating the Asian economic crisis. The crisis then facilitated the role of GEFIs in promoting good governance.

Globalization is political, technological, social, and cultural, as well as economic. It has been influenced above all by developments in communications dating back only to the late 1960s (Giddens 1999, 10). Therefore, it is a complex of intermeshing cultural, social, political, economic, and technological elements that reduces the time-space span and makes people more connected and more aware of others around the world (Giddens 1990, 64; Hall, Held, and McLennan 1992, 5–6).

Additionally, globalization itself has contingent and dialectical characteristics that can reshape society's institutions and human lives (McGrew 1992, 74; Giddens 1990, 64). It has an impact on the nation-state in three ways: it "squeezes sideways" and creates new economic and cultural regions that sometimes extend beyond borders; it "pulls away" power, including economic management, of the nation-state; and it "pushes down" by creating local autonomy (Giddens 1998, 31–31; Giddens 1999, 13).

Conceptually, the impact of globalization on governance is best described by Zygmunt Bauman (Cantell and Pedersen 1992, 144):

> The most important phenomenon in Europe today is the slow withering away of the nation-state. The nation-state was a unique institution in history which united economic management, political authority and cultural hegemony. Today, economic management is moving away from the nation-state because of the globalization of the economy. The nation-state is no longer an economic system, self-contained or self-sufficient. As far as the cultural hegemony is concerned it moves downwards from the state. The movement is not upwards like the economy, but downwards towards social movements, communities, ethnic groups and so on. What is left in the nation-state is just pure political authority without it being supported by economic management and cultural hegemony. I wonder how long this fiction can survive without its two other pillars. At any rate, we are probably coming to the end of the nation-state.

Let me deal with the aspect of culture first. By culture, I refer, as put forward by Bauman, to "the way of life" informed by the perception, meaning, and understanding of conduct. That is to say, it is a pattern of human behavior informed by one's worldview. The cultural dimension here is not to be viewed as reification in a structuralist manner—namely, that culture is relatively fixed but not rigid. Culture is predisposed to have a high degree of fixity, but over time it can be changed. Accordingly, the state's control of cultural hegemony can be challenged and then weakened by social movements in civil society. The reason for this is that culture can be a battlefield between the state and civil society and, simultaneously, a place where cooperation can construct a new and better culture.

For instance, social movements may confront the state's cultural hegemony over public policy in order to gain a more participatory role for civil society. Specifically, societal forces may question the business culture's crony capitalism, where politics and business collude in running the nation's finances and economy. They will press for greater transparency and accountability and the participation of other independent societal forces. In this context, old forms of governance in Pacific Asia are challenged by a new culture of governance.

Nevertheless, cultural struggles do not emerge on their own. Globalization, with its contingent and dialectical components, helps to push down the state's power by creating local autonomy—challenging the state's cultural hegemony and handing responsibility to civil society. Global issues, such as the environment, poverty, AIDS, women's rights, and animal rights are not just part of the larger picture, but also occur on the level of local communities. Social movements on the local level, organized through networks of civil society, can thus be driving forces in challenging old cultural values to create a new and better form of governance.

Political power as held and exercised in East Asia differs from that in Europe. That is, European countries are more democratic, and Asian nations are more patrimonial—a situation which lends itself to more autonomous rule and more concentrated power. While the role of the state in East Asia may vary further from country to country, it is evident that the impact of economic globalization has been immense—so much so that the economic crisis proved to be beyond the control of any state. In fact, the state's role in economic management had been replaced by multinational corporations, GEFIs, and the invisible hand of financial volatility, especially on the global level.

Economic globalization can directly reshape and reformulate the state's management of the economy, but, it should be noted, the state maintains its political power, which makes it distinct from a business corporation. Although some multinational corporations have budgets larger than those of some nations, and although they have great economic power, they have neither political legitimacy nor control of the means of violence within a nation. They are not military organizations, and they are not political or legal entities, which can control citizens (Giddens 1990, 70–71).

Furthermore, the nation-state should not be seen as a passive actor vis-à-vis multinational corporations or economic globalization. In the global economic context, even though "nation-states are the principal 'actors' within the global political order" and "corporations are the dominant agents within the world economy" (Giddens 1990, 71), the state can employ its political power to mobilize domestic resources against the globalizing economy. Yet the relative autonomy of the state is the result of economic globalization, and the importance of the forces of economic globalization remains.

The rapid mobility of capital in the financial system is a case in point—and particularly so as regards the economic crisis in East Asia. Giddens (1998, 30) contends that rapid financial flows have created the economic globalization that has reshaped the nation-state's economic management:

> Over a trillion dollars a day is turned over in currency exchange transactions. The proportion of financial exchanges in relation to trade has grown by a factor of five over the past fifteen years. "Disconnected capital"—institutionally managed money—has increased by 1,100 per cent on a world scale since 1970 in proportion to other forms of capital. Institutional investors based in the US alone held $11.1 trillion in assets in July 1996. Privatized pension funds, or bonds floated to fund pension schemes, are basic parts of this huge sum. In 1995 US pension funds, mutual funds and endowments held $331 billion in institutional equities.

The common thread in all financial crises—in Latin America in the 1980s, in the European exchange rate crisis of 1992, and in the Mexican bond crisis of 1994—was the volatility of capital flows (Flynn 1999, 24; Giddens 2000, 126–127).

Soros (2000, xiii) warns that the merits of market mechanisms should not be exaggerated. The law of demand and supply rarely leads to equilibrium. In fact, financial markets are unstable:

> Even in the service of individual interests, the market mechanism has certain limitations and imperfections that market fundamentalists ignore. For one thing, financial markets are inherently unstable. The theory of perfect competition takes the supply and demand curves as independently given. Where the twain meets, equilibrium is to be found. But the assumptions upon which the concept of

equilibrium is built are rarely met in the real world. In the financial sphere they are unattainable. Financial markets seek to discount a future that is contingent on how it is discounted at present. Given the imperfect understanding of the participants, the outcome is inherently indeterminate. Thus, contrary to the idea of a self-equilibrating mechanism, the stability of financial markets needs to be safeguarded by the public policy.

For Soros, the main ingredient of the economic meltdown was the international financial system, while "other ingredients" varied from country to country (2000, 210). His contentions are in line with mine, because we both argue for coordination between the external factor of economic globalization and the internal factor of domestic or regional cultural values. Nevertheless, his analysis gives prime importance to financial flows rather than what he refers to as the Asian model, while I emphasize them equally. However, as Soros leaves room for "other ingredients," this provides some open-ended flexibility.[1]

The important point is that a tremendous rise in the volume of foreign exchange transactions results in higher volatility in the exchange rate, which affects activities in the real economy (Fukushima 2000, 128) and in the political arena. However, as Soros argues, the impact of the capital flows is unique in its ability to extend the crisis across regional boundaries. This uniqueness, which is related to the openness of a country to financial markets, produces different degrees of crisis.

In the case of Thailand, it is evident that the outflow and inflow of capital played a part in causing the economic crisis.[2] But the part they played may have been central to the crisis because, in the case of inflow, had it been used productively, the crisis might have been averted. As it happened, capital inflows were put to unproductive use, which is to say, toward the domestic culture of doing business in Thailand.

For example, deregulation and liberalization of capital inflow and outflow, as carried out by the Bangkok International Banking Facilities, was launched in 1993. The aim was to increase the inflow of funds to sustain rapid economic growth and to make Thailand a regional financial center (Delhaise 1998, 83). Thus was liberalized the regulation of global capital, foreign funds, and loans to local businesses. Thai banks acted as middlemen, re-lending to local firms and benefiting from the cheaper rate of interest compared with the domestic rate (Doner and Ramsay 1999, 183; Warr 1998, 60).

Nevertheless, the Bangkok International Banking Facilities was not used according to its stated purposes. By June 1996, US$69.4 billion had been loaned, of which US$45.5 billion was in the form of one-year loans. Most loans were not hedged against currency fluctuations, and this money ration allocation was maintained until June 1997 (Flynn 1999, 25). By the time the IMF arrived with its rescue package, foreign debt was held primarily by the private sector—US$72 billion out of US$99 billion in total—(Warr 1998, 59). These loans had been misallocated to real estate and low-yielding commercial and industrial projects. Thus the financial crisis could be traced to the misuse of capital inflow, which harkened back to cultural values, or the way of doing business in Thailand. To attract foreign investment and capital inflow, the government deregulated capital control by making capital inflow, as short-term loans, easier to enter the country, and, simultaneously, by facilitating outflow as well. But the broader situation—marked by capital liberalization and deregulation, a low level of exports, a high level of foreign debt (especially in short-term loans), over-investment in real estate, speculation in the stock market, low-yielding sectors of the economy, and a high level of nonperforming loans—only kept the currency fragile. Foreign speculators therefore found it easy to attack the baht (Doner and Ramsay 1999; Flynn 1999, 25, 182; Warr 1998, 60). This, in fact, was what happened in November 1996.

Foreign investors then stopped giving new loans and withdrew their capital from the country. In 1996, capital inflow was 7.7 percent of the gross domestic product; in 1997, the same amount represented 12.6 percent of capital outflow (Fukushima 2000, 131). The Bank of Thailand was forced to float the baht on July 2, 1997. By January 1998, the baht had fallen from 25 baht per US$1 to 55 baht per US$1; a month later, it swung back to 45 baht per US$1. After that, the government had to ask the IMF for assistance. With the economic meltdown, the insolvency of banking and industrial firms resulted in the widespread closing of companies. Many workers, especially in the financial sector, found themselves without employment. Under these circumstances, the next election brought in a change of government.

In Indonesia, the country most severely affected by the crisis, the rupiah was floated in May 1998. From Rp2,500 per US$1, it reached its lowest point at Rp17,000 per US$1 in July 1997. The economic results were hyperinflation in import prices and a huge rise in the foreign debt burden, which ushered in further problems in the economy, society, and politics (Fukushima 2000, 128). In the aftermath, the country experienced malnutrition, social and political unrest, and ethnic conflict.

With financial liberalization but no prudent domestic regulations, South Korea was also affected by capital flows. But South Korea's was a liquidity crisis (Kim 2000, 115). Between 1992 and 1996, loans to South Korea increased by 158 percent, far outpacing the 44 percent rise in total lending by G10 banks[3] to other developing countries. At the end of 1996, loans to South Korea amounted to over one-quarter of all loans to East Asia. The banking sector accounted for 66 percent of all lending by international banks, while 28 percent went to the non-banking private sector and 6 percent to the public sector. In the period 1994–1996, lending to South Korea doubled from US$47 billion to US$85 billion (Smith 1998, 72). These loans were mainly short-term, and they exceeded 60 percent of South Korea's total external liabilities. This exposed the danger of liquidity shortage in the event that these loans were recalled suddenly (Kim 2000, 115). And this is what really happened. When the crisis began in Southeast Asia, international banks stopped lending to South Korea; they called in their loans, and South Korea had its crisis.

Malaysia was also hammered. From a pre-crisis 2.50 ringgit per US$1, the currency fell, by August 1998, to 4.20 per US$1—a devaluation of 40 percent. The Philippines was the least affected of the East Asia 5, with only a 35 percent devaluation of the peso between July 1997 and October 1998. This was due to its relatively low foreign debt of US$45 billion (Yusuf 2000, 163), which also implied that the Philippines had not opened itself to the global financial markets as much as had other countries.

In the transition economies of China and Vietnam, the impact of economic globalization was comparatively less. The two countries had a prudent regulation of capital inflow, which meant that the level of openness to global capital flow was low in relation to the ability to repay loans. In China, by the end of 1997, foreign debt amounted only to the moderate level of US$131 billion. In addition, over 80 percent of its foreign debt was of long maturity, with about half consisting of loans from international organizations and foreign governments (Song 1998, 105–106). Vietnam's banking system may have been no stronger than that of the East Asia 5, but the underdevelopment of its financial system, the high degree of control over foreign exchange transactions, and the restriction of private capital inflow to mainly foreign direct investment shielded the country from the crisis (Leung and Doanh 1998, 121; Turley 1999, 289).

Indeed, the transition economies by their nature, because of their kind of debt, had better prudential regulation of capital flow than did developing economies. While the debt of developing economies focused on the private sector, the debt of transition economies tended toward the development of state-owned enterprises (SOEs). Because governments in transition economies could closely oversee the capital flow, they could more easily control it.

The obverse, however, was that the close link between SOEs and their banks also meant a very weak financial sector (Rana and Lim 1999, 6). That is, with a low level of involvement in global financial markets, the transition economies experienced the effect of economic globalization to a lesser degree.

It is clear that in country after country, economic globalization, especially as regards globally integrated financial markets, was a large factor in the economic crisis. Giddens (2000, 126) writes:

> What happened resembled financial panics of earlier times, but took place with greater speed, scope and intensity because of the instantaneous character of global market reactions today. It isn't only that there can be a sudden surge of capital out of a country or area—capital can rush into favoured hot spots as well. Both processes have undesirable effects. The damage produced by rapid outflows of money has been evident in each successive crisis. But surges of capital inwards can also have destabilizing effects, leading to the over-valuation of exchange rates, rising property and asset prices, and a bubble economy.

Global financial markets are volatile, unstable, irrational, and uncontrollable. They also have an economically adverse effect on the local country. Soros (2000, xxii) may be right in claiming, in the context of financial markets, that "our understanding of the world in which we live is inherently imperfect. We are part of the world we seem to understand, and our imperfect understanding plays an active role in shaping the events in which we participate." The modern world is a juggernaut (Giddens 1990, 138–139), as is the global financial system. We cannot know all the complicated mechanisms in this modern capitalist world. As we cannot understand them, the outcome is unpredictable and uncontrollable.

Cultural Values and the Economic Crisis

Asian values, as the dominant cultural norms, played a part in the crisis as well. There are Western versions of the relationship between culture and economics, as, for example, Max Weber's *Protestant Ethic and Spirit of Capitalism*. In the East, the spirit of Confucianism in Asian values assumes the place of the spirit of capitalism. Confucianism stresses the principles of harmony, respect for authority and the elderly, loyalty, benevolence, meritocracy, literacy, and scholarship, and it is often considered as the bedrock of the economic miracles of Japan, South Korea, China, and Singapore (Flynn 1999; Han 1998; Han 1999; Kluth 2001, 4–5). This is the positive side of Asian values.

Economic growth in East Asia requires a "paternalistic state, government guidance and protection of private enterprises, a communitarian outlook and practices, and an emphasis on social order, harmony, and discipline" (Han 1999, 4). Most of these conditions could be provided by Asian values, particularly in the early period of industrialization, when such an environment proved conducive to success.

From the West's point of view, there is also a negative side to Asian values, as seen in the nepotism, favoritism, informal interpersonal relationships, patron-client networks, and corruption that gave rise to crony capitalism. These characteristics of Asian values are deemed to have been a cause of the economic crisis. In the age of globalization, which requires "transparency, accountability, global competitiveness, a universalistic outlook and practices, and an emphasis on private initiative and the independence of the private sector," these aspects of Asian values are inappropriate (Han 1998, 64).

Within the realm of Confucianism, *guanxi* existed as a way of doing business through relationships and connections. Thus was *guanxi* transposed from a cultural context to an economic one. The system of *guanxi*, which originated with the Chinese, is employed in developing Asian countries, decreasing the fixed costs of business management in relatively small firms. Compared with the rules-based system of management in developed economies, the costs of management in the *guanxi* system are cheap. However, as businesses grow and economies become more complex, the incremental costs of doing businesses also increase. At this point, the costs of the management in the *guanxi* system exceed that of the rules-based system, so in a market economy the *guanxi* system cannot be expected to survive (Kluth 2001, 18).

But before going further, let me define my terms. Asian values vary from one country to the next within a region. The larger the space, the more variety and difference in values. That is to say, although Confucian cultural values are dominant, there are also other subcultural values in the subregions of East Asia. As Han Sung-Joo argues, East Asian countries share general values, but they also have diversity in their particular subset of values (Japan Center for International Exchange [JCIE] 1998, 20). Nevertheless, there is the rubric of Asian values under which a consistency of practices falls.

It is critical that one understand how values vary within and among countries and subregions, as well as how they may be selected and combined (Han 1998, 71). The interaction and acculturation between dominant and subregional cultural values contribute to the specific and dissimilar results that can be seen. For instance, why was Singapore, with its explicit Confucian influences, less impacted by the crisis when compared with South Korea, which has a similar Confucian culture? How does one explain the situation in such East Asian countries as Malaysia, Indonesia, and the Philippines, which have cultural influences like Islam and Catholicism that do not exist in Northeast Asia?

This form of cultural analysis, first of all, enables us to study cultural values as dynamic and flexible. It can avoid what Stephanie Lawson (JCIE 2000, 12) calls a simplistic model of "static and deterministic conceptions of culture and cultural communities" that considers culture as having an enduring essence, fixed immutable identity, homogeneity, and no differences in cultural communities. If cultural values can influence the East Asian governance model that created the crisis, and if cultural values are not fixed, then civil society can join the cultural battle, employing values on the political front to challenge old forms of governance. Second, the analysis is open-ended, entertaining cultural differences and cultural adoption and adaptation. As Lawson suggests, to study culture in a fixed framework is to deny creative combination emerging from cross-cultural interaction. This also affords us a more variable explanation as to why the crisis differed from country to country.

The thrust of this analysis is that "overseas Chinese"—that is, Chinese who have emigrated from the mainland to other countries—act as carriers of dominant Asian values. In Northeast Asia, China, with its cultural and historical development, is the cradle of Asian culture. Even though its neighbors, South Korea and Japan, have cultural differences as a result of modern cultural development, they share the root of Asian culture. This is the state of affairs in Hong Kong and Taiwan, although the former is a special case, having been a part of the British Empire until 1997.

In Southeast Asia, the influence of the overseas Chinese is undeniable, even as the spread of the Chinese population may vary. For example, in Indonesia 3 percent–4 percent of the population is Chinese; in Malaysia it is 30 percent; in the Philippines, 2 percent; in Singapore, 78 percent; in Thailand, 14 percent. The ratio of overseas Chinese population to the general population matters less, however, than the economic power they exert, which is significant. In Indonesia the overseas Chinese share of market capitalization is 73 percent; in Malaysia the share is 69 percent; in the Philippines, 50 percent–60 percent; in Singapore, 81 percent; in Thailand, 81 percent (Kluth 2001, 5). With economic power so great, it is clear that the overseas Chinese business culture has a huge influence on economic development in the region.

If there are Asian values, such as Confucianism and *guanxi*, then overseas Chinese are the best medium to spread these cultural values. And if there are Asian values in the business culture of overseas Chinese, it naturally influences the way of doing business in each country where they can be found. Given that Asian values have been associated with the economies of East Asia, then there has to be a correlation between the behavior of overseas Chinese and the boom or bust of economies in the region. And so, in the same way, do overseas Chinese have an impact on the mode of governance in East Asia.

Nevertheless, this is not a game of blessing or blaming overseas Chinese for the economic boom or bust in Southeast Asia. The role played by local elites, such as politicians and bureaucrats, whose frames of reference are forged by subregional cultural values, has got to be taken into account. As such, the processes of interaction, integration, and acculturation that go on between dominant Asian values and subregional values yield a new way of doing business. This synthesis is congruent with Han (1998, 71):

> Whether Asian values have played a positive or negative role has depended largely upon which stage of political and economic development a particular country happens to be in, upon the way such values are selected and combined, and upon the dynamics among the various elements within the larger phenomenon called Asian values.

This synthesis of Asian cultural values has given rise to what Flynn calls "rule by connection," or economic management through networks of connections (1999, 3; 145–146), which manifests itself in patron-client relationships, nepotism, cronyism, collusion between business and politics, and corruption. It is this mode of governance, in combination with economic globalization, that is in part the cause of the Asian economic crisis.

Cultural interaction and acculturation can encourage certain outcomes, or they may render a clash between cultures. As regards the Asian crisis, it would seem the former was the case. While cultures may have clashed, adaptation and reintegration of values produced a certain outcome—the economic crisis. Thus, it becomes clear that cultural values are a double-edged sword. How these values are adapted and implemented in a changing environment determines whether the outcome will be beneficial or not. This may help to explain why Singapore—heavily populated by overseas Chinese and strongly influenced by Confucianism, but inclined toward social order, discipline, and community—did not suffer from economic crisis to the same degree as other countries.

Rule by connection can occur on the macro, or structural, level. Informal agreements, favoritism, close interpersonal relationships, deference to authority, and *guanxi* are transposed into a pattern of state paternalism, collusion between government and business, and government guidance and protection of private enterprises. Thus are Asian values institutionalized into a system of governance.

At the micro level, Asian values see expression as cronyism, nepotism, clientelism, and corruption among the business sector, politicians, and bureaucrats. Cultural values become habituated in human agents, informing their daily practices in business and economic affairs. What occurs on one level is often reflected in the other.

In Northeast Asia, the influences of Asian values are more direct and explicit. That is the case in Southeast Asia as well, but here they come in contact and are integrated with subregional cultural values. As a result, rule by connection assumes new characteristics, depending on the country, with different expressions on the macro and micro levels.

Today, Han (1998, 68) argues, cultural values in China are a mixture of Confucianism (along with Taoism and legalism), socialism, and pragmatism; together, these values inform the behavior, practices, and institutions of the country. At the macro level, these cultural values infuse the connection between the party-state and business, with the party-state exerting strong control over finance and investment despite the growth of the private sector and the market economy. In this respect, culture is also often influenced by politics, which is to say, communism. The factions that connect ministries, enterprises, the central bank, and provincial governments determine policies and their implementation as well as consensus and acceptance (Flynn 1999).

At the micro level, Chinese business culture is different from that of most East Asian countries because of SOEs. Because these enterprises are state-owned, private interests have less at stake (Kluth 2001, 13). There is a fledgling private business sector, and, accordingly, interpersonal relationships are not at as much of a premium as they are elsewhere in Northeast Asia. Interpersonal vested interests are overshadowed by "people interest" here, and this is one reason that foreign investment continues to flow into China.

One potential problem, however, is the transposition of cultural values to the macro level. In the absence of effective regulations, the connections among factions and the close relationships among party-state, financial institutions, and SOEs may render the system economically vulnerable. For instance, unsound lending by financial institutions to unprofitable SOEs will hurt national economic performance (Song 1998, 115; Lardy 1999, 92–93).

In Japan and Korea, Asian cultural values are transposed to the developmental state, that is, a "combination of state banks, economic planning and steering, an alliance between finance, government, and business, and pursuit of an ideology of national development" (Flynn 1999, 52). This is rule by connection at the macro level, where the values of building consensus, avoiding confrontation, and submitting to authority, with the government in the lead, are put in the service of development. In Japan, bureaucrats of the former Ministry of International Trade and Industry (MITI) played a crucial role in the direction and development of business; in South Korea, a very tight relationship existed between government and the *chaebol* (conglomerates). These connections were an important contributor to poor economic performance because government guidance and protection allowed mistakes and losses to be hidden (Flynn 1999, 13).

The same pattern of connections exists in Thailand, where the perception was that Thai banks would not be allowed to collapse despite their difficulties. This apparent invulnerability led to economic disaster (Doner and Ramsay 1999, 182–185). At the micro level in both Japan and South Korea, the close relationship between government and business is expressed through family and political party networks, sometimes both. Affiliations outside official relationships have created a network of multiple affiliations (Flynn 1999, 35), which lubricates the formal relationships in the running of the economy.

Corporate familism, over-lending by financial institutions, loan misallocations, over-investment, and investment fads became the way business was done (Jackson 1999, 5–6). In South Korea, the *chaebol* over-borrowed from institutions managed by themselves or by others closely related to them (Flynn 1999, 34–35). In Japan, at the end of 1997, Japanese banks declared some ¥76.70 trillion in nonperforming loans, many of them to companies that had been successful at hiding their insolvent assets (Asher and Smithers 1999, 38–39).

In Southeast Asia, these Asian cultural values are less dominant. Overseas Chinese are a minority in most countries, including Indonesia, the Philippines, Thailand, and Malaysia, even as they wield tremendous economic power. In Singapore, however, overseas Chinese are the majority, there has been widespread integration and acculturation, and Asian values were put to positive effect in creating the economic miracle and preventing an economic meltdown. The reason for this is that Confucian values, as discussed above, were transposed to good governance on the macro level—a government and public and private sectors that were clean and effective. Asian values on the micro level of interpersonal relationships, with practices such as clientelism, cronyism, and corruption, were less prevalent. Although Singapore has state paternalism, Asian values have impacted positively on the state on the terrain of economic management.

In Thailand, the local elite with their indigenous culture of patron-client relationships integrated and acculturated dominant Asian values that came with overseas Chinese. This established a pattern of collusion between government and business, but not in the same manner as in the developmental state; here the motivating factor was not national development but self-interest. At issue was, simply, the rule by connection, on both the macro and micro levels, for the interest of patron-client networks. Conspiracies among politicians, bureaucrats, and business were formed—a relationship described by Riggs (1966) as pariah entrepreneurship in a time of bureaucratic polity.[4]

Arriving in Thailand, overseas Chinese brought with them their Asian values as a way of doing business. With pressure from the Thai elite, which was launching its economic nationalism and "Thaification" projects during the mid-1930s to late 1940s, overseas Chinese found their place under the ruling Thai umbrella. Neatly adjusting and integrating their Asian values to the Thai patron-client way, the overseas Chinese ran their banks by being submissive, informal clients of their favorite bureaucrats and politicians. Once this interpersonal pattern of doing business was established, corruption was not far behind.

A shift in power has occurred, from bureaucrats (who reigned during the period of pariah entrepreneurship of bureaucratic polity) to provincial politician-businessmen (in a period of crony capitalism during a so-called full democracy), but this has been just a changing of actors. The core cultural values, resulting from the integration of patron-client relations, Confucianism, and *guanxi*, remain. The roots of the corrupt Thai economic culture persist in the tripartite conspiracy of bureaucrat, politician, and overseas Chinese businessmen.

As indicated above, Chinese constitute about 14 percent of the population of Thailand, but they control 81 percent of the market capitalization. In fact, in 1996, fifteen families controlled more than 50 percent of the total value of the corporate assets of the country (Kluth 2001, 6). Given these overwhelming numbers, the overseas Chinese business culture in Thailand, which was corrupt, can be said to have contributed significantly to the economic crisis. I hasten to emphasize that overseas Chinese are not to be singled out as scapegoats because the corrupt business culture could not have taken hold without the cooperation and involvement of the local elite.

This is a very similar pattern to developments in Indonesia, Malaysia, and the Philippines. In Indonesia, dominant Asian values were brought by the overseas Chinese. These cultural values were integrated into local Indonesian cultures, which Han (1999, 5) considers to be a mixture of traditional Javanese culture, Islamic influence, and the pragmatic military orientation of the "new order." Indeed, there is also acculturation among local cultures. Sukma (1999, 141) suggests that the value system of the "new order" incorporates the traditional Islamic Javanese cultural values, such as consensus and deliberation in politics, communitarianism, social order and harmony, and respect for authority and elders. However, to ensure this system, it must have compliance, which it gets through a combination of cooption, selective repression, and rewards. The result is a family-like political format that circumvents the emergence of any real competition. Into this landscape entered the overseas Chinese, who—at only 3 percent–4 percent of the population, but controlling 73 percent of Indonesia's market capitalization—were brought under the control of the local elite, with whom they established patron-client relationships.

Something similar occurred in Thailand, but while patron-client relationships there led to competitive bureaucratic and business cliques, clientelism in Indonesia led to a monopoly run by the family of President Suharto (Jackson 1999, 16–17). The combination of Asian values with Indonesian values "has worked systematically and gradually toward the creation of a noncompetitive or familylike political format that forbids the emergence of opposition" (Sukma 1999, 141). Nevertheless, for a while this system worked in both political and economic spheres. In Indonesia the fifteen wealthiest families control more than 60 percent of the total value of the country's corporate assets (Kluth 2001, 6).

Malaysia is unique in that the interaction of the indigenous cultural values of the local elite and the dominant Asian values of overseas Chinese has produced a clash, with ethnic problems resulting. Islam is ingrained in Malaysian cultural values, and the elite has employed these values to legitimize the authority of government (Han 1999, 5). Although religion can be critical of the abuse of power, religion can also be used to justify it

(Noor 1999, 173). In Malaysia's case, local cultural values have been used by the Bumiputra, Malaysians of Malay origin, to dominate political power to increase their interests over ethnic Indians, and to correct imbalances between Bumiputra and overseas Chinese (Flynn 1999, 101).

While there is xenophobia in Malaysia (Soros 2000, 202), the Chinese, at 30 percent of the population, still control 69 percent of market capitalization (Kluth 2001, 5). So the Chinese business culture continues to exert its influence on the Malaysian economy. Moreover, as regards the local elite, rule by connection through the political party United Malays National Organisation (UMNO) is strongly in evidence, with companies related to UMNO receiving government contracts for big projects (Flynn 1999, 100). Therefore, we can see that in some places the local indigenous cultures can come to play the eminent role instead of the dominant cultural value, demonstrating the complex ways, and consequences, of cultural integration.

In the case of the Philippines, the influence of Asian values is complicated by the country's long history of colonization by Spain and the United States. However, during the Ferdinand Marcos regime, the situation in the Philippines was similar to that in Thailand and Indonesia before the onset of the economic crisis. At the macro level the pattern of rule by connection backed by rule by force was predominant (Flynn 1999, 155), while corruption, cronyism, favoritism, and clientelism were explicit at the micro level of interpersonal connections. In this sense, the powerful overseas Chinese minority could be brought under the umbrella of the local elite, the result being a form of crony capitalism common to Thailand and Indonesia.

After the People Power revolt of 1986, when the Marcos government was overthrown, however, Filipino cultural values were reoriented from family interest to state interest (Romero 1999, 180, 213). Although undesirable residues of the old regime such as cronyism, special privileges, and corruption remain, there is a trend away from the old values of rule by connection backed by rule by force.

THE ECONOMIC CRISIS
AND THE COMING OF GOOD GOVERNANCE

The thesis here is that the integration of dominant Asian values with local cultural values combined with the influences of economic globalization brought on the Asian financial crisis.

As stated above, nothing much would have been wrong if capital inflows had been used productively. Nor would the economic crisis have been so severe if foreign capital inflows had been limited. These two ifs are very big, however, as neither was the case. The internal force of corrupt domestic culture acted in concert with the external force of the globalizing economy to endanger economic stability in Pacific Asia. Depending on the degree to which cultural values at both the micro and macro levels were transposed (or the degree to which the state and business were colluding) and depending on the coordination between the mechanisms of cultural values and economic globalization, the crisis left countries in the region crippled.

How could banks and financial institutions have allocated such enormous sums, borrowed from foreign entities, to domestic lenders for them to invest in unproductive and over-supply businesses (for example, the petrochemical or iron industries) for so long? The mechanisms of economic globalization and cultural values were such that decisions to allocate capital inflow were made by connection, not by considerations of the marketplace. The dark side of cultural values caused foreign capital to be misallocated. Even so, in the face of a globalized economy, it may be understandable why governments in the region chose to put their system of representative democracy to such use, because economic performance was critical to their political survival.

This was the case in transition economies like China as well. While its concern is not reelection, it is governmental legitimacy, which is conferred by successful economic development. In this environment, a "privileged position for business" is created, which governments feel a need to indulge (Lindblom 1977). The privileged position is enjoyed particularly by the financial sector, which determines the power structure of business in capitalist economy. Theoretically, this power structure is neutral; a government's indulgence to business may be good or bad depending how it was done and how much was involved. In any case, it was the cultural transposition of the rule by connection in governance that created the crisis.

The countries most damaged by the financial crisis were the emerging market economies of Indonesia, Thailand, and South Korea, all three of which exemplify the conditions indicated here. In Thailand, the relationship between politics and economics has been powerful for decades, with commercial banks servicing politicians and providing resources for commodity exports and industrial growth. This marriage of influence ensured the guarantee of the government and the Bank of Thailand that banks would not fail. Accordingly, the banks and financial companies, which were controlled by overseas Chinese, could act with impunity and continue to misallocate loans (cited by Doner and Ramsay 1999, 182–184). The banks' position at the macro level was supported by the interpersonal relationships between borrowers and lenders at the micro level. The situation with the Bangkok Bank of Commerce is a classic example. The Bank of Thailand had to support the Bank of Commerce with nearly US\$7 billion even though it had violated several directives from the central bank and had engaged in fraudulent behavior. The Bangkok Bank of Commerce had, moreover, provided loans to politicians who lacked sufficient collateral and used the funds for real estate development, which then failed (Flynn 1999, 185).

This example is just one among others. Bankers and financiers also extended loans to a closed circle of friends and relatives, especially in such nonproductive sectors as real estate and the stock market. Given the financial liberalization, deregulation, and capital inflows, the crisis might not have reached such proportions had the loans not been used so nonproductively. If internal economic fundamentals had remained solid, foreign investors would not have panicked and withdrawn their funds. At the same time, if foreign capital inflows had been limited and if the limited funds had been put to more productive use, the economic crisis would not have been so severe. With limited capital, a small economy, and fewer interrelations with the globalizing economy, the impact of the crisis might have been controlled.

In South Korea, the pattern is quite similar. Both major commercial banks were implicitly and explicitly guaranteed by the central bank. Therefore, it behooved international banks *not* to reduce their credit line, which defined the limits for entering into such transactions as currency trades and interest-rate swaps, even when they could see trouble brewing (Soros 2000, 217). Moreover, South Korea's entry into the Organisation for Economic Co-operation and Development (OECD) deregulated financial flows, especially foreign borrowings.

For over thirty years, foreign capital in South Korea had been allocated through cultural values such as "tight family control which had been exercised through the government-bank-*chaebol* network" (Flynn 1999, 66). This network produced the model of economic development of "monopolistic competition across industries." As a result, the top thirty conglomerates accounted for over half of the country's gross national product, with the top five conglomerates responsible for one-third of the country's total production (Pyo 1999, 159).

Monopolistic competition reflected the fact that the *chaebol* also monopolized foreign capital inflows, which to a large extent was a reflection of the misallocation of financial resources. A *chaebol* is a large-scale group of companies whose business activities are controlled by a single person or family or entity. With the influence of the *chaebol* so great, government provided them with abundant fiscal incentives, and the *chaebol*, having close relationships with the political authorities, were able to grow quickly (Chung and Wang 2000, 60–61). The spiral continued; by the end of 1996 the balance sheets for the *chaebol* showed debts and liabilities much larger than equity and assets (Flynn 1999, 19). International lenders called back their loans, foreign investors withdrew their investments, and South Korea was in financial crisis. However, as in the model of the developmental state, the ideology of national development afforded South Korea a comparatively stronger economic recovery than took place in Thailand, which had a higher level of individual self-interest.

In Pacific Asia, Indonesia was probably the most severely hurt by the financial crisis. In terms of business, Indonesia was also the most monopolistically controlled—by the family of President Suharto—and international loans were consistently allocated to their clients and cliques, who were involved in their various operations. In the region in 1996, Indonesia had the largest number of companies controlled by one family. In the country, the Suharto family was the largest stockholder with assets worth US$24 billion, controlling 16.6 percent of total market capitalization, even as the top fifteen families accounted for 61.7 percent. Through business groups led by Suharto's children, relatives, and business partners, many of them with political authority, the family controlled 417 listed and unlisted companies (Husnan 2000, 19–23). With such a concentration of power and resources, the degree of self-interest among the people controlling the economy was monumental. And the effects of the crisis much worse.

The crisis was less severe in Malaysia and the Philippines—compared with Indonesia, South Korea, and Thailand—as the mechanism of cultural values in creating the crisis was less prominent. One reason is that dominant Asian values were not so neatly integrated into the local culture of the elite. Another is that their level of engagement with the global financial system was relatively low. As Soros (2000, 216) observes, countries that regulate and control currency trading suffered less disruption. Thailand, with a financial system more open than Malaysia's, as reflected in their level of freely convertible currencies, therefore was hurt more. The Philippines had a low level of exposure to global finance, having less short-term debt than others of the East Asia 5. In fact, in 1993, the World Bank excluded the Philippines from the list of "miracle economies" in Asia, as it was "never one of the fastest-growing economies of the region" (Flynn 1999, 104).

In the transition economies, the crisis was less than for the East Asia 5 for two reasons. First, cultural values were less influential because of state-owned enterprises. Rule by connection was established at the macro level of party-state and business collusion, while cultural transposition to the micro level of interpersonal relationships was weakened by the interest of "the people"; that is to say, the SOEs were owned by the government. If these countries were to liberalize their economies, however, the mechanism of cultural values would, I fear, work quite effectively in generating economic crisis. That would be the case for China much more than for Vietnam because of China's higher level of engagement with economic globalization.

Second, the control and regulation of financial markets in transition economies were prudential. That was not the case with the banking systems of these countries, however. As regards China and Hong Kong, the latter's banking and financial systems were more fully developed and in place, but because the renminbi was not freely tradable, China was not hard hit. If the renminbi had been tradable, the Chinese economy would have collapsed (Soros 2000, 216).

In the small economies of Laos, Cambodia, and Myanmar, the mechanisms of economic globalization had greater influence—in the obverse—than did cultural values. There may have been mismanagement and misallocation of capital owing to Asian cultural values—including, in Laos, widespread corruption, and, in Cambodia, a lack of a legal framework for the private sector (Wescott 2001, 11, 30)—but these countries were less impacted by the crisis than either the transition economies or the emerging market economies by virtue of their nonentry into global finance and economic globalization. We hardly hear news of economic crisis in these countries, including in the closed economy of Myanmar.

Up until this point, we have seen how economic globalization and the integration of dominant Asian values with local values were the driving forces of the East Asian economic miracle. We have also observed how they were the impetus of the economic crisis. Although one may argue that both mechanisms were hidden in the economic boom and delayed the economic bust, at the end of the day they produced the crisis.

Nevertheless, both mechanisms are double-edged swords. By learning the lessons of the miracle-turned-meltdown, perhaps we can prevent the same from happening again. Good governance would seem to be the answer. Governance is "the manner in which power is exercised in the management of a country's economic and social resources." It is associated with "predictable, open, and enlightened policymaking (that is, transparent processes); a bureaucracy imbued with a professional ethos; an executive arm of government accountable for its actions; and a strong civil society participation in public affairs; and all behaving under the rule of law" (World Bank 2000). In short, there are four conditions for good governance: accountability, participation, predictability, and transparency (Wescott 2001, 1).

The wake of the financial crisis saw a growing role in the region for global economic and financial institutions, such as the World Bank, ADB, IMF, UNDP, and WTO. Countries in crisis needed rescue packages. Assistance and loans from these GEFIs came with the condition of good governance. Whether governments liked it or not, they had to practice, or at least pretend to implement, good governance. Such a condition may be risky, however, because rapid economic recovery will reduce the motivation for governments to reform (World Bank 2000, 89). For governments in East Asia, the will to reform is crucial, but nothing is simple. As has been seen in this region, the interests of the elite normally come before the interests of the nation.

However, there are positive signs, especially in the East Asia 5, which is the grouping most affected by the crisis. Governments have demonstrated reform-mindedness, and public and corporate sectors have voluntarily accepted the tenets of good governance. In Thailand, for instance, the government has adopted good governance as a national agenda, providing the thrust for reform in the public sector. It has sought to enhance the independence of regulatory agencies, corporate governance, and legal structures. Although all this comes after a crisis, such steps are immense. The perception that good governance is a required instrument for rectifying the effects of the crisis is essential.

GOOD DOMESTIC GOVERNANCE, DEEPENING DOMESTIC DEMOCRACY, AND CULTURAL STRUGGLE

Good governance, with its ideas of participation, transparency, openness, and accountability, will help to deepen domestic democracy in East Asia. To the extent that the concepts of representation and representative democracy are problematic, the participation of civil society, which is a tenet of good governance, can decrease problems that may arise. Globalization supports cultural struggles of civil society against the state. As a result, the cultural mechanism that was coopted by the state and that partly caused the crisis can be challenged.

On the other hand, following Higgott (2000), I also contend that the GEFIs' programs of good governance will de-politicize and de-democratize power relations at the global level. When these institutions employ programs of good governance, the technical concerns of public management replace the political and ethical question of equality and of who gets what, when, and how in the global economic system. In the end, the question is, Who benefits? And if richer countries use global governance to centralize their economic managerial power, regionalism leading to cosmopolitanism may be the ideal. Good governance should not stop at the national level; it should extend to the global level in the light of cosmopolitan governance and democracy, not as market fundamentalism.

The financial crisis revealed the internal workings of cultural values, which have been at the heart of corruption, nepotism, and cronyism in both the public and private sectors. To remedy the economic problems, a system must be put in place to eradicate such malpractice. In Thailand, civil society and academicians have tried to educate the public about good governance in both the private and the public spheres. The need for accountability, transparency, efficiency, responsibility, and the participation of civil society has been advocated.

This has occurred in tandem with the condition of good governance stipulated by the GEFIs for countries receiving financial assistance. Two themes have been emphasized: governance in management aimed at reform of public institutions and governance in the corporate sphere aimed at reform in the private sector.

Public governance is connected with the restructuring of institutions in order to respond with increasing democratization and globalization, which in turn require accountable, transparent, and effective public sector institutions. Institutional weaknesses, such as ineffective and overprotected SOEs, ineffectual and excessive state regulation, antiquated civil service rules, government policies preventing competition, lack of governmental accountability and probity, and abuse of public office for private gain had largely been ignored; the crisis brought these problems to the fore (World Bank 2000, 85–86).

Technical assistance can help to provide for reform in public financial management, administrative and civil services, regulatory and legal development, and anticorruption (World Bank 2000, 87–88). In the ADB's governance project in the Greater Mekong Subregion, which includes Cambodia, Laos, Thailand, and Vietnam, effective governance and public management have required reform in institutions such as the national assembly, public administration, public finance management, line ministries and departments, subnational government, and the legal and judicial system (Wescott 2001).

Corporate governance, in the ADB project, is associated with the reform of structures where governance has been weak, such as boards of directors, internal controls, audits, disclosure, and legal enforcement. Because governance has been wanting in these areas, the East Asia 5 was plagued by overcapacity, bad investments, excessive diversification by large business groups, and excessive exposure to debt, especially unhedged short-term foreign debt. To confront these problems, corporations must put into place, first of all, a set of rules that defines the relationships among shareholders, managers, creditors, the government, and other stakeholders; and then a set of mechanisms that directly or indirectly helps to enforce those rules. Both aspects vary greatly across countries depending on the interplay of political, economic, legal, cultural, and historical factors (Capulong, Edwards, and Zhuang 2000, 5).

In the post-crisis era, rules relying on connections have to be discarded and replaced by mechanisms for responsible corporate governance. Capulong, Edwards, and Zhuang (2000, 5–17) proposes the following. First, disclosure of ownership: the concentration of ownership, which reveals the distribution of power between managers and shareholders; and the composition of ownership, which identifies the shareholders and, more important, their affiliations. Second, control by and protection of shareholders: through boards of directors, which monitor management and operations; by executive compensation, which gives incentive to executives to keep ownership separate from control of the company; with minority shareholder rights, which provide opportunity for shareholders to participate in corporate decision-making; and by transparency and information disclosure, which are key to effective shareholder control and protection.

Third, monitoring and disciplining of companies: by creditors, which give recourse to creditors in the event of default on debt payments or violation of debt covenants; and through insolvency procedures, which give rights to creditors in the event of insolvency. And fourth, relying on the market: to determine control of the corporation; and to act as an external check on internal management through the possibility or threat of mergers.

Although public and corporate governance operate in different spheres, in the context of the Asian financial crisis they cannot be easily separated. Public and corporate governance can be seen as having merged for three reasons. First, when the crisis occurred, states had to use public money to resolve problems in the private sector for the sake of national economic stability. Second, many bodies that regulate corporate governance are public bodies. Third, the transposition of cultural values to the macro level of state-business collusion blurs public and private boundaries. It is strategically useful to tackle problems in public and private management separately, but at the same time we also have to be aware of the effects of the "no man's land" between them.

The practice of good governance in public and private management will be useful for social, political, and economic development in East Asian countries. The emerging market economies of the East Asia 5 could benefit most. They would gain not only by reforming public and corporate structures and institutions, but also by creating a solid base for future development under the pressures of a competitive globalizing economy—something that will benefit the emerging market economies of Hong Kong, Singapore, and Taiwan. Indeed, a country like Singapore has already gained advantage from good governance, which markedly reduced the severity of the crisis.

The crucial point is that the practice of good governance can be an instrument to counter the integration of dominant Asian culture with indigenous culture, which, as has been shown, resulted in corrupt cultural values on the macro as well as micro levels. The GEFIs' insistence on rule by the market as opposed to rule by connection is a step in that direction. By the East Asia 5 countries' having to accept the conditions of the GEFIs, it is hoped that the norms of accountability, participation, predictability, and transparency in public and corporate management will see changes in the interpersonal relationships on the micro level.

In this regard, GEFIs can also have an impact on the rising tide of civil society on the global as well as regional and domestic levels. For instance, Transparency International, a transnational nongovernmental organization (NGO), works to increase government accountability and to curb national and international corruption. Its campaigns through the Internet and international media, where it ranks countries by their levels of corruption, have been very educational.

Regional and international meetings on issues of governance, such as those held by the Japan Center for International Exchange (JCIE) and

ASEAN's Institute of Security and International Studies (ISIS), can be a means of spreading new ideas. As a consequence, new cultural processes are created in the battlefield of cultural struggles. In this sense, negative Asian cultural values can be challenged both from above (through economic globalization and the GEFIs) and from beneath (through the cultural diversity created by a globalized media, which catalyze culture locally).

Governance projects of the GEFIs, compared with the movements of civil society, however, have no direct impact on democratization because the ideology behind the project is to enhance competition in the marketplace. They involve technicalities to reform public and private institutions for that purpose specifically, but they can have the indirect, crucial impact of deepening domestic democracy.

Civil society, on the other hand, seeks to represent the interests of the citizenry more directly. While the purpose of civil society is not pure, subject as it is to its own interests and imperfections, it can act effectively as a complement to domestic democracy. In this regard, if the state opens its arms to civil society participation, the legitimacy of the state in policy initiation and implementation is enhanced.

However, from the standpoint of the state, not all East Asian countries want to have good governance and to have their domestic structure democratized. Because of political regimes or entrenched private interests, some may want the first at the expense of the second. For instance, some transition economies like China, Vietnam, and Laos may want the technicalities of public and corporate governance to enhance their capacity to compete in the global market, but they may not want to share power with a civil society that would challenge them. In the case of a closed economy like Myanmar, it may want neither. Among emerging market economies, most will accept good governance for the sake of increasing their capacity to compete in the world market. This is the case for the East Asia 5, which had to accept good governance as a condition on the basis of which they received help from the GEFIs. Democracy in these countries has got to have benefited.

GLOBAL GOVERNANCE AND COSMOPOLITAN DEMOCRACY

The importance of governance to the GEFIs lies in the fact that it increases the performance of public and corporate institutions in global market competition. Accordingly, intervention by the state in the economy should be minimized, and SOEs should be privatized in order to enhance the capacity of the enterprises to compete. Rule by connection should be replaced by rule by the market—following a model that Stephen Gill calls a "constitution for global capitalism" (Higgott 2000, 137).

Nothing is wrong with this if competition in the global market is fair and if there is no barrier between the center and periphery of global capital. However, as can be seen from Soros's comparison of the financial stability of the U.S. economy and the global economy, "the playing field of global capitalism is skewed in favor of the center" (2000, 231). As Soros again points out, a large factor in the financial crisis was the pressure by the United States and the IMF on Asian countries to open their financial markets before appropriate mechanisms were in place (2000, 217). Asian countries bore responsibility for their unhealthy domestic economic situations, but countries pressing them to liberalize their markets walked away blameless when disaster struck.

Moreover, from the domestic point of view, the IMF's rescue package appeared to bear the imprimatur of multinational corporations, which would stand to gain by the terms (Flynn 1999, 65). If the creation of effective markets in the economic globalization arena "results in unequal treatment for some states and, more importantly, exacerbates poverty for the weakest members of international society, then globalization is seen to deny justice" (Higgott 2000, 141).

Because the governance of GEFIs can be perceived as a means to an end, not an end itself, at the international level it has the effect of de-democratizing democracy. It is inadequate to the task of good global governance, external to such ethical considerations as poverty reduction, although it may claim otherwise. Giddens concludes that "we can't leave such problems to the erratic swirl of global markets and relatively powerless international bodies if we are to achieve a world that mixes stability, equity and prosperity" (1998, 153).

As Held (1995a) states, one of the problems of representation in a representative democracy is that legitimate representation within a nation is blurred by the global interconnectedness. Interests of the "relevant community" are contested and compromised by regional and global issues.

This requires us to rethink representative democracy as we have known it and to consider a more desirable cosmopolitan democracy. As defined by Archibugi and Held (1995, 13):

> The term *cosmopolitan* is used to indicate a model of political organization in which citizens, wherever they are located in the world, have a voice, input and political representation in international affairs, in parallel with and independently of their own governments. The conception of democracy deployed here is one

that entails a substantive process rather than merely a set of guiding rules. For the distinctive feature of democracy is, in our judgement, not only a particular set of procedures (important though this is), but also the pursuit of democratic values involving the extension of popular participation in the political process.

Cosmopolitan democracy introduces democratic values, especially people participation, beyond that extended by the democratic states. This model is "a system of *governance* which arises from and is adapted to the diverse conditions and interconnections of different peoples and nations" (Held 1995b, 106) [my emphasis]. Accordingly, cosmopolitan democracy represents a cosmopolitan mode of governance, which is stronger and more comprehensive than the governance propounded by the GEFIs.

Cosmopolitan democracy, linked to governance, demonstrates how democracy is compatible with governance, even as it addresses the interconnectedness of domestic and international politics. As argued above, the consequences of the practices of GEFIs' governance, especially as regards the participation of civil society, together with the dynamics of globalization, can help to deepen domestic democracy and to reduce distortions in representation. At the same time, these processes can help to create a cultural struggle, the terms of which will challenge the governance mode of rule by connection.

These same processes also help to create a new model of good governance that transcends governance in the GEFIs' mode. The purpose is to create a deeper democracy and a new stronger form of governance—cosmopolitan governance—that is effective at the global level as well. In order to achieve this, it is necessary to have transnational democracy. Giddens argues that to deepen democracy in democratic countries we need to democratize above—as well as below—the level of the nation; that is to say, to consolidate democracy it is necessary to encourage it at both the international and national levels (1999, 75).

Similar to the national level where governments should recognize NGOs and their movements in civil society, the participation of global civil society in global policy must be strengthened and recognized by global policy managers and international institutions. There are regional and global issues that exist in the vacuum between sovereign nations and regional and global organizations, and global civil society can advance these institutions by mobilizing national and international civil culture through the media. Greenpeace and animal rights movements are two such examples.

Organizations in civil society, however, should stand for assistance, not resistance. They should not be seen merely as players in the policy process necessary for the "legitimation of the liberalizing agenda" (Higgott 2000, 143). Civil society balances the interests of the political and economic spheres. In democratic society, in fact, as Giddens (1999, 78) contends, state control cannot be so easily replaced with markets.

If civil society participation in global policy processes is developed, it is certain that, as in domestic democracy, the problems of representation at the global level will be reduced. While one can envision the deepening of democracy at the global level, as at the national level, global civil society will have to address broader concerns. Compared with the sovereign state, as Higgott points out, NGOs and other non-state actors have no legitimacy or authority in policy making. Second, paradoxically as well, their internal organizations are less democratic than their external participation. This makes domestic and global civil society less democratically accountable than states or interstate organizations. Third, any implementation of solutions taken in global negotiations by the interstate organizations must be carried out by the sovereign state (Higgott 2000, 15–16). These are challenges if national and global civil society is to be strengthened in both national and global policy processes.

At the same time, although the state's power is reshaped by the globalization forces, it remains a political force. The state, with its participation in regional and international institutions, is still a main component of cosmopolitan democracy. To have democracy at the international level may be a utopian dream, as power relationships and interests would be more complex than at the national level. A pluralistic model of interest groups further complicates relations in the global context.

Moreover, the state itself does not act as referee anymore, but as an interest group so as to protect its national interests. Therefore, a vision of cosmopolitan democracy should be realistic, modest, and achievable step by step, built on the base of a concrete global political economy. The first step should be taken by the states as they participate in regional institutions.

In the East Asian context, cosmopolitan governance and democracy are the highest ideals, but finding the means to achieve these goals is not easy. Globalization has had an immense impact, but there are different levels of democratic development. Compare, for example, Thailand and Myanmar. At the same time, the level of democracy in a country, however different it may be from that of another country, can determine the will toward cosmopolitan democracy. If the will varies too greatly, then East Asian countries may prefer the GEFIs' model of governance.

For my part, I optimistically believe that the misfortune of the economic crisis can shift the mindset of East Asian countries so they will realize the importance of cosmopolitan governance. Different countries were affected by the crisis to different degrees depending on how the mechanisms of cultural values and economic globalization were combined, but all were affected in significant ways. This renders them ready to see the cruel world of economic globalization, especially the instability of financial markets. One good sign is that ASEAN has enlarged into ASEAN + 3, demonstrating that countries have taken a further step toward regional cooperation. Cooperation in helping each other, even if for self-interest, is an invaluable starting point from which to create a better regional economic and political policy. In this process, regional governance can act to confront both regional and global issues.

NOTES

1. Soros' notions of closure and openness of financial markets and of other ingredients enable us to understand, as in X theory, the various degrees of impact from the capital flow to the crisis, and, then, different degrees of the development of good governance in each country in Pacific Asia. Accordingly, it is useful for showing how capital flow impacts the situation at different levels in different countries. At the same time, this analysis provides us with a way to look at how cultural values interact with economic globalization in producing a crisis.
2. It is impossible, and not my aim, to explain the economic crisis in terms of comprehensive macroeconomics. The point that I will concentrate on is the impact on the financial crisis of capital flows related to economic globalization.
3. G10 refers to the Group of 10, which is made up of the Group of Seven—Canada, France, Germany, Italy, Japan, the United Kingdom, and the United States—plus Belgium, the Netherlands, Sweden, and Switzerland; the group actually comprises eleven countries.
4. In the heyday of the bureaucratic polity, where top bureaucrats, especially from the military, dominated the Thai political arena through political positions in the cabinet, "pariah entrepreneurship" was established. Bureaucrats acted as patrons, protecting overseas Chinese businessmen as clients. The overseas Chinese reciprocated, offering bureaucrats shares and positions on the company boards (Riggs 1966, 242–310).

Bibliography

Ake Tangsupvattana. 1999. "Social Causality, Sex Tourism and Environmental Degradation in Thailand: An Application of the Philosophy of the Social Sciences to Relations between the Thai State and the Business of Tourism." Ph.D. thesis, Department of Sociology, University of Essex.

Archibugi, Daniele, and David Held. 1995. "Editors' Introduction." In Daniele Archibugi and David Held, eds. *Cosmopolitan Democracy: An Agenda for a New World Order*. Cambridge: Polity.

Asher, Davis L., and Andrew Smithers. 1999. "Japan's Key Challenges for the 21st Century." In Karl D. Jackson, ed. *Asian Contagion: The Causes and Consequences of a Financial Crisis*. Singapore: Institute of Southeast Asian Studies.

Cantell, Timo, and Paul Podell Pederson. 1992. "Modernity, Postmodernity and Ethics—An Interview with Zygmunt Bauman." *Telos* 93: 133–144.

Capulong, Ma. Virginita, Davis Edwards, and Juzhong Zhuang, eds. 2000. *Corporate Governance and Finance in East Asia: A Study of Indonesia, Republic of Korea, Malaysia, Philippines, and Thailand, Volume I*. Manila: Asian Development Bank.

Chung, Kwang S., and Wang Yen Kyun. 2000. "Republic of Korea." In Juzhong Zhuang, David Edwards, and Ma. Virginita Capulong, eds. *Corporate Governance and Finance in East Asia: A Study of Indonesia, Republic of Korea, Malaysia, Philippines, and Thailand, Volume II*. Manila: Asian Development Bank.

Delhaise, Philippe F. 1998. *Asia in Crisis: The Implosion of the Banking and Finance Systems*. Singapore and New York: Wiley.

Doner, Richard F., and Ansil Ramsay. 1999. "Thailand: From Economic Miracle to Economic Crisis." In Karl D. Jackson, ed. *Asian Contagion: The Causes and Consequences of a Financial Crisis*. Singapore: Institute of Southeast Asian Studies.

Falk, R. 1995. "The World Order between Inter-State Law and the Law of Humanity: The Role of Civil Society Institutions." In Daniele Archibugi and David Held, eds. *Cosmopolitan Democracy: An Agenda for a New World Order*. Cambridge: Polity.

Flynn, Norman. 1999. *Miracle to Meltdown in Asia: Business, Government and Society*. New York: Oxford University Press.

Fukushima Kiyohiko. 2000. "Regional Co-operation: Security Implications of the Instability in International Finance." In Mely C. Anthony and Mohamed Jawhar Hassan, eds. *Beyond the Crisis: Challenges and Opportunities, Volume I.* Kuala Lumpur: Institute of Security and International Studies.

Garnaut, Ross, and Ross McLeod. 1998. "The East Asian Crisis." In Ross H. McLeod and Ross Garnaut, eds. *East Asia in Crisis: From Being a Miracle to Needing One?* London and New York: Routledge.

Giddens, Anthony. 1990. *The Consequences of Modernity.* Cambridge: Polity.

———. 1998. *The Third Way: The Renewal of Social Democracy.* Cambridge: Polity.

———. 1999. *Runaway World: How Globalisation Is Reshaping Our Lives.* London: Profile Books.

———. 2000. *The Third Way and Its Critics.* Cambridge: Polity.

Hall, Stuart, David Held, and G. McLennan. 1992. "Introduction." In Stuart Hall, David Held, and Tony McGrew, eds. *Modernity and Its Futures.* Cambridge: Polity.

Han Sung-Joo. 1998. "Asian Values: An Asset or a Liability?" In *Globalization, Governance, and Civil Society.* Report of the Global ThinkNet Tokyo Conference, February. Tokyo and New York: Japan Center for International Exchange .

———. 1999. "Asian Values: An Asset or a Liability?' In Han Sung-Joo, ed. *Changing Values in Asia: Their Impact on Governance and Development.* Tokyo and New York: Japan Center for International Exchange.

Held, David. 1995a. *Democracy and the Global Order: From the Modern State to Cosmopolitan Governance.* Cambridge: Polity.

———. 1995b. "Democracy and the New International Order." In Daniele Archibugi and David Held, eds. *Cosmopolitan Democracy: An Agenda for a New World Order.* Cambridge: Polity.

Higgott, Richard. 2000. "Contested Globalization: The Changing Context and Normative Challenges." *Review of International Studies* 26: 131–153.

Husnan, Saud. 2000. "Indonesia." In Juzhong Zhuang, David Edwards, and Ma. Virginita Capulong, eds. *Corporate Governance and Finance in East Asia: A Study of Indonesia, Republic of Korea, Malaysia, Philippines, and Thailand, Volume II.* Manila: Asian Development Bank.

Jackson, Karl D. 1999. "Introduction: The Root of the Crisis." In Karl D. Jackson, ed. *Asian Contagion: The Causes and Consequences of a Financial Crisis.* Singapore: Institute of Southeast Asian Studies.

Japan Center for International Exchange. 1998. *Globalization, Governance, and Civil Society*. Tokyo and New York: Japan Center for International Exchange.

———. 2000. *Values and Identity*. Tokyo and New York: Japan Center for International Exchange.

Kikuchi Tsutomu. 2001. "The Political Economy of 'ASEAN+3'/East Asian Cooperation—Toward Better Regional and Global Governance." Paper presented at the 15th Asia-Pacific Roundtable, Kuala Lumpur, 4–7 June.

Kim Kihwan. 2000. "Stabilising Asian Financial Markets: What Needs to Be Done?" In Mely C. Anthony and Mohamed Jawhar Hassan, eds. *Beyond the Crisis: Challenges and Opportunities Volume 1*. Kuala Lumpur: Institute of Strategic and International Studies.

Kluth, Andreas. 2001. "Asian Business." *The Economist*, 7 April.

Lardy, N. R. 1999. "China and the Asian Financial Contagion." In Karl D. Jackson, ed. *Asian Contagion: The Causes and Consequences of a Financial Crisis*. Singapore: Institute of Southeast Asian Studies.

Leung Suiwah and Le Dang Doanh. 1998. "Vietnam." In Ross H. McLeod and Ross Garnaut, eds. *East Asia in Crisis: From Being a Miracle to Needing One?* London and New York: Routledge.

Lindblom, Charles E. 1977. *Politics and Markets: The World's Political-Economic Systems*. New York: Basic Books.

McGrew, Anthony. 1992. "A Global Society?" In Stuart Hall, David Held, and Anthony McGrew, eds. *Modernity and Its Futures*. Cambridge: Polity.

Noor, Farish. 1999. "Values in the Dynamics of Malaysia's Internal and External Political Relations." In Han Sung-Joo, ed. *Changing Values in Asia: Their Impact on Governance and Development*. Tokyo and New York: Japan Center for International Exchange.

Pyo, Hak K.1999. "The Financial Crisis in South Korea: Anatomy and Policy Imperatives." In Karl D. Jackson, ed. *Asian Contagion: The Causes and Consequences of a Financial Crisis*. Singapore: Institute of Southeast Asian Studies.

Rana, Pradumna B., and Joseph Anthony Y. Lim. 1999. "The East Asian Crisis: Macroeconomic Policy Design and Sequencing Issues." In S. Ghon Rhee, ed. *Rising to the Challenge in Asia: A Study of Financial Markets*. Manila: Asian Development Bank.

Riggs, Fred W. 1966. *Thailand: Modernization of a Bureaucratic Polity*. Honolulu: East-West Center Press.

Romero, Segundo E. 1999. "Changing Filipino Values and the Redemocratization of Governance." In Han Sung-Joo, ed. *Changing Values in Asia: Their Impact on Governance and Development*. Tokyo and New York: Japan Center for International Exchange.

Rosenau, P. M. 1992. *Post-modernism and the Social Sciences: Insights, Inroads, and Intrusions*. Princeton, N.J.: Princeton University Press.

Smith, H. 1998. "Korea." In Ross H. McLeod and Ross Garnaut, eds. *East Asia in Crisis: From Being a Miracle to Needing One?* London and New York: Routledge.

Song Ligang. 1998. "China." In Ross H. McLeod and Ross Garnaut, eds. *East Asia in Crisis: From Being a Miracle to Needing One?* London and New York: Routledge.

Soros, George. 2000. *Open Society: Reforming Global Capitalism*. New York: Public Affairs.

Sukma, Rizal. 1999. "Values, Governance, and Indonesia's Foreign Polity." In Han Sung-Joo, ed. *Changing Values in Asia: Their Impact on Governance and Development*. Tokyo and New York: Japan Center for International Exchange.

Turley, W. 1999. "Viet Nam: Ordeals of Transition." In Karl D. Jackson, ed. *Asian Contagion: The Causes and Consequences of a Financial Crisis*. Singapore: Institute of Southeast Asian Studies.

Warr, Peter G. 1998. "Thailand." In Ross H. McLeod and Ross Garnaut, eds. *East Asia in Crisis: From Being a Miracle to Needing One?* London and New York: Routledge.

Wescott, Clay G., ed. 2001. *Key Governance Issues in Cambodia, Lao PDR, Thailand, and Vietnam*. Manila: Asian Development Bank.

World Bank. 2000. *Reforming Public Institutions and Strengthening Governance: A World Bank Strategy*. Washington, D.C.: World Bank.

Yamamoto Tadashi. 2001. "Good Governance: Key Issues Confronting the Asia Pacific Region." Paper presented at the 15th Asia-Pacific Roundtable, Kuala Lumpur, 4–7 June.

Yusuf, Z. A. 2000. "Can We Tame the Menacing Financial Phantoms?" In Mely C. Anthony and Mohamed Jawhar Hassan, eds. *Beyond the Crisis: Challenges and Opportunities, Volume I*. Kuala Lumpur: Institute of Security and International Studies.

7

Toward a New Security Order in Pacific Asia

YOON YOUNG-KWAN

It has almost become a cliché to say that international relations among East Asian countries can be characterized as a balance-of-power system similar to nineteenth-century Europe (Friedberg 1993/1994, 5–33; Kissinger 2001, 25–26). East Asia has had no effective institutional mechanism to provide nation-states with norms, rules, or standards that regulate state behavior and stabilize international relations. In contrast, countries in Europe today enjoy stable international relations with the help of useful international institutions such as the North Atlantic Treaty Organisation (NATO), the European Union (EU), and the Organization for Security and Co-operation in Europe (OSCE).

In the East Asian system of balance of power, states frequently face a so-called security dilemma. The lack of institutions makes a state suspicious about the intentions of other states. A state that acts to strengthen its defensive posture tends to be regarded as aggressive by other states, which in turn leads to an escalation in arms competition. Similarly, without an effective institutional mechanism, information flows are much less perfect, and the likelihood of one state overreacting to another increases the possibility of conflict. In East Asia, bilateral alliances balanced by the United States fill the vacuum left by the lack of institutional mechanisms, and these alliances work as the only tool to assure security among nations.

The level of danger associated with the security dilemma in East Asia has varied, reflecting changes in the international political situation in the past few decades. In the cold war, the existence of the common enemy, the

---

This chapter reflects the author's personal opinion and has nothing to do with the official position of the South Korean government.

Soviet Union, was reason for major actors in East Asia to be more cooperative. The end of the cold war, however, brought the security dilemma to the fore. With the threat of the Soviet Union gone, the major powers in the region grew less cooperative and more suspicious of one another. The September 11, 2001, terrorist incidents in the United States have had considerable implications for the level of the security dilemma in the region as well. However, while the attacks altered the landscape of international politics, they have not contributed much to stabilizing security relations among East Asian nations.

What can be done to make the region a more secure place in the twenty-first century? In addressing this question, the analysis here will focus on the conceptual framework of the security dilemma.

THE IMPACT OF THE END OF THE COLD WAR

The collapse of the Soviet empire and the end of the cold war have affected the nature of the East Asian security order in various ways. First of all, the disappearance of the Soviet Union as the communist power in Asia has changed the nature of the U.S. military commitment in the region. Formerly, this commitment had been geared to the deterrence and containment of the Soviet threat in the region. Since the collapse of the Soviet Union in 1991, however, the United States has focused more on its role as a stabilizer among East Asian nations.

Initially, there were internal debates within the United States as to whether the military commitment should be continued. Scholars like Chalmers Johnson argued for withdrawal; Japan had risen as an economic powerhouse and, in the absence of the Soviet Union, was capable of looking after its own security (Johnson and Keehn 1995).

Other points of view were also voiced. Joseph Nye, himself a policy maker at the time, argued for a continued commitment. The region's major powers, Japan and China, were experiencing rapid changes of power, and as a result, there was an increase in instability. The role of the United States in East Asia would be best served, therefore, as that of a stabilizer, or balancer, of international relations. According to Nye, it was a role most East Asian nations welcomed (1995, 90–102). The Nye initiative became the official policy of the United States, reflecting the change of the basis of U.S. commitment in East Asia from deterrence to stabilization (U.S. Department of Defense 1995).

Secondly, the disappearance of the Soviet threat has reduced the incentive for the United States and China to cooperate closely (Campbell 2001, 371–385; Shambaugh 2001, 50–64). Until the 9-11 incident, neither country could find a rationale for strategic cooperation. The inconsistency between the Bill Clinton administration and that of George W. Bush over how to define China from a strategic perspective was itself a reflection of this impasse. While the Clinton administration saw China as a strategic partner, the Bush administration viewed it as a strategic competitor—at least until the 9-11 attacks.

Thirdly, it is now conventional wisdom that, since the end of the cold war, Japan has sought a more responsible role in East Asian security. The Japan specialist Michael Green (1995) has elaborated on the long process of Japan's trying to redefine U.S.-Japan security relations in pursuit of more autonomy, even as it has maintained strong security ties with the United States. On April 17, 1996, a few months after the Taiwan Strait crisis, Clinton and Japanese Prime Minister Hashimoto Ryutaro, in a joint communiqué, announced a revitalization of the U.S.-Japan alliance to guarantee security over a wider geographical scope of Asia Pacific than had been the case before. Japan promised to increase logistics, strengthen rear-area support, and cooperate in the study of a ballistic missile defense system.

In September 1997, the Guidelines for Japan-U.S. Defense Cooperation were revised to include the provision of "operational cooperation" for Japan's Self-Defense Forces (SDF) at times of regional conflict in the form of surveillance, intelligence gathering, etc. It is noteworthy that the Chinese government was very much concerned about the new defense guidelines, President Jiang Zemin going so far as to say that China was on "high alert" (Christensen 1999, 63).

Finally, the end of the cold war has significantly changed the nature of the North Korea problem. The collapse of the Soviet Union and the transformation of other socialist countries abruptly decreased the inflow of foreign economic aid to North Korea, especially energy, and this dealt a severe blow to the country's economy. In the mid-1990s, the economy had been reduced by half; the country experienced famine on a massive scale. This dire situation forced North Korean policy makers to gradually open up their economy, while surreptitiously developing nuclear weapons, the cause of great international concern.

The international crisis caused by suspicions surrounding North Korea's nuclear development was first resolved by the 1994 Geneva Agreed Framework. In the agreement, North Korea promised to freeze its nuclear development, for which the United States agreed to provide two nuclear light-water reactors through the Korean Peninsula Energy Development Organization (KEDO) project. North Korea also promised that it would allow an inspection team from the International Atomic Energy Agency (IAEA) before the delivery of key parts of the light-water reactors. The timing of the inspection had been the sticking point of the U.S.–North Korea confrontation—until the second crisis broke out in October 2002, when North Korean authorities admitted to continued development of nuclear weapons through a uranium-enrichment program.

On October 3–5, U.S. Assistant Secretary of State James Kelly was in Pyongyang for the resumption of the dialogue between the two countries. When Kelly confronted officials with evidence that North Korea had a clandestine nuclear weapons program, Kang Sok-ju, the first vice minister of foreign affairs, replied angrily to the effect that: "Your president called us a member of the axis of evil. . . . Your troops are deployed on the Korean peninsula. . . . Of course, we have a nuclear program" (Karon 2002).

Before talks broke down, North Korea urged the United States to assure its security and to conclude a nonaggression pact, in reply to which the United States demanded that North Korea dismantle its nuclear development program (Struck 2002). Each side insisted on its conditions being met first. Resolution of the security dilemma on the Korean peninsula continues to be critical.

Overall, the end of the cold war in 1991 has intensified the security dilemma among the East Asian states. While the three major powers, the United States, Japan, and China, managed to cooperate with each other in order to deter the Soviet threat, their relations have since become more complex and less secure, especially U.S.-China and Japan-China relations. The fact that Japan and China have been undergoing rapid changes in their relative power has added to the difficulty and uncertainty of East Asian security relations.

THE IMPACT OF THE 9-11 INCIDENTS

U.S. foreign policy has experienced significant changes since the 9-11 attacks. They, together with the fear of more to come, have provided the United States with a strong motive for international activism. Policy makers and ordinary citizens in the United States had thought themselves safe from events going on in the rest of the world. Indeed, the United States is geographically protected from other regions by oceans on both sides, and even in the age of nuclear intercontinental ballistic missiles (ICBMs), the country thought that it was safe because of the success of its nuclear deterrence. In the age of terrorist attacks, however, these assumptions prove to be no longer valid.

In 1997, Richard Haass, a U.S. security specialist, referred to the United States as "the reluctant sheriff." Today he sees the United States as becoming "the resolute sheriff" (Haass 2002). With its primacy in power, the United States is now willing to exercise its influence more freely in making rules, in intervening in world affairs, and in punishing its enemies with or without the approval/consent of other nations/its allies.

The opposition of formidable powers such as China and Russia functioned as a constraint on U.S. attempts to exercise leadership in international relations. The 9-11 incidents saw an important change in this regard. The United States was able to mobilize the support of China and Russia in its antiterrorism campaign, and, consequently, Washington's bilateral relationships with both countries improved significantly. In the case of China, the tensions that had existed over Taiwan, human rights, weapons proliferation, and other issues appear to have been smoothed over. For instance, immediately after 9-11, the Chinese government strongly condemned the terrorist acts, shared intelligence about Osama bin Laden's Al Qaeda network, and cooperated with other Asia Pacific nations in furthering the antiterrorist cause at the Asia-Pacific Economic Cooperation (APEC) meeting in Shanghai in October 2001. In return, the Bush administration dropped references to China as a "strategic competitor" (Shorrock 2001). It is uncertain, however, how long this cooperative relationship between the two countries will continue. It is true that in the United States not a few still view China as a rising power and a future threat to U.S. interests, particularly in East Asia.

Post–9-11, Japan, as a traditional ally of the United States, may have been even more cooperative than China. The Japanese government, through the political initiative of Prime Minister Koizumi Jun'ichiro, passed a law that circumvented Article 9 of the Constitution and enabled the dispatch of the Maritime Self-Defense Force overseas. It is evident that real political constraints continue to work domestically against Japan's pursuit of "remilitarization," even as Japan's neighbors tended to view the dispatch of SDF personnel abroad with concern.

While the U.S.-Japan alliance remains solid and the U.S.-China relationship has strengthened in the wake of 9-11, the bilateral relationship between

Japan and China, in terms of security, is still very difficult. Japanese policy makers are concerned about China's rapidly rising economic capability, its military budget in recent years, and the implications of all this for the security of Japan. At the same time, Chinese policy makers tend to view the Japanese search for an expanded security role in the region as a threat. As a result, any dialogue in the realm of security issues between the two countries has been very limited. In other words, 9-11 has done nothing to resolve the security dilemma between the two major Asian powers.

In fact, 9-11 might even have had a slightly negative impact on intra-East Asian relations. First of all, as U.S. policy makers focus single-mindedly on the war against terrorism, they have much less time to mull over key issues in Asia. According to Kurt Campbell of the Center for Strategic and International Studies, speaking at a forum organized by the Sasakawa Peace Foundation, this should be a matter of concern for U.S. allies in Asia (Shorrock 2001). Secondly, 9-11 might have distracted the attention of most East Asian policy makers from their own regional security agendas. Thus, should any of these regional issues explode, policy makers would be less prepared to resolve them. Even as regards terrorist activities in Southeast Asia, overcoming differences of policies and positions remains a difficult task.

MAJOR AREAS OF CONFLICT IN EAST ASIA

The Korean Peninsula

In the past several decades, North Korea has been regarded mainly as a security problem. However, it is no longer merely a security problem but simultaneously an economic, humanitarian, and international political problem. All these factors are intermingled. North Koreans view weapons of mass destruction (WMD) as the last card with which they can emerge from economic disaster, international isolation, and an insecurity complex as a nation.

The complicated nature of the North Korea problem requires a comprehensive approach through which both sides take action. In other words, once North Korea gives up development of WMD, countries such as the United States, South Korea, and Japan will have to provide economic aid, diplomatic normalization, and security assurance to North Korea. If they are willing to do that, the involved parties will benefit from the peaceful resolution of the North Korea problem in terms of security improvement, economic prosperity, and refugee issues. A version of the Marshall Plan for North Korea would thus be called for.

Regarding North Korea policy, South Korea, the United States, and Japan have worked closely together through the Trilateral Coordination and Oversight Group (TCOG). However, once these countries come to a final agreement and a Korean version of the Marshall Plan is initiated, it is critical that a multilateral forum be established for dialogue among the two Koreas, the United States, Japan, China, and Russia. Even at a time when the North Korean refugee issue has attracted international attention, the affected countries have had no forum for dialogue on this matter at all. The United States and North Korea, unable to overcome their mutual suspicions, had no diplomatic contact for almost two years—until the unsuccessful attempt at dialogue in October 2002. A similar deadlock existed between Japan and North Korea until the September 2002 summit talks in Pyongyang.

The Taiwan Strait

China is steadily growing more impatient with the status of Taiwan; the past several years have seen a rapid increase in the Chinese military buildup focused on Taiwan. The number of short- and medium-range ballistic missiles targeting Taiwan has risen from forty or fifty in 1995–1996 to over three hundred. Taiwan, for its part, has been experiencing great democratization in recent years, and a growing percentage of the population identifies itself more as Taiwanese than Chinese, leading to a stronger voice for Taiwanese independence. The United States, while supporting China's one-China policy, has made it clear that the policy should be achieved through diplomacy, not by force. The strong will of the United States on this matter was revealed when, in the 1995–1996 Taiwan Strait confrontation, it dispatched two aircraft carriers to the area. One issue, however, is that the United States lacks a clear concept about what it would do in a military crisis. The U.S. government calls its position "strategic ambiguity."

From China's point of view, the renewed alliance between the United States and Japan and their cooperation in missile defense have important implications for the Taiwan issue. In particular, China worries that, should Taiwan be included in the Asian theater missile defense (TMD) system, Taiwan would be more resistant to China's demand for unification. TMD would strengthen Taiwan's defensive posture and lessen its vulnerability to China. With these stakes, suspicions run high among the major powers and "[p]erhaps nowhere else on the globe is the situation so seemingly intractable and the prospect of a major war involving the United States so real" (Campbell and Mitchell 2001, 15). Even as the policy makers of these countries are paying attention to the war against terrorism, the Taiwan issue remains volatile and dangerous.

Terrorism in Southeast Asia

Currently, the most urgent security issue in Southeast Asia is terrorism. In Indonesia, a country with the largest Muslim population in the world, several terrorist networks, such as Jamaah Islamiah (JI) and Kumpulan Mujahideen Malaysia (KMM, or the Malaysian Mujahideen Group), are believed to have ties with Al Qaeda and to have committed terrorist acts in recent years. However, the Indonesian government has been reluctant to act resolutely against these networks for fear of a Muslim backlash. It interrogated Abu Bakar Baashir, the leader of JI, but soon released him claiming no substantial evidence—despite allegations from Singapore and Malaysia.

In the past two years, Malaysia too experienced terrorism, where tourists on the island of Sipadan, off the coast of Sabah, were abducted by the Abu Sayyaf Group. In contrast to the inaction of Indonesian President Megawati Sukarnoputri, the response by Malaysian Prime Minister Mahathir bin Mohamad was firm and decisive. Immediately after 9-11, Mahathir condemned the terrorist attacks, and Malaysian police forces moved to detain more than sixty alleged terrorists under the country's Internal Security Act (Balfour 2002). These steps earned him the gratitude of U.S. President Bush for his "stirring response in the global campaign against terror" (U.S. Department of State 2002). Mahathir, however, has strongly opposed direct military intervention by the United States, calling instead for a more prominent role for the Association of Southeast Asian Nations (ASEAN) in cracking down on terrorism.

The government of the Philippines has been the most aggressive in Southeast Asia in its actions against terrorism, inviting the direct involvement of the U.S. military. In the southern Philippines, Abu Sayyaf, which was founded by one of bin Laden's top associates, has kidnapped tourists and held them for ransom. There are other terrorist groups active as well.

In June 2002, an attempt to rescue the hostages by the Philippine military, with the assistance of U.S. forces, ended with the death of several of the terrorist captors as well as two of the three captives. Manila's call for a coalition with Malaysia and Indonesia for counterterrorist cooperation has resulted in a trilateral agreement to counter terrorism and transnational crime (San Juan 2002).

The United States has deep concerns about terrorist networks and activities in Southeast Asia. Southeast Asian governments, however, are not the Taliban and have been opposed to terrorist groups for a long time. Instead of seeking to take charge of the antiterrorist campaign in Southeast Asia, the United States might find it prudent to let regional governments take the antiterrorist initiative themselves. The more direct the military intervention the United States may attempt, the stronger the backlash of the Muslim population in the region will be, and the more complicated the domestic and international political situation will become.

Thus, it is important to strengthen collaborative regional efforts to that end. At the ASEAN summit in Brunei in November 2001, member countries adopted the ASEAN Declaration on Joint Action to Counter Terrorism. The major test will be the coordination of the various governments' antiterrorism policies, which vary greatly, as can be seen from the aforementioned situation in Indonesia, Malaysia, and the Philippines. After the terrorist bombing of a nightclub in Bali in October 2002, the Indonesian government was pressured to take decisive antiterrorist action (Dillon 2002). Indonesia, however, as Southeast Asia's largest country and the world's most populous Muslim nation, must tread carefully within its own borders. Moreover, if there is to be any regional coordination, getting Indonesia's cooperation is indispensable, as it retains veto power over any measure that ASEAN proposes.

Once ASEAN countries succeed in overcoming these difficulties and producing an effective common policy on terrorism, ASEAN and the ASEAN Regional Forum (ARF) will be able to function as meaningful institutional mechanisms for security cooperation from a medium- and long-term perspective.

LIMITATIONS OF THE EAST ASIAN SECURITY ORDER

The main characteristic of the East Asian security order, as noted, is that it is based on a bilateral alliance centered on the United States. Like the nineteenth-century European system, where the balance of power was achieved through alliances, the current situation is ridden with security dilemmas. International relations are unstable, and states are suspicious about the deeper intentions of other states. Without an effective institutional mechanism that can provide principles, norms, or standards, it is difficult to regulate the behavior of the states.

In this kind of security arrangement where the United States is the hub and East Asian states are the spokes, the United States has taken on the role of stabilizer, as the relationship between the United States and its allies tends to be stable. However, the relationship between countries other than the United States, such as Japan and China, tends to be underdeveloped and in many cases rather volatile. One way to overcome the drawbacks of this hub-and-spoke security arrangement would be to foster a multilateral institutional mechanism.

A multilateral institution would complement the bilateral security system in East Asia today. In the past five decades, decision-making procedures among East Asian states regarding security issues have been heavily skewed toward the United States, and this orientation has become a source of anti-U.S. feeling especially since the end of the cold war. By establishing a multilateral security institution in addition to the existing bilateral alliances, the decision-making procedures will become more democratized, and, as such, anti-U.S. sentiment might be lessened substantially.

There is another reason that a multilateral security institution would be beneficial. In East Asia, changes in a country's power relative to other countries' occur very rapidly. South Korea, China, Taiwan, and other countries have experienced rapid economic growth, and as a result, the changes in their power vis-à-vis their neighbors has had significant implications for international security. The gap between a nation experiencing such growth and its international role is sometimes wide, and in turn instability tends to increase. A security system based only on a bilateral alliance will not be able to adjust smoothly to this structurally caused instability. With a multilateral system, states will be able to adjust the gap between their relative power and the role of rising states more easily (Doran 1991). New norms, principles, and rules will make the adjustment process smoother, and the increased information flow will help to reduce suspicion and tension among states.

Europe has absorbed the structural impacts of the end of the cold war through such incidents as the unification of Germany, the collapse of the Warsaw Pact, the dissolution of Yugoslavia, and the political upheavals in the Balkans. However, in East Asia, there has been no comparable structural adjustment. It seems likely that the region will have to undergo this process in the coming decade on the Korean peninsula or even in China. Addressing these challenges peacefully will be of utmost importance. This is another reason that an effective institutional mechanism for security cooperation in the region must be established.

The only multilateral security institution in East Asia is the ARF, which was created in July 1994. East Asian nations, in the new international environment after the end of the cold war, recognized the need for some kind of forum to deal with regional conflicts, to address security concerns such as environmental problems, drug dealing, and terrorism, and also to build mutual confidence among nations. In a response that contrasts with that of the earlier Bush administration, the U.S. State Department under the Clinton administration expressed the view that a multilateral institution comparable to the Commission on Security and Cooperation in Europe (CSCE) be formed. The ARF was the result.

The ARF has accomplished its goals, providing an important forum for security issues and contributing to confidence building among member states. It has been able to induce China, which had been rather skeptical about multilateral security cooperation, to join the forum. And it was China's participation in the ARF that opened up the possibility of multilateral discussions on such complicated issues as the dispute over the Spratly Islands. In 2000, North Korea joined the ARF, affording the foreign ministers of the United States and North Korea a fifteen-minute dialogue for the first in July 2002.

These positive results notwithstanding, the ARF has its weaknesses. Instead of influencing and regulating the behaviors of member states in a meaningful way, the ARF has been nothing more than a forum for dialogue. It did not, for instance, contribute to the resolution of the East Timor conflict in any substantial manner.

Searching for a New Security Order for Asia Pacific in the Twenty-First Century

A security specialist once identified four important tasks for Asia Pacific nations to build peace in the region: establishing a democratic domestic political system, enhancing economic interdependence among nations, strengthening international institutional mechanisms, and adopting sound balance-of-power policies (Segal 1997). The first two tasks, establishing a democratic political system and enhancing economic interdependence, however, are not targets that policy makers can pursue in the short term. Even so, as witnessed from the experience of World War I, it is dangerous to depend totally on balance of power.

The task of strengthening international institutions thus takes on greater urgency. In this regard, there are two suggestions: The first is to expand the role of APEC in the field of security. In 2001, the United States actually utilized APEC as a forum to mobilize cooperation and public opinion against terrorism. Even China, which had avoided discussion of political security issues in a multilateral setting, signed on to the communiqué promoting cooperation against terrorism.

Establishing an entirely new multilateral institution will take a great deal of energy, time, and political capital. It might be easier and less costly to broaden the role of APEC gradually and to develop it into something akin to the OSCE in addition to its economic function. Now would seem the right time to formulate ideas for such an institution since the United States, eager to mobilize countries for its war on terrorism, has greater incentive to cooperate.

More than major powers, middle powers—such as Australia and New Zealand, which have close security ties with the United States through the Australia–New Zealand–United States (ANZUS) treaty—may now be in a position to mediate or facilitate a broader role for APEC. Moreover, in Australia's efforts to solidify its economic relationship with Northeast Asia and to improve political relations with the ASEAN countries, APEC has been a valuable instrument. With its display of diplomatic leadership in East Timor in 1999, Australia would seem well suited to mediate APEC's larger role.

The second suggestion is to set up a multilateral forum to deal with Northeast Asian security issues. The ARF could then concern itself with Southeast Asian security issues and leave such matters as the North Korea problem to a new institutional mechanism concerned specifically with Northeast Asian security cooperation. This multilateral body might be composed of the two Koreas, the United States, Japan, China, and Russia. While it would make sense for South Korea, the United States, and Japan to take the initiative in the North Korea problem, other important security issues, such as refugees and an international guarantee for peace on the Korean peninsula, require the participation of all neighboring countries. This institution could also address other Northeast Asian security issues such as measures for military confidence building, arms control, and so on.

Both the ARF and this proposed Northeast Asian security forum could function as major sub-regional multilateral institutions in addition to APEC, as a newly fortified international economic and security organization. Certainly, it will not be an easy task to broaden the role of APEC into a security forum, or to create a six-power institution for Northeast Asian security. However, without strengthened international institutional mechanisms, East Asia will not be able to resolve the security dilemmas that are rampant in the region's international relations. Unless preparations are made for the inevitable political changes of the twenty-first century, the cost to the region may be very dear.

BIBLIOGRAPHY

Balfour, Frederik. 2002. "Malaysia: A Surprising Ally in the War on Terror." *Business Week,* 6 May. <http://www.businessweek.com/magazine/content/02_18/b3781073.htm> (30 July 2003).

Campbell, Kurt M. 2001. "The Cusp of Strategic Change in Asia." *Orbis* 45(3): 371–385.

Campbell, Kurt M., and Derek Mitchell. 2001. "Crisis in the Taiwan Strait?" *Foreign Affairs* 80(4): 14–25.

Christensen, Thomas J. 1999. "China, the U.S.-Japan Alliance, and the Security Dilemma in East Asia." *International Security* 23(4): 49–80.

Dillon, Dana Robert. 2002. "Military Engagement with Indonesia in the War on Terrorism." The Heritage Foundation, executive memorandum 818, 12 June. <http://www.heritage.org/Research/AsiaandthePacific/EM818.cfm> (1 August 2003).

Doran, Charles F. 1991. *Systems in Crisis: New Imperatives of High Politics at Century's End.* New York: Cambridge University Press.

Friedberg, Aaron L. 1993/1994. "Ripe for Rivalry: Prospects for Peace in a Multipolar Asia." *International Security* 18(3): 5–33.

Green, Michael. 1995. *Arming Japan: Defense Production, Alliance Politics, and the Postwar Search for Autonomy.* New York: Columbia University Press.

Haass, Richard N. 2002. "From Reluctant to Resolute: American Foreign Policy after September 11." Remarks to the Chicago Council on Foreign Relations, Chicago, Illinois, 26 June. <http://www.state.gov/s/p/rem/11445.htm> (30 July 2003).

Johnson, Chalmers, and E. B. Keehn. 1995. "The Pentagon's Ossified Strategy." *Foreign Affairs* 74(4): 103–114.

Karon, Tony. 2002. "How Do You Solve a Problem Like Korea?" *Time* (18 October).

Kissinger, Henry. 2001. *Does America Need a Foreign Policy?* New York: Simon and Schuster.

Nye, Joseph S., Jr. 1995. "The Case for Deep Engagement." *Foreign Affairs* 74(4): 90–102.

San Juan, Joel R. 2002. "Gloria, Mahathir sign counter-terrorism accord." *The Manila Times* (8 May). <http://www.manilatimes.net/national/2002/may/08/top_stories/20020508top5.html> (1 August 2003).

Segal, Gerald. 1997. "How Insecure Is Pacific Asia." *International Affairs* (Spring): 235–250. <http://segal.org/g/site/ia1.htm> (1 August 2003).

Shambaugh, David. 2001. "Facing Reality in China Policy." *Foreign Affairs* 80(1): 50–64.

Shorrock, Tim. 2001. "Ties Warmer after Sept. 11, But Focus on Asia May Blur." <http://www.spf.org/spf_e/spffeatures/china-us.html> (30 July 2003).

Struck, Doug. 2002. "Nuclear Program Not Negotiable, U.S. Told N. Korea." *Washington Post* (20 October).

U.S. Department of Defense. 1995. *United States Security Strategy for the East Asia-Pacific Region* (also known as the Nye Report). Policy report. Washington, D.C.: Office of International Security Affairs.

U.S. Department of State. 2002. "State's Kelly Praises Malaysia for Aid Against Terrorism." International Information Programs, 15 April. <http://usinfo.state.gov/topical/pol/terror/02041600.htm> (30 July 2003).

8

Attempts at a Regional Architecture

SIMON S. C. TAY

The promise for Pacific Asia in the 1990s was that cooperation and increasing parity would be the mark of relationships among nations in the region. The common wisdom of that period was that Asia would grow to be coequal with North America and Western Europe. To achieve this, the "Asian miracle" established a menu of policies and a path of development for export-led industrialization and growth (World Bank 1993; Wade 1990). In this, even as Japan and the newly industrialized economies (NIEs) were seen to lead, the flying-geese pattern of development included the near-NIEs of Southeast Asia and the formerly closed economies of China and Vietnam. Accordingly, the vision of an Asia Pacific community suggested a group of countries around a rim of ocean, cooperating on the basis of greater parity and equity (Godement 1997).

Looking back, we can note the several assumptions that were built into this vision either explicitly or implicitly. The first of these was that while the United States was recognized as a major power in Asia Pacific and as a leading partner, it was not considered to be in a position of dominance or primacy. A second assumption was that Asia would have increasing coherence and linkages, but it would be an "open regionalism," not closed or limited as was the European Union. A third assumption was that member states of the Association of Southeast Asian Nations (ASEAN) would collectively or individually play a major role in the dynamics of the region; hence, the attempt to imbue the region with ASEAN-based modes of interaction like the "ASEAN way" and the early significance of the Bogor

The assistance of Chan Ji-Quandt, a researcher at SIIA, in the preparation of this chapter is acknowledged with thanks.

Declaration, in which Indonesia and other ASEAN members took the lead (Anatolik 1990; Haas 1989; Tay and Talib 1997; Tay 1999).

A decade later now, the Asia Pacific ideal of regionalism has been altered by events and trends. Since 1997, many if not most of the economies of Asia have lost their promise, growing more slowly or uncertainly, even experiencing stagnancy, decline, and instability. The storm of the Asian financial crisis has dispersed the flock of flying geese and destroyed the pattern of their flight (Montes 1997; Radelet and Sachs 1998; Godement 1999; Agenor et al. 2000).

The status of the United States, with its long period of sustained growth, has been reasserted in the world in both economics and political security (Brooks and Wohlworth 2002; Emmott 2002). Against this backdrop, China's economic dynamism has continued, carrying wider political implication for the region. China's promise attracts envy and some concern, but also the largest share of economic investment (Lardy 2002). In comparison, the economic attractiveness of ASEAN members, as well as their political influence, has diminished (Funston 1998; Tay, Estanislao, and Soesastro 2001).

The ideal of parity in Asia Pacific has consequently dissipated. Relations and frameworks for relationships are undergoing reconsideration and reconfiguration. Likewise, the miracle formula of export-driven growth, pushed on by centralized governments' mix of authoritarianism and the market, has come under scrutiny (Stiglitz and Yusuf 2001).

This turn of events leaves us with several questions: How did this sense of East Asian regionalism arise? What are the prospects for this regionalism—its promise and its limits? What new architectures of regionalism are emerging, and how do they coexist?

The primary point here is that a new sense of East Asian regionalism has arisen to link ASEAN and Northeast Asia. This is expressed most notably in the ASEAN + 3 process that brings together the ten ASEAN countries with China, Japan, and South Korea. The process has provided East Asian economies with greater unity and confidence, and it has the potential to assist them in the areas of relations with the United States as well as economic and other forms of globalization.

This chapter, however, argues that this process alone is not sufficient to meet the needs of the region and that it is not the only path of regionalism that might be pursued. There are contemporaneous movements that involve some but not all of the ASEAN + 3 countries. And there is the suggestion that links to non-ASEAN + 3 countries in the region—for example,

Australia, New Zealand, Taiwan, Hong Kong, even India—are also needed, in some form or other.

Yet, while the impulse is toward greater regional linkages, there are opposite, divisive factors. One is the significant difference between the larger economies of Northeast Asia and the small-to-medium–sized economies of ASEAN. This specter of a northeast-southeast divide is especially vivid if we consider the high growth rates seen in China and, most recently, South Korea—which are well above those of ASEAN states.

Divisiveness also exists within ASEAN itself. While the group now includes ten members, four of these—Cambodia, Laos, Myanmar, and Vietnam—are new to the association. The CLMV countries, as they are often called, are also less developed than the six older ASEAN members, with less experience in managing a market economy that is relatively open to the world economy. But a two-tier ASEAN is problematic, requiring that scholars as well as ASEAN officials address these concerns (Tay, Estanislao, and Soesastro 2001).

These several issues—along with the efforts by ASEAN to create an economic community among its own ten members, and the efforts by some to reach bilateral arrangements with other Asian nations—are the subject of examination here.

What unites the region is no less important that what may divide it. Indeed, the future of East Asian regionalism is at stake: an identity for East Asians, the ability to manage their own affairs, and the hope of greater equity among themselves and greater parity abroad.

THE RISE OF REGIONALISM IN PACIFIC ASIA

The trend away from the nation-state and toward globalization and regionalism has grown since the end of the cold war. Improvements and lower costs for technology, telecommunications, and transport have enabled this trend. Trade and economic integration have fueled it. Europe's experiment in the European Union as well as the more limited arrangements of the North American Free Trade Agreement (NAFTA) have exemplified it (Ohmae 1995).

Yet for some time, Asians did not proceed with any institutionalized form of regionalism akin to the European Union or NAFTA. Most Asian economies preferred to plug themselves in directly at the global level, emphasizing bilateral ties, especially with the United States, which has been the main source for foreign investment and the main market for Asian exports.

Export-led development in East Asia and its role in East Asia's integration into the world economy were primary to the rapid economic development of the region. East Asian economies relied heavily upon the markets of Europe and North America, a fact that lead to relatively weak regional economic integration. However, since the mid-1980s, several forces have served to strengthen regional integration: the liberalization of trade and investment regimes of many Southeast Asian countries; the increase of Japanese investment in Southeast Asia; the increase of regional involvement by the newly industrialized economies of Asia; and the emergence of China as an industrial location for regional firms. With each of these changes, East Asian economic integration has progressed (Park 2002).

Intraregional trade intensity, which is defined as the share of trade flows within a region, appears particularly high in East Asia, with exports in 2000 reaching 41.5 percent. Intraregional trade intensity among ASEAN members, however, is significantly lower. The three Northeast Asian countries of China, Japan, and South Korea have been the engine of growth for the region, but it is notable that trade among them is relatively low as well, in a range of 15 percent–20 percent. Thus the sub-region of Southeast Asia can be seen to constitute a very important trading partner for Northeast Asia (Park 2002).

Despite such trade intensity, however, no strong movement was made toward an institutional framework for the region. In some ways, this should not come as a surprise. Asia has no enduring history of unity and accepted commonality, whether in polity, culture, language, or religion. The antecedents of East Asian regionalism have been brief and contested. One period was in the fifteenth century, when the Ming empire of China ruled the waves and, in pre-colonial times, extracted an acceptance of suzerainty from most of the kingdoms in East and Southeast Asia. A second period was the Japanese co-prosperity sphere during World War II. Neither set a happy precedent for East Asian regionalism.

Why, then, should there be one now?

Several factors are at play. The first, and most important, was the trigger of the Asian financial crisis in 1997. The crisis exposed inherent weaknesses in financial and economic structures and demonstrated how events in one country can spread, like contagion, to another, with little regard to the differences in economic fundamentals. Countries afflicted by the crisis had little in the way of a coordinated response. Even as the crisis ebbed and assistance was provided by international financial institutions, especially the International Monetary Fund (IMF), there was resentment in East Asia over solutions that were felt to be inappropriate to the circumstances and "imposed" by the "Washington consensus." The United States, which is perceived to dominate the world of international monetary and financial affairs, has been the focus of this resentment (Tay 2001, 208–209; Bergsten 2000).

Now, even as the crisis has ended, competition on the global level has grown more intense. The difficulties surrounding Asian integration have not diminished. Indeed, by a number of indicators, they have grown. The perception that Asians need ways to foster intra-Asian cooperation has grown commensurately, as the financial crisis brought into question the effectiveness of ASEAN and the Asia Pacific Economic Cooperation (APEC) forum, neither of which was prepared to respond.

ASEAN lacked sufficient economic weight and political unity—a situation that became especially clear as Indonesia, the association's largest member, was at the epicenter of the crisis and buckled under wide-sweeping economic and political strain. In this regard, ASEAN's sacrosanct principle of mutual noninterference in the internal affairs of its members proved another factor in the association's impotence. ASEAN members had embarked on a free trade agreement to reduce tariffs prior to the crisis, but fuller economic integration and financial harmonization had never been on its agenda. The association also could offer no response to the massacre in East Timor after it had voted for independence from Indonesia, and it could do nothing to stem the Indonesian forest fires that cloaked the region with haze in 1997–1998 (Tay 2001; Than 2001).

As for APEC, that the organization was not designed for crisis management may have been true, but many viewed that as unacceptable. Given the involvement in APEC by the United States and Japan, there would have been sufficient weight to intervene if there had been political will. All possible APEC initiatives to address the crisis were felt to be undermined by U.S. insistence that any means other than that prescribed by the IMF could not be supported.

APEC, which in many ways is dominated by the United States, thus provided no help during the crisis. With this experience, many East Asians feel a need to make their own arrangements. While these will not be a substitute for international institutions, or for APEC, they may gain for East Asia greater leverage vis-à-vis the United States (Munakata 2002).

But more fundamentally, some analysts feel that APEC is inadequate, even aside from its lack of help in the crisis. With the organization's broad agenda, the high level of political and economic diversity among APEC's member states is no longer manageable; nor has the leadership of the United States and Japan proven to be strong or cohesive enough. Instead, APEC has been embroiled in disputes among its membership over such issues as trade liberalization. This has tended to split the organization in half, with many East Asian economies lining up on one side with Japan, and the United States and its supporters on the other (Krauss 2000, 473).

But another factor worthy of consideration is a growing sense of Asian identity. This is not so much a revival of Asian values—which were articulated in the early 1990s arguing that Asian versions of democracy differed from Western democracy—as a more general sense of identity.[1] Asians are becoming more international at the same time that they are becoming more aware of themselves as a people. A new generation is emerging that—through education, travel, the Internet, satellite television, and commerce—has an understanding of the United States and U.S.-influenced international standards that is second nature.

Instead of Asia becoming homogenized like a McDonald's franchise, however, this suggests that the increasingly individualized interconnections with the West will result in hybrid recognitions of culture. Subtler mixes will arise that leave behind traditional Asian forms even as they insist on a difference from the West. A region will arise that is modern and still, somehow, "Asian." In many ways, this will mirror the realignments in Western cultures themselves. Asian and other minorities there have sought to reclaim their own identity, rather than to be absorbed into a largely white mainstream. The process has enriched the texture of metropolitan cities in the United States and elsewhere.

Asia's accommodation of what is universal, Western, and rooted in the United States holds similar promise. Its richness, moreover, stands to be magnified by the sheer number of people and the cultural diversity of the continent. In this process, Asian values will not be silenced, but there will be no ready return to the state-centered discourse of Asian values. What is emerging will instead be negotiated at the level of individuals and communities, not by governments of political leaders. The new Asian culture will therefore not be found in a museum of Confucian analects or in the speeches of octogenarian party cadres—but in the streets of Shanghai, Singapore, and Shibuya. My guess is that it is emerging with influences of J-pop, films by Ang Lee, and California roll sushi. It will grow as new Asians meet and communicate their similarities, differences, and interdependencies. And, in all likelihood, they will do so in English, with their own particular accent.

This nascent pan-Asian culture has lacked a strong institutional or political foundation, unlike the earlier state-driven debate about Asian values. Here the orientation is toward consumption and the market, but institutional expression is not entirely out of the question. In part, this possibility was expressed in the convening of the Asia-Europe Meeting (ASEM). East Asian states were interested in encouraging European investment in Asia, and the European Union was interested in improving access to East Asian markets. Both sides shared the desire to curb the unilateralist propensities of the United States.

By its co-sponsorship of ASEM, the European Union was making the implicit statement that it recognized East Asia as a "distinct geographical and economic entity" (Tay 2002). And thus the initiative had the unintended consequence of fostering cooperation among East Asian states.

On their part, East Asians understand the need to strengthen their negotiating position vis-à-vis the European Union and the United States. Since 2000, the European Union has expanded to include several economies of Eastern Europe, and the proposal for the free trade area of the Americas, as exemplified by NAFTA, has seemed to be gaining momentum. The desire to create an Asian entity, then, has been referred to as a "counter-regionalism factor." Support has strengthened as the trend toward regionalism has grown geographically as well as functionally (Munakata 2002, 2).

Cooperation based on geography is not unimportant. For one thing, proximity, where dense business networks are in place, reduces transaction costs. Thus, it can be argued that East Asian regionalism came about due to the economic interaction and integration process that had been accelerated by globalization and technology. These forces, known as the "local economic factor," have also strengthened considerably over time (Munakata 2002, 3).

CHALLENGES FACING EAST ASIAN REGIONALISM

It has been more than a decade since Malaysian Prime Minister Mahathir bin Mohamad proposed the formation of the East Asian Economic Group. The organization was conceived to be an informal regional organization that would serve as a consultative forum for East Asian economies as the need arose. The proposal was rejected by East Asian countries, as well as by the United States, because of fears it would bring about divisiveness in the Pacific and challenge the fledgling APEC process. To address these concerns, the proposed forum was softened to become a caucus that would work within APEC. To this day, there have been no formal meetings or institutions of the so-called East Asian caucus.

Even as East Asians are being drawn together economically and politically, there remain factors that stand as challenges or obstacles to regionalism. The major factor is the importance of the United States to the region as a whole and to certain countries in particular. Since the end of World War II, the United States has been the foundation and guarantor of security in the region. Japan and South Korea in Northeast Asia and Thailand and the Philippines in Southeast Asia have defense alliances with the United States. Singapore, while not a formal ally of the United States, has developed close economic and security ties with it. This Asian receptiveness to U.S. presence in the region owes not to the grudging acceptance of power as much as to the acknowledgement that, in large part, the United States has played a relatively benign role as a guarantor of peace and stability.

The United States, moreover, has been and continues to be a major investor in the region. The U.S. role in security and economic development was especially important during the cold war and for the original ASEAN members who feared Vietnamese expansionism. It must be remembered that, in the 1960s, many saw the region as a troubled "drama" beset by poverty and instability.

As such, while some in China and Vietnam may see hegemonic and neo-imperialistic tendencies in the United States, many others in ASEAN and Northeast Asia have known the United States in a different light. Without U.S. engagement in the region, many fear the loss of the security balance. This is not a matter of the exercise of great power. Given the history of the region, where no collective framework for peacekeeping and other such measures exists, the U.S. presence has been stabilizing.

Concerns persist, however, over U.S. hegemony and its history of alternating between ignorance and unilateral intervention in its dealings with the region. The U.S.-led war against terrorism since the tragic events of September 11, 2001 (9-11), has exacerbated these concerns, and the war against Iraq has left many in Asia—as well as Europe and elsewhere—questioning the thrust of U.S. foreign policy. The rise of anti-U.S. sentiment may drive East Asian regionalism toward taking a more independent stance. But it should be noted that other sentiments are also evident: the governments of Japan, South Korea, the Philippines, and Singapore have supported the U.S. action, and most of those who have not supported U.S. intervention have at least sought to contain and limit their differences.

Simon S. C. Tay

As such, the United States remains the vital nonregional actor in East Asia's new regionalism. If the United States strongly opposes the institutional identity of the region, then it will fail, in the same way that Mahathir's proposal for an East Asian Economic Group did. If the United States is comfortable with the idea, or even supportive of it, the chances increase significantly, even if there is still no guarantee of success.

The second factor that may be an obstacle to East Asian regionalism is China-Japan relations. The relationship is troubled by suspicion and differences, notwithstanding the high levels of Japanese investment in China. In part, of course, this is because of historical reasons that derive from World War II. It is a sensitive issue, but the politics of apology and amnesia has been troubling to Japanese ties with South Korea and ASEAN nations as well.

On this point, ASEAN has stressed a pragmatic and forward-looking emphasis on trade and investment. This is in sharp contrast to the 1970s, when the visit of the Japanese prime minister to Southeast Asia was marked by street protests. South Korea, under President Kim Dae Jung, has also taken steps toward reconciliation, although to a far lesser extent than has ASEAN. Between China and Japan, however, relations have seen little fundamental improvement.

In large part, this is because the differences are not only historical but also present and prospective. Present-day relations are often adversely impacted by the role of the United States. Japan is dependent on the U.S. alliance for its security. When China-U.S. relations are strained, the Chinese may view Japan as a junior partner of the United States or, to state it less kindly, a pawn. Conversely, when China-U.S. relations show improvement, Japan fears that its special situation with the United States is overshadowed. Needless to say, the nascent sense of East Asian unity could be easily undermined by these tensions. Prospectively too, the path of China-Japan relations may be rocky, as the two giants of East Asia engage in a contest for preeminence. This trend was observable in their respective responses to the Asian financial crisis.[2]

All this points to the central need for reconciliation between China and Japan as a cornerstone for a regional East Asian architecture. Without rapprochement, any positive emerging trends of regionalism can easily falter. In this context, Japan must come to terms with its history. And further, it must build a future for itself in the region that includes its neighbors as partners.

Japan's role, to be sure, is complicated by its decade-long recession and attempts at reform. With mixed economic indicators, the verdict on the government's efforts, which focus on massive public spending, is still out.

Japanese public opinion itself grows divergent. Among nonbureaucratic elites, there are calls for radical reform and the "internationalization" of Japan, as seen in the work of Sakaiya Taichi (1991) and the report of the Prime Minister's Commission on Japan's Goals in the 21st Century (The Prime Minister's Commission 2000). Such steps would include private-sector reform, an emphasis on individual creativity and self-responsibility, and the increased use of English.

Another quite different strand of reform can be characterized as a narrow nationalism, typified by the advocacy of the governor of Tokyo, Ishihara Shintaro, which would likely have a negative effect on any reconciliation between Japan and its neighbors. Another promise of reform is also personified by the prime minister, Koizumi Jun'ichiro, who was swept into office on a slate of reform. Yet it remains unclear what precise reform can be agreed on and carried out by the government, and the great hopes that initially greeted his election have faded. Prime Minister Koizumi has caused some consternation among Northeast neighbors by his visits to war shrines. The steps his government has taken in the wake of 9-11 to support U.S. military actions have also taken the Japanese defense forces to a high point of activity and stirred debate about the relevance of the country's post–World War II pacifist constitution.

Until the internal debate is decided about the country's reform and future directions, Japan's ability to contribute significantly to the leadership of the region must be questioned. Extensive discussion of an Asian monetary fund and a common currency has occurred in Japan, but, assuming that Japan would be a major actor in such initiatives, sentiment is divided between whether this would be a positive influence or but a bankrolling of dubious policies. Reservations notwithstanding, East Asian countries understand the continuing importance of Japan in the region.

A third factor in the way of East Asian regionalism is that the small and medium-sized countries of the region may play a greater role than befits their strength. An instance of this can be seen in the arena of bilateral free trade agreements, where South Korea, Singapore, and Thailand have been active, reaching out beyond the region to Australia, India, and even Mexico. ASEAN as a whole has been negotiating a trade agreement with China and, separately, is looking into ways to strengthen ties with Japan as well. But there are limits to the leadership that these countries can offer the region. For one thing, ASEAN is an association without a present economic integration of its membership. Thus, some have spoken of ASEAN's having a leading role in the ASEAN + 3 process by default—its importance deriving not from the association's strength and unity, but from the disunity and division among others.

A fourth factor limiting East Asian regionalism is the apparent choice of governments in the region to exclude economies outside the ASEAN + 3 process. The economies excluded, for different reasons, are Australia, New Zealand, India, Hong Kong, and Taiwan. Short of full inclusion in ASEAN + 3, there are many ways that links could be strengthened with these economies (of that more later), but the point to be made is that as they are excluded, any East Asian regionalism is weakened.

The case of Taiwan, in particular, is politically problematic for the region—and not only because of its relationship with China. The China-U.S. relationship, ties with Japan and with ASEAN, and the overall economic significance of Taiwan all complicate the equation.

In theoretical terms, there are, according to political economist Walter Mattli (1999a), preconditions for successful regional integration.[3] The first is strong market pressures for integration, which will arise where there is significant potential for economic gain from market exchange in the region. If there is little potential for gain—either because countries do not complement each other or because the regional market is too small to offer economies of scale—the process of integration may not work.

Another precondition is that of undisputed leadership. There must be a benevolent leading country in the region, one that serves as a focal point in the coordination of rules, regulations, and policies and that may also help ease tensions arising from inequitable distribution of gains from integration. Attendant to this precondition would be the provision in an integration treaty for the establishment of commitment institutions, such as the centralized monitoring of third-party enforcement that will help to catalyze the integration process.

Economic difficulties constitute a background condition of integration. Political leaders would sacrifice their political power and autonomy if economic difficulties convince them that they can survive in office only by promoting regional integration, which is essential to improved economic performance. Regions with strong market pressure for integration and undisputed leadership are most likely to experience successful regional integration, while regional groupings that do not satisfy either of the conditions are least likely to succeed.

Mattli's observations are based on his study of integration in Europe, but his theories are not without relevance or insight for East Asia. His first precondition, that of strong market pressure for integration, is satisfied by the experience of the Asian financial crisis and the ongoing frustrations with ASEAN and APEC. East Asian countries do feel the need for integration and liberalization for the additional benefits they would bring. However, although there is high intraregional trade within East Asia, the largest export markets for East Asian economies have been the United States and Europe.

As regards the precondition of undisputed leadership in the region, the issue is not so settled, as Japan and China vie for preeminence (Iriye 1992). Japan may be the second largest economy in the world, but, as stated, it has suffered under recession and stagnation for over a decade. When the financial crisis struck East Asia, however, Japan did step forward to offer loans to economies in need. China, on the other hand, is a growing economic might that would seem poised to outgrow Japan in the future.

Should political circumstances in the region change, perhaps then there will be stronger, faster, more ambitious steps taken toward an East Asian regional architecture. Otherwise, as obstacles remain, what can be done?

DIFFERENT FRAMEWORKS FOR REGIONALISM

The ASEAN + 3 process has taken center stage in much of the discussion on East Asian regionalism. While the process is notable, despite its limitations, other ongoing institutional initiatives are worthy of note. Some include a broader base of countries than does ASEAN + 3, especially in respect to economic and trade cooperation.

Furthermore, the "minilateral" and bilateral undertakings among East Asian countries must be looked at. While these arrangements are seemingly ad hoc and, it may be argued, detract from a more inclusive regionalism, their dynamic with ASEAN + 3 has complexity and nuance.

APEC

The Asia Pacific Economic Cooperation forum was founded in 1989 to address economic issues in the region. APEC member nations account for nearly half the world's merchandise trade, half the global gross national product, and approximately half the world's population. The forum, which operates from a secretariat in Singapore, sponsors regular meetings and annual summits of senior government officials and heads of states.

Additionally, there are informal track-two events involving experts and businesses, such as the Pacific Economic Cooperation Council and the APEC Business Advisory Council.

APEC operates by consensus rather than through binding agreements or the kind of legalism evident in NAFTA and the European Union. APEC members define broad regional goals through a formula of "concerted unilateralism," but the specifics of implementation are left to each nation, with little or no supervision (Gershman 2000).

APEC provides three occasionally overlapping agendas. The first is economic and technical cooperation promoting human resources development, or "eco-tech." The second is trade and investment liberalization. The third, and the weakest, is the agenda of sustainable development—an effort characterized by a flurry of small-scale building projects and little beyond statements of principle (Gershman 2000; Lincoln 2001).

Of the three, trade and investment liberalization has garnered the most attention. The agenda emerged in 1993, when then U.S. President Bill Clinton invited the eighteen leaders of APEC member nations to Washington for the first APEC Economic Leaders Meeting. This was followed the next year by the Bogor Declaration, which proclaimed the elimination of all trade and investment barriers by 2010 for APEC's wealthier members and by 2020 for its poorer members.

At the 1997 meeting, APEC leaders agreed to negotiate, on a fast-track basis, mandatory liberalization targets in nine sectors covering US$1.5 trillion in trade—a project known as Early Voluntary Sectoral Liberalization. The relevant sectors encompassed a range of products, but Japan's opposition to the inclusion of fisheries and forestry, and the insistence of several countries (including the United States) that they be kept on the agenda, effectively torpedoed the broader initiative. Since then, liberalization through APEC has been stalled. This, and the Asian financial crisis that same year, have combined to demonstrate the limits of the APEC process.

Subsequent APEC summit meetings have failed to bring leaders together in the same spirit of optimism that was the basis of the Bogor meeting. Although the APEC forum has declared its support for free trade, many members oppose mandatory implementation schedules for comprehensive reduction of tariff and non-tariff barriers. This is understandable, given the diverse economies and perspectives on trade and investment regulation. Some countries, especially Malaysia and Japan, have argued that the liberalization goals be nonbinding and have opposed the U.S. demand that all economic sectors be open to foreign trade and investment. Countries that oppose the

U.S. drive to convert APEC into another free trade area would prefer APEC remain a consultative organization that facilitates technical cooperation on economic matters (Gershman 2000; see also Flamm and Lincoln 1997).

The 1999 APEC meeting in Auckland was dominated by discussions of the crisis in East Timor and proposals by the Group of Seven (G-7) to reform the international financial architecture. The 2000 meeting in Brunei focused on technical issues associated with facilitating e-commerce. There was some forward motion, especially as regards economic and technical cooperation, but it did not compensate for the lack of progress in trade and investment liberalization or the overall ideal of a Pacific Asia community. In the face of APEC's apparent immobility and failure to act, countries in East Asia have begun to pursue bilateral and regional initiatives outside the APEC framework (discussion of which will appear later).

The modus vivendi presently emerging is that the gathered heads of state focus on bilateral meetings among themselves, paying little attention to the APEC-wide process. This seems to make the best of an inherent limitation, using the forum's lack of cohesion to reap the benefits of the informality that exists at these meetings.

In response to the events of 9-11 and the U.S.-led war on terrorism, the 2001 summit in Shanghai produced a statement, signed by all members, to condemn terrorism. This was followed by the announcement by the United States, at the 2002 summit in Los Cabos, Mexico, of its initiative for ASEAN: an economic undertaking with geostrategic implications, one informed by the events of 9-11 and the concern that Southeast Asia might constitute a second front for the U.S.-led war on terrorism.

While these issues are no doubt important, they stand well outside the purview of APEC, highlighting questions about the forum's continuing relevance. The present usefulness of APEC seems to be limited to an occasion for leaders from the region to meet and discuss a series of general matters, rather than to focus and help drive an existing, coherent agenda. As such, while APEC is likely to continue, increasing numbers of observers have sought to think of ways to revitalize and perhaps reorient the process.[4]

ASEAN and the ASEAN Free Trade Area

At its inception in 1967, ASEAN talked of fostering economic ties among its members. In truth, however, ASEAN's first priority was to increase political and security confidence and to reduce tensions among its members. Only in 1992, twenty-five years later, did ASEAN begin its first real, sustained economic effort, with the ASEAN Free Trade Area (AFTA).[5]

To a considerable degree, the timing of AFTA was indicative of the perception that, after the end of the cold war and the peace accords in Cambodia, an enlarged, deeper conception of regionalism was needed. To remain relevant in the changed geopolitical context, ASEAN embarked in 1992 on a path to have the existing six members—original members Indonesia, Malaysia, the Philippines, Singapore, and Thailand, plus Brunei—joined by Cambodia, Laos, Vietnam, and Myanmar to comprise the ten members of ASEAN. This enlarged grouping was, moreover, challenged to deepen their economic links with AFTA to reduce tariffs. An ASEAN Investment Area agreement was also launched to facilitate the flow of capital.

The implementation of AFTA was brought forward from 2005 to January 1, 2003, and, after the Asian financial crisis, the date was further accelerated. In January 2002, AFTA came into effect for the older six members of ASEAN. The newer members are scheduled to begin to implement their AFTA obligations by 2007. Proponents of AFTA declare its success in bringing down tariffs for a broad range of products.

Yet, somewhat like APEC, the AFTA arrangement may already be showing its limitations. Countries have backtracked on the liberalization of some of their products. Malaysia, in particular, has sought to slow liberalization in the automotive sector, in which the government has promoted and protected national manufacturers.

Elimination of intraregional tariff and non-tariff barriers on the agreed-upon goods is only one aspect of ASEAN's efforts to sharpen its competitive advantages (Soesastro 2002; Stubbs 2000). But beyond these concerns, AFTA faces other challenges. First, the pace and scope of tariff reductions worldwide have increased, thus putting pressure on AFTA to diminish the number of products that remain on its list of exempt goods. Second, and perhaps more importantly, experts, officials, and businesses recognize that the reduction of tariffs is only one component in easing business across borders. The need for liberalization in services and capital investment as well as for the facilitation of trade through the movement of people and the agreement of mutually accepted standards are other items that ASEAN must seek to address in moving beyond AFTA and toward economic integration and even an ASEAN economic community (Stubbs 2000; Yeo 2002a). ASEAN leaders reinforced this intention at their summit in 2003, calling for the creation of an ASEAN Economic Community as a next step forward from AFTA.

In this regard, commentators like Hadi Soesastro of Indonesia argue that AFTA's life cycle will not be very long once it has been established; the agreement would have reached its objectives if it is no longer needed. AFTA, as such, should be viewed essentially as a training ground, an intermediate phase in the efforts of ASEAN to integrate member nations into the world economy. But even as the training continues, wider regional arrangements have emerged with partners in Northeast Asia and elsewhere.

ASEAN + 3 and ASEAN + 1

Efforts at cooperation among the members of ASEAN + 3 have been increasing. To date, the most important cooperative effort achieved by the process has been in the financial and monetary sectors. At the Chiang Mai meeting of finance ministers in May 2000, the ASEAN + 3 governments agreed to what has become known as the Chiang Mai Initiative, marking the beginning of a new era of East Asian regionalism. They committed to exchange data on capital flows, to review the financial policies of member nations so as to monitor regional finance, and to expand the existing arrangement among some ASEAN members to engage in bilateral currency swaps. An additional support system is also being developed through the bilateral swap arrangements and repurchase agreements with China, Japan and South Korea (Tay 2001).

Progress for the ASEAN + 3 framework has been gradual. The first informal meeting of ASEAN + 3 leaders was held in November 1997. The second was held in December 1998 in Hanoi, where members were determined to strengthen regional dialogue and cooperation. A meeting for East Asian deputy finance ministers was formalized, as was the East Asia vision group. The third summit, held in Manila in November 1999, marked a significant step for the organization. ASEAN + 3 was formally institutionalized in the first gesture toward an East Asian regional architecture.

In the formation of ASEAN + 3, leaders expressed the shared need to accelerate trade and investment and technology transfers; to encourage technical cooperation in information technology and e-commerce; to promote industrial and agricultural cooperation and tourism; to strengthen the banking and financial system; and to develop the Mekong River Basin. With these goals in mind, leaders established a human resources development fund and the ASEAN action plan on social safety nets (ASEAN Secretariat 1999).

Simon S. C. Tay

In 2002, Malaysia proposed locating the secretariat of ASEAN + 3 in Kuala Lumpur. Members, however, were not in favor of the idea of an ASEAN + 3 secretariat at all, fearing that it would undermine the efforts of the ASEAN secretariat in Jakarta toward reinventing and integrating ASEAN economically. Having invested more than three decades in ASEAN, these Southeast Asian leaders were careful not to give any appearance of detracting from it.

Thus, the approach of the group seems to be twofold: to proceed with closer ASEAN cooperation and integration at the same time that it fosters the ASEAN + 3 framework. In ASEAN + 3, moreover, the processes that bring all member states together is being complemented by processes that bring the ASEAN members together with one or another of the Northeast Asian states, in what has been called ASEAN + 1 arrangements.

In this context, China's offer to come to a free trade agreement with ASEAN was an initiative of great significance. On November 4, 2002, the Framework Agreement on Comprehensive Economic Cooperation was signed by China and ASEAN, committing them to begin negotiations in 2003 on the creation of an ASEAN-China Free Trade Area. These negotiations have been proceeding apace.

The target date for realization of the ASEAN-China Free Trade Area is 2010 for the six older members of ASEAN, and 2015 for Cambodia, Laos, Myanmar, and Vietnam. This agreement is aimed at liberalizing trade in goods and services in addition to promoting a transparent and liberal investment regime.

The establishment of the ASEAN-China Free Trade Area will open up a market of 1.7 billion consumers with a combined GDP of US$1.5 trillion to US$2 trillion and two-way trade of US$1.2 trillion (ASEAN Secretariat 2002;"Premier Zhu Spells Out" 2003). China's willingness to push ahead with these plans is an unprecedented political move—and a significant departure from its historical stance toward Southeast Asia. This is the first time in its history that it has found in Southeast Asia a point of common political and economic interest. For both China and ASEAN, this may be a form of political confidence building (Macan-Markar 2002; Katzenstein 2000, chapters 1 and 3).

China's initiative has sparked similar proposals by the major East Asian economies of Japan and South Korea. There have also been proposals for an East Asian free trade area and Northeast Asian free trade agreement.

During a trip to Singapore in 2002, Japanese Prime Minister Koizumi (2002) delivered a speech proposing the further integration of the region.

He spoke of partnership, of comprehensive economic cooperation between Japan and Pacific Asia, and of his hopes that the Japan-Singapore Economic Partnership Agreement would be a launching pad for these goals. This bilateral "new age" agreement, concluded in 2002, may have implications for other ASEAN member states in their ties with Japan.

Koizumi also proposed initiatives in other areas. These included designating 2003 as the year of Japan-ASEAN Exchange and opening discussions on several fronts: an initiative for a Japan-ASEAN comprehensive economic partnership, an initiative for development in East Asia, and enhanced security cooperation between Japan and ASEAN. The ASEAN-Japan summit at the end of 2003 not only marked the decades of relations and cooperation between ASEAN and Japan, but also launched detailed discussions on separate, bilateral trade agreements between Japan and some ASEAN members, including Thailand and Malaysia. Koizumi's broader goal is to create an East Asian "community that acts together and advances together" and some believe that this East Asia cooperation should be founded upon the Japan-ASEAN relationship to make good use of the ASEAN + 3 framework, and increase the cooperation among the Northeast Asian states of China, Japan, and South Korea.

Looking beyond East Asia, Koizumi expressed the hope that the United States, Australia, and New Zealand would become a part of this community. Critics responded that such a grouping, which they called ASEAN + 5 (Japan, China, South Korea, Australia, and New Zealand) + 1 (United States), would not be very different from APEC and that it might be even more difficult to realize than ASEAN + 3 (Lim 2002; Jain 2002). But whatever the aims for regionalism might be, Koizumi's policy is interesting in that it is based on the belief that initiatives such as the China-ASEAN Free Trade Area and ASEAN's agreements with Australia and with New Zealand will contribute to the strengthening of the East Asian economic region.

The Japanese proposal is seen by analysts as an attempt perhaps to ward off economic stagnation at home, and also to prevent China from snatching the role as the economic leader of the region ("Japan Pushes" 2002; "Asia" 2002; Okamoto 2001). This competitiveness can be healthy and, one hopes, result in closer economic ties between ASEAN and Japan and between ASEAN and China, with the greater prospect of knitting the whole region together.

Simon S. C. Tay

Beyond ASEAN + 3: ASEAN's External Relations

In addition to the ASEAN + 3 and ASEAN + 1 processes with Japan and with China, ASEAN has made overtures to countries in the region which have remained outside these associations.

The special administrative region of Hong Kong is not represented separately, nor is the economy of Taiwan. Thus far, neither has concluded a free trade agreement with any ASEAN member state. For ASEAN there is obvious value in economic relationships and cooperation with them, given the size and strength of their economies and their capital flow to both ASEAN and China.

Taiwan of course has political and security motives for emphasizing such links. It has sought, without success, to be admitted to various regional processes, including the ASEAN + 3 and the ASEAN Regional Forum (ARF), the leading multilateral security process in the region. But even without such considerations, it is clear that based on finance, trade, and investment, there are grounds for allowing Taiwan's inclusion as a separate, substantial economy. Additionally, we should recognize that ASEAN + 3 would be enhanced by cooperation with Taiwan on financial matters, but only if arrangements are suitable. After all, the Asian crisis that began in 1997 deepened and spread further when Taiwan's currency, too, was devalued.

Currently, Taiwan is also seeking to enter into bilateral trade agreements with countries in Asia, including ASEAN countries. Given its membership in APEC and the World Trade Organization (WTO), this should be economically rational and politically acceptable, provided that Taiwan does not in the process seek to demand recognition beyond what the countries in the region already admit.

On its part, Hong Kong is negotiating bilateral free trade agreements with New Zealand and China. There could be a possible Japan–South Korea free trade agreement and a South Korea–Chile free trade agreement (Tsang 2003; Park 2002, 13). These developments demonstrate the fecundity and variability of free trade agreements in Asia and between Asian and non-Asian economies. For even as these developments are unfolding in East Asia, overtures are being made to actors outside East Asia—Australia, New Zealand, and even India. In August 2002, Australia signed a memorandum of understanding regarding the ASEAN-Australia Development Cooperation Programme (AADCP). This US$45 million initiative will be jointly implemented by ASEAN and Australia, and it will help to strengthen regional economic and social cooperation and regional institutions and to assist the newer ASEAN members integrate into the association. The core components are, one, a series of medium-term activities that address issues of economic integration and competitiveness and will contribute to the broader objectives of "strengthening ASEAN economic integration" and "enhancing ASEAN competitiveness"; two, the Regional Partnerships Scheme, a flexible mechanism for smaller collaborative activities; and three, the Regional Economic Support Facility, a policy research unit now in operation within the ASEAN Secretariat, focusing on economic issues (35th ASEAN Ministerial Meeting 2002).

New Zealand too has a mechanism for development cooperation with ASEAN, known as the ASEAN-New Zealand Economic Cooperation Programme. Formerly the ASEAN Regional Programme, this mechanism has two major long-term goals: to achieve sustainable development for ASEAN countries and to facilitate linkages between New Zealand and ASEAN in various fields of trade. ASEAN is one of New Zealand's main recipients of funds for development (ASEAN Secretariat 1996).

Australia and New Zealand have reached an agreement for a broader framework for economic cooperation, called the Closer Economic Partnership. A framework for this partnership was adopted in September 2001, providing a formal structure for promoting trade and investment, including tariff and non-tariff issues. While the Closer Economic Partnership sets a base for relations, some countries have proceeded to negotiate bilateral agreements with higher levels of cooperation and economic liberalization. Singapore, for example, has concluded a free trade agreement with New Zealand and, separately, with Australia. Thailand is another ASEAN country that has held discussions with Australia.

ASEAN's ties with India have taken a significant step forward recently, with the ASEAN-India Summit in November 2002. In addition to cultural and security ties, the possibility of an India-AFTA link is being considered as a step toward the longer-term goal of an India-ASEAN regional trade and investment area.

India and Singapore, in April 2003, announced that a comprehensive free trade agreement was under negotiation, again demonstrating how an individual ASEAN member might establish bilateral ties before the association does. The arrangement will have free trade aspects as well as possible enhancements in the area of services, especially air services.

Simon S. C. Tay

Observations, Implications, Complications

In this flurry of trade and other activities, several observations may be offered.

The first is that while ASEAN + 3 is perhaps the central process for East Asian regionalism, it is certainly not the only one. The second observation is that ASEAN remains a key player in the regional processes, notwithstanding its small economic size (even when combined) and its loss of prestige and momentum following the 1997 financial crisis. The establishment of ASEAN + 3, ASEAN + 1, and other initiatives makes it clear that ASEAN is central to the emerging regionalism.

Third, bilateral free trade agreements are taking place or under consideration. The most active country in this regard is Singapore. Apart from being a member of AFTA, it has already signed agreements with New Zealand, Japan, the European Free Trade Area, and Australia. Final negotiations have also been completed with the United States, pending legal finalization and approval by the U.S. Congress ("Everyman for Himself" 2002; Zoellick 2002).

Among other ASEAN members, Thailand has also begun to be very active, pursuing bilateral agreements with Australia and China. Malaysia of late has indicated that it wishes for a free trade agreement with Japan and the United States, thus reversing its opposition to Singapore's push for bilateral free trade agreements, which Malaysia believed could undermine AFTA (Kassim 2002).

In Northeast Asia, the activities of China and Japan have been noted, as have the efforts of Hong Kong and Taiwan. South Korea too has been active in free trade agreements on a bilateral basis. Thus far, however, it has preferred to initiate these with countries outside Asia.

This proliferation of free trade agreements may be a sign that countries in the region are moving toward the creation of an economic bloc and free trade bloc. One of the most important questions that has arisen amid the flurry of free trade agreements is whether they would lead to regionalism or undermine it (Okamoto 2001).

A fourth observation may be made about Asian or ASEAN agreements with countries outside ASEAN + 3. As surveyed, there are different developments between ASEAN and Australia, between ASEAN and India, and between ASEAN and Taiwan, which invests heavily in Southeast Asia. At a later stage, there may be an agreement between ASEAN, or some of its member states, and the United States. All this activity demonstrates the interdependency of countries in the region; it also indicates the support that countries outside the region have for East Asian regionalism (Abidin 2001).

All this is recognition of East Asia's importance in the trade and politics of countries outside Asia as well. The developments underscore the fact that if East Asian countries do not participate in the shaping of the emerging regional institutions, they could very well be disadvantaged. Yet, these developments are also recognition that the new East Asian regionalism cannot and should not be "fortress Asia," that it cannot afford to isolate itself from the rest of the world. Thus there seems to be an operative principle of "open regionalism," carried over from the APEC process.

COMPLEXITIES FACING THE DEVELOPMENT OF EAST ASIAN REGIONALISM

The task of fostering and deepening regionalism in East Asia or even within ASEAN will not be easy. Political and economic rivalries within the region are barriers to effective cooperation between the states. On the larger stage, there is, notably, the rivalry and distrust between China and Japan, as both countries are now clearly competing for the leadership of Asia. There are rivalries on the more microeconomic level as well. To name the most prominent: Hong Kong and Singapore are vying to become the financial hub of East Asia; Korea and Taiwan compete vigorously in global markets in a number of sectors; and Malaysia and Singapore have bilateral disputes over a number of issues, despite their strong economic interdependence. And then there is the no small matter of relations between China and Taiwan.

Huge differences in political systems underlie these contentions. China—as well as Vietnam and Myanmar—are trying to maintain highly authoritarian regimes even as they embrace the market economy. By contrast, Japan has been a practicing democracy for fifty years. Most East Asian countries fall somewhere in the middle of the spectrum, tilting toward the democratic end but sometimes with relatively weak variants of democracy and usually without deep democratic roots. These political differences would, at a minimum, complicate any Asian integration effort. Nor are these differences without history.

Japan remains the largest and richest economy in Asia, but as its economy has been stagnant for a decade, there is uncertainty within the region about the effectiveness of any leadership role to which Japan might aspire. The rest of Asia, furthermore, has yet to accept Japan as a true partner. Upon the end of World War II, Japan concentrated on its economic reconstruction—and succeeded admirably—but it was absent when it came to formulating the postwar world economic order. Japan also has serious "history" issues, that is to say, amnesia about its historical role in the region, and this does not sit well with Asians who suffered under Japanese occupation. Even government-to-government settlement of the history issue does not guarantee public support, upon which the ultimate resolution depends. If Japan hopes to gain the confidence of its neighbors, it needs to address its history fully, and it needs to articulate both its national strategy and the role that it wishes to play in the region.

China, on the other hand, is on the rise, its economy growing at a remarkable rate. While some—in Japan and elsewhere—worry that China will become a threat to Japan's economic primacy and will overwhelm the smaller ASEAN economies, others perceive the complementary nature of bilateral economic relations and see huge opportunities in the Chinese market and abundant labor force. Economic strength, however, has also afforded China an increase in its military expenditures, which, together with issues related to Taiwan and the activities of Chinese research ships in Japanese waters, creates a growing nervousness in Japan. Suspicions of China's intentions are widespread in the region.

From the Chinese point of view, Japan's unwillingness or inability to come to grips with its history has only nurtured grass-roots suspicion of Japan, justifying Beijing's repeated demands for an apology, which in turn provoke Japanese resentment. Some in China are also worried that the U.S.-Japan security alliance is part of a U.S. strategy to encircle China. But at the same time Beijing also appreciates the U.S. security presence in the region as it prevents Japanese rearmament.

The role of the United States, as discussed above, is an important, extra-regional factor. If the United Sates strongly opposes the nascent institutional identity of the region, the regional effort is certain to fail, much as the Asian Monetary Fund and East Asian Economic Grouping did. If the United States is comfortable with the idea, or even supportive, there is still no guarantee of success, but the chances will increase significantly.

In the 1990s, U.S. Secretary of State James Baker expressed support for a new Asia Pacific architecture, one that would comprise a framework for economic integration, a commitment to democratization, and a revamped defense structure for the region. The Clinton administration subsequently embraced the concept of multilateral security dialogue as a pillar of the "new Pacific community," and expressed support for several potential areas of dialogue including APEC (Bergsten 2000).

Camilleri (2000) contends that there were several considerations for Washington's shift in policy, but none more important than the realization that the United States could no longer perform the coordinating role characteristic of the cold war. The two traditional pillars of U.S. predominance in Asia—economic muscle from its markets and overall financial presence, and security muscle from its bilateral alliances and military bases—were both diminishing assets. However, while a continuing U.S. presence in Pacific Asia might not be enough to contain China, offer a comprehensive guarantee of regional security, or cope with the region's increasing economic interdependence and realignment of power, the United States has been the foundation and guarantor of security in the region. It has always been and forseeably will continue to be the major investor in the region (US-ASEAN Business Council 2003)

A hopeful scenario would be to draw China into a multilateral security dialogue, or into an institution where regional members can monitor developments and have checks in place. Each member, including China, would thus be obliged to act according to the interests of the institution as a whole, thus providing some reassurance to the region (Krawitz 2002). At the moment, settling upon a benevolent leading country of the region does not seem feasible. One alternative, which has already come to fruition, is that of the middle powers taking the initiative to form a multilateral institution. ASEAN's efforts to date can be interpreted as taking on that role for its members as well as others in East Asia.

One of the main reasons for ASEAN + 3 is that ASEAN, by drawing China into a multilateral institution, would have China as a partner rather than a threat to its economic security. In his speech to the U.S. Chamber of Commerce, Singapore's Trade and Industry Minister Yeo (2002b) stated his belief that an integrated ASEAN is the only viable response to an economically rising China. ASEAN countries have to work toward closer regional economic integration, and if there is no free movement of goods and services and investments within the region, Southeast Asia will lose out to China. If Southeast Asia is able to make a common economic space, it will have integrity vis-à-vis China, it can stake out its own areas of strength, and it can benefit from China's economic growth.

China, on the other hand, sees engagement with ASEAN as an opportunity to convey the message that it is not a threat to its neighbors and instead offers a hand of cooperation and friendship. The proposal of the ASEAN-China free trade agreement, linking the region together, is a demonstration of its good intentions. Japan and other countries, such as the United States, Australia, and New Zealand, have also seen the benefits of ASEAN + 3, and have expressed their support for it. But the question remains: Which of the many frameworks are East Asians likely to adopt?

The support given to ASEAN + 3 has been inspiring, particularly as the region seeks to integrate in other ways. For example, the northeast-southeast divide within Asia continues to pose difficulties, with ASEAN countries much poorer than Japan, South Korea, Taiwan, and Hong Kong. With China growing at such rapid pace, ASEAN could well lose vital foreign direct investment to China. The Asian financial crisis had the effect of widening the northeast-southeast divide further. Recovery from the crisis in Northeast Asia was quick, whereas some countries in Southeast Asia were mired in it, and in Indonesia the financial crisis turned into a political crisis.

Within ASEAN itself, there are divisions. In comparison to the older members of the association, Cambodia, Laos, and Myanmar are much poorer, less developed, and their economies much less liberalized. Regional economic integration may thus be of less benefit to them. An effort must be made to enhance their competitiveness in all fields, or new ASEAN members will not be able to gain from the region's economic liberalization and integration. Such disparity, combined with the serious challenge of poverty within Southeast Asia, has to be addressed if ASEAN is to lead the region into an institutional bloc. Moreover, the economic and development gap within East Asia itself is even wider than that within ASEAN. Despite the challenges, ASEAN has pushed forward cooperation with Japan, South Korea, and China in the framework of ASEAN + 3 to attract more investment and technology.

The example of the European Union, while different in many respects, should encourage East Asia to pursue regional integration. In Europe, trade integration between north and south has succeeded as differences were reconciled. Economic integration has helped to overcome deep-seated political animosities, where the history of France and Germany has been as bloody as that of China and Japan. Economic rationality, political will, and a concern about coping with globalization are key factors for those who believe in closer East Asian regionalism.

The Prospects for East Asian Regionalism

From the observations of the driving forces and limitations of the nascent regionalism of East Asia, several principles suggest themselves as incumbent to the process.

First, it should be an open and flexible caucus, not an exclusive group or bloc. There is no need for another institution, given the many that already exist in the region. Nor would it serve the region well to exclude the United States, or other countries, especially as many nations in the region rely on the United States for both security and economic reasons. The new East Asian regionalism might therefore serve as a forum for discussion and agreement on positions that would then be taken before larger institutions. Approached in this way, East Asian regionalism would not detract from other Asia Pacific and international institutional efforts, but serve to make them more effective and representative (Tay 2001).

Second, East Asian regionalism should have functionality, not political fixity. It is important that, in the face of integration and globalization, there be regional management and cooperation. This will test the tendency to include and exclude members on political grounds. For example, in the arena of economic and financial cooperation in the region, which the ASEAN + 3 process has emphasized, ASEAN + 3 has both more and less members than this function would require. If ASEAN + 3 is to have a fixed structure, then important economies such as Hong Kong, Taiwan, and Australia, would have to be excluded in preference to smaller and more isolated economies. The new regionalism should instead be inclusive, with reference to the function that a country can bring to the issue (Tay 2001).

Third, the leadership of East Asian regionalism should focus on issues and not on the leadership of great powers. If we look at traditional modes of regionalism, central leadership is critical. However, without a historical reconciliation between China and Japan, this will not be possible in East Asia. The region lacks a single leader that is acceptable and able. In addition to issue-specific leaderships, there are suggestions that ASEAN and small and medium-sized countries, such as South Korea, might therefore lead the region. Their role may be larger and more special than normally expected, but they cannot offer permanent and strong leadership of the traditional type in the region.

East Asian regionalism therefore might have to look at newer and more limited forms of leadership. This could be achieved by having different leaders on different issues. Leadership would arise from the initiative and interests of different states; for example, Singapore might be able to lead on free trade initiatives, Malaysia and Thailand on peacekeeping, Japan as regards the G-8. Such issue-specific leadership would be consonant with the ideas of flexibility and functionality. And it would also be more aligned with principles of equality than the idea of "great power" leadership. In this way, the new East Asian regionalism would voice the aspirations of ASEAN and Pacific Asia (Tay 2001).

These principles, in toto, suggest that East Asian regionalism should not be a fixed bloc or union with permanent membership and permanent leaders. Instead it should be a framework for what we may call "coalitions of the willing." These coalitions can arise from certain issues or even events. They may then dissolve or evolve to tackle new issues. As the need arises they would work with existing regional and subregional institutions. The idea of coalitions might extend beyond East Asia, and raft together other countries such as Australia and New Zealand (Tay 2001).

CONCLUSION

The emergence of the various free trade agreements in the region can be seen as a reflection of the failure of the WTO to continue with multilateral free trade talks. Multilateralism is indisputably superior to bilateralism as it offers much more; however, one has to look for other means to promote free trade and other options for its economic growth if further trade liberalization talks are not in progress. Now that we have an idea of the different frameworks and agreements trying to create an East Asian regional bloc, we see a large number of free trade agreements crisscrossing the region, a network that also stretches beyond the region. Countries are hopeful that these various frameworks will bring about deeper integration within the region, as well as contribute to the development of East Asian regionalism. As these free trade agreements are in place, further integration would be much easier. But the number of free trade agreements also highlights the fact that the countries in East Asia are not united and are in many ways fragmented, and that they have found it difficult to work together within an institution toward the creation of AFTA. There is a divide not only between Northeast Asia and Southeast Asia, but also within each as well.

There are those who are skeptical that the frameworks discussed here can bring about East Asian regionalism. This skepticism exists in and about ASEAN itself, even if it is the current focal point which many hope can lead to greater East Asian institutional identity. ASEAN member countries are not united and there are many underlying tensions between the countries. In the absence of a benevolent leading country, it is doubtful that there could be a strong framework for East Asian regionalism. The dependency on the United States for economic and military security also affects the movement toward East Asian regionalism. If the United States is in support of it, its chances are boosted.

For whatever the complexities and challenges going forward, it seems clear that there has been a new and sustained impulse since 1997 toward developing arrangements for East Asian regionalism as well as a greater recognition that the stakes for developing cooperation and institutional identities are considerable.

NOTES

1. Cultural influences as well as the commerce of goods have started to flow among East Asian countries. When many, like the American Joseph Nye, write of "soft power" and influence, few observe how Japanese trends, artifacts, and fashion have permeated other Asian countries. Signs of this include the spread of karaoke, toys, and the clothing of younger Asians, especially females. Increasing cross-flows of culture may also be noted in terms of the spread of tropical architecture and traditional forms that have been quite successfully adopted as the basis for vacation resorts and a comparable lifestyle (Tay 2002; for a more academic treatment, see Han 1999).

2. The contention was observable in Japan's giving of aid but also in its failure to provide market reform at home to absorb Asian imports and its failure to defend the idea of the developmental state, as compared to the free market ideas of the IMF and the World Bank. China's response was to maintain its currency without devaluation and thus to help avoid a second round of competitive devaluations.

3. For this section of the chapter, the work of Chan Ji-Quandt is particularly acknowledged.

4. As for the United States, it is interesting that APEC is only mentioned in the national strategy statement of the George W. Bush administration, released in October 2002, as an institution that can assist with security issues.

Simon S. C. Tay

5. In 1992, at the 4th ASEAN Summit in Singapore, ASEAN heads of governments signed the Singapore Declaration and the Framework Agreement on Enhancing ASEAN Economic Cooperation, which provided the basis for the establishment of AFTA.

BIBLIOGRAPHY

Abidin, Mahani Zainal. 2001. "ASEAN and Its External Economic Linkages." In Mya Than, ed. *ASEAN Beyond the Regional Crisis*. Singapore: Institute of Southeast Asian Studies.

Agenor, Pierre-Richard, et al. 2000. *The Asian Financial Crisis: Causes, Contagion, and Consequences*. New York: Cambridge University Press.

Anatolik, Michael. 1990. *ASEAN and the Diplomacy of Accommodation*. New York: M.E. Sharpe.

"ASEAN-China Dialogue." 2002. <http://www.malaysia-china.com.my/forum_eng/aboutforum/acdialogue.htm> (4 October 2002).

ASEAN Secretariat. 1996. "ASEAN-New Zealand Dialogue." Joint press statement of the 13th ASEAN–New Zealand Meeting, Hanoi, 28 October. <http://www.aseansec.org /5841.htm> (16 July 2003).

———. 1999. Joint Statement on East Asia Cooperation, Manila, 28 November. ASEAN Documents series 1998–1999.

———. 2002. "ASEAN and China Sign Economic Pact." News release, Jakarta, 4 November. <http://www.aseansec.org/13169.htm> (16 July 2003).

"Asia: Koizumi's Depreciation Tour; Asian Diplomacy." 2002. *The Economist* (19 January).

Ball, Desmond, and Amitav Acharya. 1999. *The Next Stage: Preventive Diplomacy and Security Cooperation in the Asia Pacific Region*. Canberra: Australian National University.

Bergsten, Fred C. 2000. "The New Asian Challenge." Working Paper for the Institute of International Economics. <http://www.iie.com/publications/wp/2000/00-4.pdf> (16 July 2003).

Brooks, Stephen G., and William C. Wohlworth. 2002. "American Primacy in Perspective." *Foreign Affairs* 81(4): 20–33.

Camilleri, Joseph A. 2000. "Regionalism and Globalism in the Asia Pacific: The Interplay of Economy, Security and Politics." Paper presented at the 41st Annual Convention of the International Studies Association, Los Angeles, 14–18 March.

Clark, Cal. 2000. *Growing Pains: ASEAN's Economic and Political Challenges.* New York: Asia Society.

Emmott; Bill. 2002. "A Survey of America's World Role." *The Economist* 29 June: 3–28.

"Everyman for Himself." 2002. *The Economist* (2 November).

Flamm, Kenneth, and Edward Lincoln. 1997. "Time to Reinvent APEC." Policy Brief No. 26, Foreign Policy Studies Program. Washington, D.C.: Brookings Institution.

Funston, John. 1998. "ASEAN: Out of Its Depth?" *Contemporary Southeast Asia* 20(1): 22–37.

Gershman, John. 2000. "Asia Pacific Economic Cooperation (APEC)." In Tom Barry and Martha Honey, eds. *Foreign Policy In Focus* 5: 39 (November).

Godement, Francois. 1997. *New Asian Renaissance from Colonialism to the Post–Cold War.* London: Routledge.

———. 1999. *The Downsizing of Asia.* New York: Routledge.

Haas, Michael. 1989. *The Asian Way to Peace.* Westport, Conn.: Praeger Publishers.

Han Sung-Joo, ed. 1999. *Changing Values in Asia: Their Impact on Governance and Development.* Tokyo: Japan Center for International Exchange.

Iriye Akira. 1992. *China and Japan in the Global Setting.* Cambridge, Mass.: Harvard University Press.

Jain, Purnendra. 2002. "Koizumi's ASEAN Doctrine." *Asia Times Online* 10 January. <http://www.atimes.com/japan-econ/DA10Dh01.html> (24 February 2002).

"Japan Pushes Own ASEAN Trade Plan." 2002. CNN (11 May). <http://www.cnn.com>.

Kassim, Yang Razali. 2002. "The Paradox of Asia's FTAs." *The Business Times* (Singapore) 18 December.

Katzenstein, Peter J. 2000. *Asian Regionalism.* Ithaca, N.Y.: Cornell University Press, East Asia Series.

Keidanren (Japan Business Federation). 2002. "Urgent call for Implementation of the Initiative for Japan-ASEAN Comprehensive Economic Partnership." *Nippon Keidanren*, 17 September. <http://www.keidanren.or.jp/english/policy/2002/054.html> (16 July 2003).

Koizumi Jun'ichiro. 2002. "Japan and ASEAN in East Asia—A Sincere and Open Partnership." Speech in Singapore, 14 January. <http://www.mofa.go.jp/region/asia-paci/pmv201/speech.html> (16 July 2003).

Simon S. C. Tay

Krauss, Ellis S. 2000. "Japan, the US, and the Emergence of Multilateralism in Asia." *Pacific Review* 13(3): 473–494.

Krawitz, Howard M. 2002. "China's Trade Opening: Implications for Regional Stability." *Strategic Forum*, no. 193 (August).

Lardy, Nicholas. 2002. *Integrating China into the Global Economy*. Washington, D.C.: Brookings Institution.

Lim, Hua Sing. 2002. "Koizumi Unclear on Asian Economic Initiative." *Asahi Shimbun* (22 February).

Lincoln, Edward J. 2001. "Taking APEC Seriously." Policy Brief No. 92, Foreign Policy Studies Program. Washington, D.C.: Brookings Institution.

Macan-Markar, Marwaan. 2002. "ASEAN-China FTA: Boon for Whom?" *Asia Times* (22 October). <http://www.atimes.com/atimes/Southeast_Asia/DJ22Ae05.html>.

Mattli, Walter. 1999a. "Explaining Regional Integrational Outcomes." *Journal of European Public Policy* 6(1): 1–27.

————. 1999b. The Logic of Regional Integration: Europe and Beyond. Cambridge: Cambridge University Press.

Montes, Manuel F. 1997. "The Economic Miracle in a Haze." In Manuel F. Montes, Kevin F. Quigley, and Donald Weatherbee. *Growing Pains: ASEAN's Economic and Political Challenges*. New York: Asia Society.

Montes, Manuel F., Kevin F. Quigley, and Donald Weatherbee. 1997. *Growing Pains: ASEAN's Economic and Political Challenges*. New York: Asia Society.

Munakata Naoko. 2002. "Whither East Asian Economic Integration?" Working paper, Center for Northeast Asian Policy Studies, Brookings Institution, Washington, D.C., June. <http://www.brook.edu/fp/cnaps/papers/2002_munakata.htm> (16 July 2003).

Ohmae Kenichi. 1995. *The End of the Nation State: The Rise of Regional Economies*. New York: Free Press.

Okamoto Jiro. 2001. "Japan and the ASEAN Plus 3 Process." East Asia: Regional Development and Outlook, APEC Study Centre, Institute of Developing Countries, JETRO, Taipei, September. <http://www.npf.org.tw/symposium/s90/900921-te-3-2.htm> (16 July 2003).

————. 2002. "Seeking Multilateralism Friendly FTAs: The Research Agenda." Working Paper Series 01/02, No. 1, APEC Study Centre, Institute of Developing Countries, JETRO, Chiba, Japan, March.

Park Sung-Hoon. 2002. "East Asian Economic Integration: Finding a Balance Between Regionalism and Multilateralism." Briefing Paper,

European Institute for Asian Studies, Belgium, February.

"Premier Zhu Spells Out 5 Point Proposal on ASEAN+3 Cooperation." 2003. *People's Daily* (19 March). <http://fpeng.peopledaily.com. cn/200111/05/print20011105_83944.html> (16 July 2003).

The Prime Minister's Commission on Japan's Goals in the 21st Century. 2000. *The Frontier Within: Individual Empowerment and Better Governance in the New Millennium.* Tokyo: Office for the Prime Minister's Commission on Japan's Goals in the 21st Century.

Radelet, Steven, and Jeffrey Sachs. 1998. *The East Asian Financial Crisis: Diagnosis, Remedies, Prospects.* Cambridge, Mass.: Harvard University Press.

Sakaiya Taichi. 1991. *The Knowledge Value Revolution.* New York: Kodansha America.

Soesastro, Hadi. 2002. "The ASEAN Free Trade Area: A Critical Assessment." *Journal of East Asian Affairs* 16(1): 20–53.

Stiglitz, Joseph E., and Shahid Yusuf. 2001. *Rethinking the East Asian Miracle.* New York: Oxford University Press.

Stubbs, Richard. 2000. "Signing on to Liberalisation: AFTA and the Politics of Regional Economic Cooperation." *Pacific Review* 13(2): 297–318.

Tay, Simon S. C. 1999. "Preventive Diplomacy in the ASEAN Regional Forum: Principles and Possibilities." In Desmond Ball and Amitav Acharya, eds. *The Next Stage: Preventive Diplomacy and Security Cooperation in the Asia Pacific Region.* Canberra: Australian National University.

———. 2001. "ASEAN and East Asia: A New Regionalism?" In Simon S. C. Tay, Jesus Estanislao, and Hadi Soesastro, eds. *Reinventing ASEAN.* Singapore: Institute of Southeast Asian Studies.

———. 2002. "Asian Values Revisited." *The Edge Malaysia* (29 April).

Tay, Simon S. C., Jesus Estanislao, and Hadi Soesastro. 2001. *Reinventing ASEAN.* Singapore: Institute of Southeast Asian Studies.

Tay, Simon S. C., and Obood Talib. 1997. "The ASEAN Regional Forum: Preparing for Preventive Diplomacy." *Contemporary Southeast Asia* 19(3): 252–268.

Than, Mya, ed. 2001. *ASEAN beyond the Regional Crisis: Challenges and Initiatives.* Singapore: Institute of Southeast Asian Studies.

35th ASEAN Ministerial Meeting. 2002. "ASEAN and Australia Launch New Partnership under ASEAN-Australia Development Cooperation Programme (AADCP)," news release, 1 August. <http://www.aliesha. com/amm35/ADDCP.htm> (16 July 2003).

Tsang, Joseph. 2003. "Free Trade Agreements in Asia." <http://www.joet-

sang.net/pta/pta.html> (16 July 2003).

US-ASEAN Business Council. 2003. "ASEAN and Its Importance to the United States." <http://www.us-asean.org/2003_policy_recommendations.asp> (16 July 2003).

Wade, Robert. 1990. *Governing the Market: Economic Theory and the Role of Government in East Asian Regionalism*. Princeton, N.J.: Princeton University Press.

World Bank. 1993. *The East Asian Miracle: Economic Growth and Public Policy*. Policy Research Report. New York: Oxford University Press and World Bank Group.

Webber, Douglas. 2001. "Two Funerals and a Wedding? The Ups and Downs of Regionalism in East Asia and the Asia Pacific after the Asian Crisis." *Pacific Review* 14(3).

Yeo, B. G. (NS) George. 2002a. "Building an ASEAN Economic Community." Speech at AFTA (ASEAN Free Trade Area) Seminar, Jakarta, 31 January.

————. 2002b. "How ASEAN Can Hold Its Own against China." *Straits Times Interactive* (12 November). <http://www.straitstimes.com.sg> (16 July 2003).

Yusuf, Shahid. 2001. "Globalization and the Challenge for Developing Countries." Working paper for the World Bank Group, Washington, D.C., June.

Zoellick, Robert. 2002. "Unleashing the Trade Winds." *The Economist* (7 December).

9

Conclusion:
Some Scenarios for Pacific Asia

Simon S. C. Tay

The chapters in this volume have offered insights about the region on specific issues. The effort here is to offer neither a summary nor a ready conclusion about the future of Pacific Asia. Rather, the purpose is to sketch a number of scenarios for the region, consideration of which may be helpful in the policy making and governance of states. To close with such speculations may perhaps seem unconventional. It is, however, inevitable, given the nature of the subject.

The future is, after all, contingent. This seems especially so today when Asia and the Pacific region have been tossed and turned in the wake of a series of changes and challenges—from the Asian financial crisis that began in 1997 to post–9-11 concerns with terrorism. This sense of contingency is amplified by the unexpected and potentially discontinuous nature of these changes and challenges.

In view of this, the scholars who have contributed to this volume do not only offer current analyses and straight-line extrapolations into the future. They have tried, within their subject areas and the limitations of space, to speculate as well about the broader significance of the issues observed. The broader significances and, more, the interplay of different possible events are the focus of this final chapter.

Cross-Cutting Issues

From the analyses of the region in the preceding chapters, there are a number of broader cross-cutting issues that arise. These include the following.

Simon S. C. Tay

Growing Gaps in Development

Growing development gaps between less developed and more developed countries in the region can be vividly seen. The region has always been diverse. The economic and technological differences between Japan, at one end, and the least developed countries, at the other, are perhaps greater than in any other region in the world, and certainly well beyond the gaps that exist in Europe. In Pacific Asia, the gaps, moreover, seem to be growing.

The promise of technology affords late-developing countries the where-withal to leapfrog these gaps, but there is no evidence yet of this taking place. Instead, the trends in areas like information and communications technology (ICT) show an increase and acceleration in the gaps between the most developed and least developed countries. Trends in investment and trade, too, show something of the same phenomenon. While all countries may benefit from freer trade in goods, volumes increase most when free trade is fostered between developed and larger economies. The trends in the early twenty-first century favoring bilateral trade agreements augment this differentiation; the countries most active and successful in negotiating and effecting these agreements are already the most active and successful traders.

The growing gaps will test the sense of community and solidarity in Pacific Asia. Between states, the sense of community and mutual assistance has not been strong. Except for Japan, there is no significant record of aid being rendered among Asian countries, although to a lesser degree Australia and New Zealand do offer aid and assistance programs. The lack of a tradition of assistance may be attributed to the relatively low economic development of the larger countries, like China and Indonesia, and the small size of the more developed economies, like Brunei and Singapore. The ambitions of economic cooperation, and of win-win liberalization, have instead been emphasized for "trade, not aid." There are truths behind this mantra, but the gaps that are emerging will test solidarity, and it will be increasingly important if regionalism is to proceed for each state to see the benefits of moving ahead.

The trend within each country also shows growing gaps between the rich and poor. In some countries, like China, the differences are geographic as well as social. Coastal cities aggregate much of the growth and economic benefits, while inland communities and the countryside fall further behind. Within larger cities, stark differences are observable, too. The whole region bears witness to the phenomenon of gated communities for the rich and squatter communities for the poorest—often within short distance of each other.

Within some states and societies, the sense of solidarity and community has been quite strong. The crisis years demonstrated this, as the impact on the poor was not as dire as had been predicted. But elsewhere, the elites have been shown to be self-serving and without a sense of wider responsibility for society as a whole.

The State and Governance: Necessary and Insufficient

The importance of the state and of governance has been reinforced in recent years. This has been contrary to the prediction, made in the early 1990s, that the state would wither away from the pull and push of globalization, with greater sovereignty being devolved to both international regimes and sub-state–level institutions. The challenges and changes of the years since 1997 have brought the state back into sharp focus. Even as it grapples with globalization, the state remains the primary and essential focal point for addressing the various phenomena that arise. It is clear today that no state can deal with all its concerns on its own. It is also clear that there can be no solution that does not bring the state into the equation.

While the state may be necessary, it is by no means apparent that governments within the region have been sufficient to the tasks they have faced. Questions about their effectiveness, especially in times of crisis, have emerged—from the 1997 financial crisis to the 2003 outbreak of Severe Acute Respiratory Syndrome (SARS). These questions have been compounded by questions of legitimacy.

Corruption, cronyism, and nepotism—KKN, as the phrase is known in Indonesia—remain to be dealt with. There has been some progress in addressing corruption and promoting transparency and accountability—seen perhaps most starkly in the trials of three incumbent leaders—Joseph Estrada of the Philippines, Abdurrahman Wahid of Indonesia, and Thaksin Shinawatra of Thailand—with the first two since having been relieved of office. However, the systemic problems of corruption have not been resolved. For too many societies, the problems remain rooted as an "enemy within."

Democracy adds another layer of issues to governance. In the years of the Asian miracle, what was known as the "soft authoritarianism" of many states in the region achieved a certain legitimacy, based on their economic performance, the central importance of the developmental state in orchestrating growth, and the idea of Asian values. But after 1997, in many countries—Indonesia especially—the wish for democracy has emerged more strongly than before. Questions regarding legitimacy of government have gone far beyond anything experienced before.

Beyond legitimacy, the effectiveness and strength (or fragility) of the states have also received scrutiny. Within the region, a wide range can be observed. Some governments have been relatively effective and capable in implementing the policies and measures that their political systems decree. In others, even when political promises are made at the highest level, there may be gaps in implementation because of a lack of capacity or a lack of central supervision over the bureaucracy or decentralized provincial authorities.

As regards these issues of governance—corruption, democratic legitimacy, and effectiveness and strength of the state—there are sharp differences among the states in the region. On corruption, Singapore is rated among the least corrupt societies in the world. Others, like Indonesia and Vietnam, are rated among the most corrupt in the world.

On democratic legitimacy, Australia, New Zealand, and Japan lie on one end of the spectrum, as mature democracies. At the other end are states like Myanmar, Brunei, Laos, and Vietnam, which are, in varying ways, outside the democratic tradition. Other countries are democracies in the making, with Thailand, Indonesia, and the Philippines moving dynamically and perhaps chaotically toward that end, and Malaysia and Singapore moving more incrementally.

On effectiveness and strength too, some states have demonstrated their ability to deal with crises. Malaysia under Mahathir bin Mohamad demonstrated considerable administrative capacity during the financial crisis in managing the fixed exchange rate mechanism. Singapore similarly showed its ability to control its border as a public health measure during the SARS crisis in 2003, without shutting down the inflow of visitors. On the other hand, Cambodia and Indonesia have been ineffective at controlling their borders and containing both the transboundary flow of illegal products, such as drugs, weapons, timber, and workers, as well as the trade in women. These issues are essential to governance in the region, but not all states have been sufficiently equal to the challenge. These weaknesses will be tested further in the future, whether in the regional efforts against terrorism or other cross-border phenomena.

Growth and Development, States and Markets

Financial and macroeconomic impacts were part and parcel of the Asian financial crisis, as were its effects at the level of households and individuals. The poorest in society were the most vulnerable, but the consequences of the crisis have been farther reaching. Even in countries that have re-achieved their pre-1997 levels of growth, there has been no ready return to the status quo of those earlier years. Part of what has changed is the way development is viewed, as well as the actors and policies that foster that development.

During the period of rapid growth, the newly industrialized economies (NIEs) achieved a relative equity, even as economic growth was the primary, or even the sole, goal of development in many states. The crisis has since led many to consider the human goals of development, moving beyond economic growth to include concerns of equity and social and environmental issues. There has been a new orientation toward "human development," as per the United Nations Development Programme (UNDP), and toward "sustainable development," as called for in the United Nations Conference on Environment and Development (the Earth Summit in Rio).

Pre-1997, the state was accepted as the main actor in the Asian miracle and accorded a central role in economic and related spheres. Japan's example of what observers called the "developmental state" was widely influential in the region. This was a departure from the emphasis on free-market forces that international organizations and developed economies in the West have held dear.

Generally, the role of the state in Asia has been larger and broader than that of states in the West, but it is uncertain if this will continue in the wake of the 1997 crisis. The influence of international institutions and of market reforms has tended to recommend models of governance that are more along Western lines, with a clearer division between the private and public sectors.

The Japanese model of the developmental state is now gone, but no dominant model has emerged to take its place. The reforms that have been instituted in the region are not uniform. South Korea, for example, under the supervision of the International Monetary Fund (IMF) and a reform-minded government, has taken a different path from Malaysia, which has consciously avoided IMF tutelage and continued with the same premier and government. Thailand has similarly exited IMF tutelage and, with new leadership under Prime Minister Thaksin, has placed greater emphasis on domestic demand and development of its rural economy.

Countries less affected by the crisis have not significantly changed direction either. China has continued with its experiment in a socialist market economy. Australia and New Zealand, which had never followed the Japanese model, have continued with their own models of development, which are more aligned to Anglo-American traditions.

With these differences in concepts of development and the relationship between the state and the market, prospects for regional cooperation grow more complex.

China and the Rest

China is progressing on a path of openness and development that can be traced most recently to the opening of the country under the leadership of Deng Xiaoping. In the view of some, the opening can be traced back further to the late nineteenth century, when China grappled with its weakness vis-à-vis colonial powers. In any case, it would not be correct to suggest that what we see of China today is something entirely new.

What has changed has been China's position in relation to other countries in the region. The Asian financial crisis that began in 1997 spread like contagion throughout the continent, especially among members of the Association of Southeast Asian Nations (ASEAN), but the crisis did not substantially affect China. On the other hand, Japan, by far the wealthiest country in the region and the largest donor of aid to Asia, was so mired in its own economic stagnancy that it seemed powerless to help its neighbors, let alone itself, notwithstanding substantial amounts of financial aid. Thus, Japan was forced to cede some of its leadership role in the region to China. The economic climate after the crisis has been much more competitive than before the crisis, with low-cost countries like Indonesia and higher-cost economies like Japan, Singapore, South Korea, and Taiwan all struggling. Yet China continues to generate growth and attract investment—much of it, indeed, from its higher-cost Asian neighbors.

Over the past five years, the flow of foreign direct investment, which once preferred the ASEAN economies to China, has come to heavily favor China. China showed astute management of its economic foreign policy by not devaluing its currency during the Asian crisis, thus avoiding another round of competitive devaluations and gaining credit as a stabilizing force. The initiative for an ASEAN-China free trade agreement is another situation that speaks well for China, indicating China's predisposition and willingness to cooperate with its neighbors. This has helped mitigate tensions from economic competition with these countries, especially the less developed economies of ASEAN.

In addition to economic concerns about China, there are also strategic and security issues. Attitudes on this score differ from one country in the region to another. Some have past or present points of contention with China. The continuing historical debate over World War II remains a gap that separates the two giants of the region, Japan and China. Disputes over the Spratlys and other islands in the South China Sea call for resolution between China and the multiple claimants to the islands, the Philippines and Vietnam among them.

By and large, however, the states of the region have studiously sought to avoid treating China as an enemy or strategic competitor. Indeed, many of the efforts at institutionalizing the region, including the ASEAN + 3 process (ASEAN plus China, Japan, and South Korea), have been initiated, at least in part, to accommodate China and to encourage its peaceful integration into the region.

There is, however, no guarantee that this will continue. Developments in the internal politics of China—with new leadership, a rising nationalism, and the necessary lubrication of growth—may bring change. External factors, including economic and political competition with its neighbors, are a potential source of uncertainty—as is China's evolving relationship with the United States.

The Necessary but Resented United States

The role of the United States cannot be underestimated. Although not part of Pacific Asia, the United States has been a critical element in the region since the end of World War II. Even during the 1980s, when American economic strength seemed to ebb and there was talk of Japan as number one, the U.S. presence in terms of security was deemed irreplaceable. Considerable effort was made by many in Asia to persuade the United States, especially during the Bill Clinton administration, to remain in the region, both physically and economically. One attraction of the Asia-Pacific Economic Cooperation (APEC) forum was that it served to anchor the United States to the region in a multilateral process. From the 1990s onward, U.S. primacy in economic and security issues has reasserted itself and confirmed the importance of the United States to Asia.

Simon S. C. Tay

Relations with the United States, however, differ from one state to another. Australia, Japan, South Korea, the Philippines, and Thailand have formal security alliances with the United States. Singapore, too, maintains a close friendship with the United States, having a long-term agreement that allows the U.S. fleet to use its deep-sea harbor facilities. For Vietnam and China, there has been a history of conflict with the United States. For Malaysia and Indonesia, there is sometimes the rhetoric of independence and resentment but also tacit acceptance of a U.S. role in the region and a reliance on American interest on many issues.

Economically, the United States has no rival as a destination for Asian exports and a source of foreign investment. Yet, while the United States is an essential part of Asia's landscape, its presence is by no means without consequence, whether present or potential.

The primary relationship in this regard is with China. In the longer arc of history, U.S.-China ties have been strong. But since the end of World War II and the rise of the communist rule on the mainland, the relationship has been uneasy. This tension was seen most recently in the early days of the George W. Bush administration, when U.S. leadership seemed to regard China as a "strategic competitor."

For the United States, there are recurring themes in the China relationship with which each administration must deal. The Clinton administration also came into office on an election promise to be tougher with China. While that relationship warmed into talk of China being a "strategic ally," the bombing of the Chinese embassy in Belgrade in the NATO-led intervention over Kosovo undid much of the progress overnight.

Beyond particular incidents, the U.S.-China relationship has to contend with a number of perennial issues. From the U.S. point of view, there are the issues of democracy, human rights, and Taiwan, which are reinforced by more general suspicion over the rise of China as a rival in the long term, and one with a different ideology.

On China's part, efforts have been made to foster the relationship and to draw closer to the United States on several fronts. This was particularly noticeable after the events of 9-11 and in the run-up to the change of Chinese leadership. Much of this was calculated to be necessary for the overarching wish for political stability that will allow China the best conditions to open up to the world and consolidate its domestic politics and society.

But with China's growing sense of nationalism and its demand for a fair multipolar world, there are uncertainties that may arise. Intimations of this could be seen in the Chinese response to the Belgrade embassy bombing and the subsequent collision of the American EP3 "spy plane." The status of Taiwan continues to be a lightning rod as well, with Chinese feelings no less intense than those of the United States.

Post–9-11 America has also awakened a broader questioning of the U.S. role in Pacific Asia. Public sentiment in Malaysia, Indonesia, and even U.S. allies South Korea and Thailand turned sharply from sympathy to resentment and charges of U.S. bullying. The U.S. interventions in Afghanistan and Iraq have been controversial. Among states in the region, only Australia, Japan, the Philippines, and Singapore openly supported the war against Iraq. Even Thailand, South Korea, and New Zealand demurred.

Support for the United States has also created divisions. Australia's suggestion that it was Washington's "deputy sheriff" and its support of the use of preemptive force in Iraq were met with diplomatic fury and derision, especially by Malaysian Prime Minister Mahathir.

As the Bush administration continues its campaign against international terrorism, Asians will experience changes with the developments that unfold. This will be not only in terms of external security alliances and arrangements but, given the nature of terrorism, in internal policies and actions taken within their own borders. Indonesia, for example, after 9-11 experienced the cost of U.S. dissatisfaction.

More fundamentally, even beyond 9-11 issues, Pacific Asia at present is incomplete without the United States. As the states that comprise the region do not share a uniform response to U.S. concerns and demands, however, the United States is the "price setter" and Pacific Asian states the "price takers."

Nascent Regional Identity and Institutions

Even as Pacific Asia may be an incomplete region, the chapters in this volume have considered regional phenomena in politics, economic cooperation, and other areas that demonstrate a real interdependence and a nascent regional institutionalization.

Some interdependencies do not appear well managed. There are gaps in institutional arrangements among governments in concerns such as the environment, investment, and the movement of people. Even in finance, where progress has been made, the efficacy of the arrangements remains untested.

In these circumstances, the neofunctionalist thinking on regionalism suggests that forms of supranational integration must emerge if the maximum welfare is to result for the most people. The ASEAN + 3 process is, in most analyses, the leading framework for this effort. Yet even as the process is undertaken, there are limits, as has been noted, to how far the road will lead. The ASEAN + 3 process, in this regard, is typical of the intergovernmental processes that can be an alternative approach to regional arrangements and integration.

In such intergovernmental processes, the central, sometimes exclusive role is assigned to governments—particularly to heads of governments. These political elites guard their sovereignty jealously, carefully sacrificing what they must to attain their common goals. Under such circumstances, the more powerful and larger states will exert the greater influence on the pace and direction of regional integration.

In Pacific Asia, however, given the difficulties between the two giants of China and Japan, efforts at regional integration are likely to advance slowly, if at all. For even when we look beyond governmental processes, there is no shared understanding among the states in the region. There is no vision or pursuit of values that would be associated with a community in the deeper sense of the word.

Observations in this volume suggest future challenges to a greater institutionalization of Pacific Asia. In the overview this is referred to as the X factor, an anticipation of the divergence between those states that are successful in dealing with challenges and those that are struggling.

In this regard, an Asian miracle in which all or most of us prosper would seem unlikely. There are going to be winners, true. But with globalization and increased competition, there will, more than ever, also be losers. As such, this X factor may strain regionalism when there are insufficient institutions to address regional interdependencies, and no vision and sense of community to knit the sense of a region together.

Four Scenarios

Against these cross-cutting issues, this concluding chapter suggests four scenarios for Pacific Asia that can be envisioned along two main axes of geostrategic issues.

The first axis is that of the United States and China. We must look not only at the relationship between these two giants. The allegiance of other states needs also to be considered. To put it starkly, we might ask: Will Pacific Asia continue to be dominated by the United States or grow to be more China-centered?

The second axis emphasizes not international relations but the internal dynamics of each state in the region. We must consider the degree to which each state is capable and willing to undertake efforts in increased regional cooperation and affiliation. Again, to frame the issues simply, we would ask: Will Pacific Asian states have sufficient internal capacity and cohesion and favor external cooperation, or will they suffer internal weakness and generate external instabilities?

Transposing these two axes gives us four possible scenarios. In scenario A, states experience internal weakness and generate external instabilities, and accordingly continue to rely on the United States as a guarantor of stability and economic progress. This scenario seems entirely possible, given the harsh conditions and the challenges that have emerged since 1997, the different capacities of states to meet them—the X factor—and the weak regional institutions and processes for cooperation.

In scenario B, the dominant role of the United States continues, but in an environment where more rather than fewer states are more capable of dealing with economic, political, and other challenges, and more willing to cooperate with each other. This outcome is possible, or even probable, if the ASEAN + 3 and other regional processes and nascent institutions continue to grow. If this occurs, states will be better able to coordinate their responses to a number of issues, including the engagement of China.

In scenario C, states possess internal cohesion and proceed with similar cooperation as in scenario B, but the United States does not dominate the picture. Instead, China emerges as the center of their regional relationships. This scenario is foreseeable if China continues its rapid progress of the past few years and rises to stature, and if the United States should diminish its presence or interest in Asia, for whatever reason.

In scenario D, the states look increasingly toward China as the center of the region. This reorientation, however, is based on weakness rather than strength. The states find themselves lacking confidence in their own ability to address the multiple challenges facing them and unable to come together on significant issues, including the rise of China.

We cannot here, for the constraints of length, debate at length the likelihood of these four different scenarios. They are offered in an attempt to aggregate the different issues surveyed in this volume.

It can, however, be briefly said that scenarios B and C would appear to be more desirable in several ways. As regards the states in the region, these two scenarios assume strength rather than weakness and an improved ability to cope with challenges. They share the optimism of Pacific Asia as a more coherent and cooperative region, having greater confidence. Working together, the states, especially the smaller and medium-sized ones, may be seen better able to influence the course of their destiny. Whether they will be more or less reliant on the United States, or more or less centered on China is a decision in which they have some influence and choice, rather than having it imposed upon them. In comparison, scenarios A and D share the dismal prospect of weak states and, accordingly, slimmer prospects for regional cooperation.

If it is a choice between scenario B or scenario C, many may prefer B. This is a preference that essentially extrapolates from the status quo. For the last several decades, many have hoped that the United States would extend its influence for stability, its investment for economic progress, and its markets for Asian exports. Profiting from this, they have hoped that internal cohesion would progress as would regional cooperation toward shared prosperity and common security. As this has yet to happen, many would resist any scenario in which the United States grows more distant. More than ever, this would be the response if they felt that the region would look more and more to China while suffering the loss of the United States, a power that has proven itself relatively benign.

With this in mind, scenario C is approached with some caution. It would mark a shift from the regional order we have known to an order for which there is no happy precedent. The manner of this shift, too, is indeterminate. It is possible, for example, that a lesser U.S. presence and interest in Pacific Asia could arise quite suddenly in response to domestic politics. The United States has always been said to have an isolationist streak, notwithstanding that its substantial engagements with parts of Asia, like Japan and China, go back to the nineteenth century. The American desire for isolation from a troubled world can be seen in the controversial proposal for missile defense in the early days of the current Bush administration. This was, in considerable part, propelled by the idea that the United States could withdraw behind such a shield, once constructed.

The character of a China as the vital center for the region is also uncertain. In these past decades of rapid change, China has been seen at times to be astute, confident, and sensitive to the needs and concerns of its neighbors. Yet at other times, over certain issues that threatened its sovereignty and the rule of its governing party—for example, Taiwan, Falun Gong, and the disputed territories in the South China Sea—China has been seen to have acted imperiously.

We need not, however, see scenario C with the misgivings of some Pacific Asian states. In contrast to scenario D, scenario C begins from a position of greater regional strength, capability, and combined weight vis-à-vis China. In this regard, perhaps the ideal future for many would be for scenario B to serve as precursor to scenario C.

This would mean that the United States would allow, encourage, and even enable a growing sense of regionalism among both its allies and non-allies in Pacific Asia. It would then, gradually and with still a residing interest, wean itself from the region and the region from its dominance. In this, suspicions of a rising China would be given time to be assuaged, with an underlying hedge of U.S. alliances with regional partners, such as Japan and Australia. China might thus not dominate the region, as some fear, but might take its place as a respected leader in a region that would be more comfortable with itself.

UNEXPECTED SHOCKS AND UNPREPARED ACTORS

Yet, while these scenarios may be desirable to some, there is no guarantee that they will eventuate. Among the recent changes and challenges that the region has faced, one is struck by their unexpected nature and their sudden impact. The possibilities of recurrence and intensification are not far behind.

The events and aftermath of 9-11 are an example of this. While the events took place in the United States, literally on the other side of the world, they have had a sharp and enduring impact on Pacific Asia, and it has come home to many states. The Bali bombing at the end of 2002 demonstrated this all too tragically.

For Southeast Asia, the threat of terrorist acts, which once seemed confined, has spread with international links. Indonesia alone did not feel the impact of the Bali bombing. Malaysia and Singapore, given their close connections with and proximity to Indonesia, also experienced increased security alarms. In the southern Philippines and the Indonesian province of Aceh, pre-existing conflicts between the capital and its peripheries are now viewed in a different light, and accorded different responses.

In Japan and Australia, the events of 9-11 and the interventions in Afghanistan and Iraq have also had political impact. In Japan, they have allowed the Koizumi Jun'ichiro government to win approval for deployment of defense forces that in normal circumstances would have been unimaginable. In Australia, the John Howard government's stance allying itself firmly with the United States has perhaps increased its international profile but also sharpened its differences with Asian neighbors Indonesia and Malaysia.

Amid these differences, however, forms of cooperation have been found. Some of these are limited to political statement. Others extend to the sharing of sensitive information, which, in the case of Malaysia and Singapore, have continued despite political differences.

The concerns with international terrorism are, however, not a thing of the past. The possibility of more incidents cannot be ruled out. And it behooves one to recall that political commitment on 9-11 issues in Indonesia before the Bali bombing was very different after the tragedy. The state's position on cooperation on security issues changed sharply, as did the political space for Muslim moderates to speak up against radical groups and to take action against groups with links to international terrorist networks.

Yet while the response to the Bali tragedy was, in these respects, positive, there is no guarantee of a similar response in all instances of concern and loss. New and different political impacts have got to be expected.

Another example of a sharp and unexpected impact is the public health crisis that erupted in the region in 2003 with the outbreak of SARS. Public health concerns are not new to the region. Indeed, some strains of influenza cause more deaths each year than did SARS. While the outbreak is perhaps too recent to analyze the regional cooperation on SARS definitively, some early observations can be offered.

We may be disappointed at the modes of regional cooperation. Some states in the region may have overreacted with the instinct to ban or otherwise irrationally discriminate against travelers or nationals from some countries with SARS, while other states were felt to have initially underreacted in identifying and reporting the outbreak within their borders and seeking international cooperation and assistance.

Some reports suggest that information was not received expeditiously from China and that the Chinese government denied the existence of the crisis. Beijing authorities seemed to recognize this with their decision to replace the health minister and the strong measures taken to contain the further spread of SARS. Other SARS-affected areas experienced problems in their response as well. Authorities in Hong Kong and in Taiwan faced criticism from their own citizens for their lack of effective action.

When realization about SARS did come, the response of some states could also be criticized. Instead of introducing screening measures, they issued blanket bans against travelers from SARS-affected areas.

Yet the crisis also witnessed a new effort in regional cooperation. Consultation among health ministers was held at the initiative of ASEAN, and included the Northeast Asian countries of China, Japan, and South Korea, as well as the World Health Organization. As such, SARS witnessed another use of the ASEAN + 3 framework. Measures among these states were harmonized over time for cross-border regulations and movements of visitors, although policies of the states continued to differ to a considerable degree.

The region has faced many unexpected challenges—financial crisis, the Bali bombing, SARS. The future, viewed through the lens of present uncertainties, is fraught with difficulties. The only thing these challenges have in common is their unpredictability and their suddenness.

All we can hope is that the actors—states, regional agreements and institutions, international organizations, and even nongovernmental actors—will be better prepared to deal with whatever comes, taking the necessary action both within each state and among the states. The record does not commend us well—either in our preparation for these contingencies or our understanding of our regional neighbors.

REGIONAL ORDER AND AN ORDERLY REGION

The early easy predictions of an Asia Pacific community and an Asian century seem now to belong to a distant history, rather than to the 1990s.

In this short time, we have lost faith in a Japanese miracle and an Asian miracle. Many now rush to China but, even if we wish China well, we should be aware of the challenges China will face. There are no miracles, and there is no Chinese miracle.

Given that we cannot predict the nature of future challenges, we would do better to emphasize the need to increase capacities, improve governance, and strengthen our societies.

In many ways, national concerns should be paramount in this. Each state in the region must put its own house in order. Yet if each state overemphasizes efforts at the national level, the region as a whole may run the risk of being overlooked. Nation building should not inadvertently contribute to the neglect of the wider vista of regional interdependence, increased cooperation, and integration. If it does, Pacific Asia will not cohere as a region or community, with beneficial systems of dialogue, cooperation, and solidarity.

Simon S. C. Tay

The regional dimensions of assistance and cooperation can prove vital. This is especially the case as the challenges are large and overwhelming. No state in the region—whether large and influential or small and weak—can successfully resolve all the challenges it faces without addressing its interdependencies with other states. The present moment contains a nascent sense of regionalism, especially with the ASEAN + 3. In this, to use Arnold Toynbee's phrase, "history is on the move." So it is across the world.

This movement of history is not assured or predetermined. Competing visions of the international order range from the realist idea of a U.S.-centered architecture to the several non-realistic conceptions, like Samuel Huntington's clash of civilizations, the liberal community of peace stressed by Michael Doyle and others, and the neoconservative vision of a U.S.-led "empire lite."

Will Pacific Asia be more democratic and move toward Western models in governance and society? Will the region continue to rely on the United States as a guarantor of peace and stability? Will the diverse cultures and civilizations in Pacific Asia lead to conflict, or will increasing dialogue lead to increased confidence, shared norms, and the acceptance of the peaceful settlement of disputes?

Such questions loom when we think of international order and the regional order that follows. The fate of Asia Pacific is not immune from these global and U.S. influences. Indeed, these visions can be major determinants for the future of the region.

Yet for Pacific Asia, there is also an increasing sense that regional factors will be a significant part of the calculations. The concept, initial steps, and progress of a Pacific Asia, as opposed to an Asia Pacific that includes the United States, signal the importance of those regional elements in making up the future.

In this, the questions of international order and the corresponding regional order are perhaps secondary to the recognition that there is a need for Pacific Asia to be an orderly region; one that is better able to manage its already existing and still increasing interdependencies.

In thinking about possible future scenarios for Pacific Asia, perhaps the value lies not in the veracity of each prediction, but the process itself. For we thereby imagine possible orders for the Pacific Asian states not merely as physically contingent territories, but as a diverse but increasingly interdependent and integrated region.

Bibliography

Han Sung Joo, ed. 1999. *Changing Values in Asia: Their Impact on Governance and Development.* Tokyo: Japan Center for International Exchange.

Katzenstein, Peter J. 2000. *Asian Regionalism.* Ithaca, N.Y.: Cornell University Press, East Asia Series.

Krauss, Ellis S. 2002. "Japan, the US, and the Emergence of Multilateralism in Asia." *Pacific Review* 13(3): 473–494.

Mattli, Walter. 1999. "Explaining Regional Integrational Outcomes." *Journal of European Public Policy* 6(1): 1–27.

Stiglitz, Joseph E., and Shahid Yusuf. 2001. *Rethinking the East Asian Miracle.* New York: Oxford University Press.

Tay, Simon S. C., Hadi Soesastro, and Jesus Estanislao. 2001. *Reinventing ASEAN.* Singapore: Institute of Southeast Asian Studies.

Wade, Robert. 1990. *Governing the Market: Economic Theory and the Role of Government in East Asian Regionalism.* Princeton, N.J.: Princeton University Press.

Webber, Douglas. 2001. "Two Funerals and a Wedding? The Ups and Downs of Regionalism in East Asia and the Asia Pacific after the Asian Crisis." *Pacific Review* 14(3).

About the Contributors

SIMON S. C. TAY, Chairman, Singapore Institute of International Affairs, Singapore; Associate Professor, National University of Singapore

AKE TANGSUPVATTANA, Assistant Professor and Deputy Dean for Student Affairs, Faculty of Political Science, Chulalongkorn University, Thailand

JAMUS JEROME LIM, Department of Economics, University of California, Santa Cruz, United States

LOUIS LEBEL, Director, Unit for Social and Environmental Research, Chiang Mai University, Thailand

OKAMOTO YUMIKO, Professor of Economics, Department of Policy Studies, Doshisha University, Japan

YAP CHING WI, The Necessary Stage, Singapore

YOON YOUNG-KWAN, Visiting Fellow, Asian Pacific Research Center, Stanford University, United States; former Minister for Foreign Affairs and Trade, South Korea

YU XUEJUN, Director General, Department of Policy and Legislation, National Population and Family Planning Commission of China

The Japan Center for International Exchange

FOUNDED IN 1970, the Japan Center for International Exchange (JCIE) is an independent, nonprofit, and nonpartisan organization dedicated to strengthening Japan's role in international affairs. JCIE believes that Japan faces a major challenge in augmenting its positive contributions to the international community, in keeping with its position as one of the world's largest industrial democracies. Operating in a country where policy making has traditionally been dominated by the government bureaucracy, JCIE has played an important role in broadening debate on Japan's international responsibilities by conducting international and cross-sectional programs of exchange, research, and discussion.

JCIE creates opportunities for informed policy discussions; it does not take policy positions. JCIE programs are carried out with the collaboration and cosponsorship of many organizations. The contacts developed through these working relationships are crucial to JCIE's efforts to increase the number of Japanese from the private sector engaged in meaningful policy research and dialogue with overseas counterparts.

JCIE receives no government subsidies; rather, funding comes from private foundation grants, corporate contributions, and contracts.